The profound crisis affecting our societies is obvious. Ecological disturbances, social exclusion, the rampant exploitation of natural resources, the frenetic and dehumanizing quest for profit and the widening of inequalities lie at the heart of our contemporary problems. Nevertheless, men and women everywhere are coming together around innovative and original projects with a view to opening up new prospects for the future. There are solutions. Novel proposals are being made all over the planet, often on a small scale, but always with the aim of bringing about real change in our societies.

TOMORROW

Photographic credits

© Move Movie: 67, 74, 102, 106, 109, 116, 123, 130–31, 152–53, 194, 250–51, 288–89, 304
© Laurent Cercleux: 18, 64, 98
© Cyril Dion: 54, 190–91
© Grima Irmudottir: 312
© Emmanuel Guionet: 34–35, 217, 257, 263, 266, 274–75, 295
© Alexandre Léglise: 2–3, 49, 225, 242, 318–19
© Sylvie Peyre: 182

© Actes Sud, 2017
ISBN 978-2-330-07909-3
www.actes-sud.fr

CYRIL DION

TOMORROW

ALL OVER THE GLOBE,
SOLUTIONS ALREADY EXIST

ACTES SUD

INTRODUCTION

July 27, 2012. It's early. I'm staring up at the slats in the attic where my family and I are sleeping. My head feels fuzzy, still groggy from sleep, a bit dazed by the heat. I need some fresh air. I get up quietly, pull on some clothes and slip outside. Nature smells good. I move slowly through the tall grass, barefoot. A myriad of insects is buzzing around the bushes. The first light of day does me good.

We're spending our family vacation at a cousin's farm, which has recently converted to organic farming. Behind the garden hedge, a few cows, pigs, and horses are grazing on the lush grass. I put on my shoes and walk for nearly an hour, connecting with the dense, tranquil life that's thriving in the thickets, the trees, the ponds.

Back in the attic, I turn on my computer to check the news. On *Le Monde*, I notice an article with an unusual headline, topping the list of the texts "most-shared" by Internet users: "The end of the world in 2100?" It's a blog post by environmental journalist Audrey Garric. Scanning it first, then reading it more carefully, I realize that she's writing about the possible extinction of multiple forms of life, including a large proportion of human beings, within just a few decades. I find it hard to believe. The information comes from a study published in the journal *Nature* by twenty-two researchers from around the world. It compares dozens of other studies concerning pollution, climate change, deforestation, soil erosion, population growth, biodiversity collapse, and concludes that we are near a tipping point, where the mass deterioration of ecosystems could entirely change the biological and climate equilibrium of the planet. This change could be so severe that many living organisms would not be able to adapt.

I'm in a state of shock for several hours. When everyone wakes up, I don't say anything. I don't know what to say. I watch my children eat breakfast, their eyes still puffy from sleep; I look at the others (my companion, her cousins) and the mechanical gestures they make to get up and running for the day. Everything that would have looked normal to me yesterday now seems totally out of sync. I don't know how to share with them what I have just read. And I don't really want to. Maybe I'll wait an hour and then tell them about it. As best as I can, without being too emotional. Taking care to nuance it as much as possible. But still, let them know just how much this news upsets me. No one reacts as I had expected (I only spoke to the adults). The conversation started something like this: "We all know it's catastrophic—yet, what do you want us to do about it?" At one level, I am appalled, while at another, I completely understand. Because ultimately, what are you supposed to do with news like this?

Ten days later, the study made the front page of the French daily *Libération*. On a slow news day in August, environmental journalist Laure Noualhat managed to get the headline and four inside pages. I talked about it again with my partner. This time she paid more attention. Yet I was fascinated by the lack of any real reaction to this information. Including my own. It doesn't change anything about our everyday lives, even though we're talking about a series of events whose impact would be as, and probably far more, serious than a world war.

On March 31, 2013, I was one of the guests on Stéphane Paoli's radio news show on France Inter. While preparing for the broadcast, I talked to him about the study and shared my dismay. No other major media had seriously reported on the issue since the *Libération* article of August 9, 2012. On air, he discussed this absurd lack of media coverage, decisively. And yet the 1:00 p.m. news program—in the middle of his own show on public radio, considered to be a serious, left-leaning broadcast where many top-notch journalists have been working for years—only discussed a handful of current events and a few squabbles among politicians. Nothing important. Ultimately, this information that should have been the top news in all the newspapers, all the radio shows, all the national televisions broadcasts, was relegated (with the notable exception of *Libération*, thanks to Laure Noualhat's stubborn insistence) to a blog post in one of the major French dailies, a sidebar in *Alternative Économiques*, and two articles on the Internet (as far as I know, on the websites of *Échoes* and *Psychologie* magazine). How was this possible?

I spent more than six years thinking long and hard about this paradox. In late 2006, I was asked to create a movement, Colibris, inspired by the agroecologist and writer Pierre Rabhi. I remained its director through August 2013, a period during which we were trying to understand what inspired individuals, entrepreneurs, and elected officials to act—or to not act. The alarming predictions had been increasing for decades, coming from authors such as Fairfield Osborn in 1949, Rachel Carson in 1961, reports from the Club de Rome in 1972, the IPCC[1] since 1988, the first summit in Rio in 1992 (and all those that followed), documentaries, television shows, NGOs, and even some politicians—but none of them resulted in any significant initiatives. Governments continued to pursue short-term plans, regularly basing their decisions on heavyweights from the economic and financial spheres, and on their obsession with getting reelected; most businesspeople espoused the logic of growth and capitalism, for better or for worse; and most individuals continued to nourish the consumer machine, caught in the trap of their everyday lives and financial hassles. Meanwhile, half the wildlife populations were disappearing, global temperatures continued to rise, mounds of garbage were piling up, one billion people did not have enough to eat, and nearly 1.5 billion were obese—and eighty-five people had as much money as 3.5 billion others. What would it take for us to act?

After pondering these questions, I realized two things. First of all, we are suffering from an increasing virtualization of reality, from an inability to link our actions to unseen and unfelt consequences: climate change caused by our extravagant use of energy;

1. Intergovernmental Panel on Climate Change.

the suffering of slaves in distant countries who assemble our telephones and sew our clothes; the depletion of resources used to manufacture our goods; the suffering of unending lines of animals sent through mechanized slaughterhouses so that we can stuff ourselves with steak, hamburgers, and hot dogs; and the thousands of wild species that we wiped from the surface of the Earth to build parking lots, hotels, and supermarkets, to grow the corn and soy that feeds our cattle, our chickens, and our pigs that we keep imprisoned in immense warehouses. Time and time again, I have tried to explain to my children why I refuse to take them to the fast-food restaurants where all their friends routinely go, like we go to the movies or the bakery. But the things I keep harping about—the same things I used to hear years earlier, without it having any impact on me—are only words, abstract ideas. The razed forests are only numbers, sometimes images, that we forget as soon as a new distraction pushes them out of our minds. I am well aware of just how hard I have to work to regularly reconvince myself about the decisions I've taken: the necessity of not eating meat, not going to the supermarket, not taking airplanes too often. And how often I fall short. How useful are all these good intentions faced with the influence of mass culture and habits? What hope is there when everything about our lifestyles, everything in the way our world is organized, is speeding us along in the opposite direction. And yet, what other choice do we have?

The second thing I realized is our lack of vision. Starting in 2007, I could see just how much we were lacking a positive vision of ecology, of a sustainable world. We spent our time (like most of our colleagues working for other NGOs) asking stakeholders to change the way they lived, yet without offering them exciting global alternatives. We were urging them to step off the edge. And few people are brave enough or have the means to make such a leap into the unknown. We had to offer a life raft, solid and reassuring ground from which we could collectively build the future. Or at least try.

The conferences and events that we organized were full of people all repeating the same thing: "What can we do?"

But proposing isolated measures isn't enough. Especially when they seem to be out of sync with the magnitude of the problem. It is hard to believe that "taking a shower instead of a bath" can have any impact on the depletion of water resources, once you realize that 70 percent of our water is used by agriculture and livestock breeding.[1] There is something incongruous about comparing the enormous issue of climate change with the light you just turned off or the car trip you avoid taking. Especially when you know how much greenhouse gases are emitted by Chinese coal power plants and tar sand oil extraction in Alberta. These reasons that are constantly trotted out as excuses not to act (because there is always a bigger polluter somewhere in the world) are unworthy of us, of our humanity. But they express something crucial: some part of us believes that these acts won't do any good. And no one wants to put out any effort for nothing in return. Maybe these initiatives need to be part of a master scheme. As if we were drawing up plans for a new house, a new society, with instructions as to how everyone could participate by helping to lay the foundations. Perhaps we first need to devise meaning, build enthusiasm, and create stories that speak to our minds as well as to our hearts.

Sometime in 2008, I discovered a book that had a profound impact on me: *The Tale-Tellers: A Short Study of Humankind,* by novelist and essayist Nancy Huston. The book opens with these lines:

> Humans alone, of all the terrestrial animals, know how they were born, and that they will die.
>
> These two things give us what even our closest relatives (chimps and bonobos) do not have—namely, the notion of *a lifetime.*

1. "Eau et agriculture," Le Service Public d' Information sur l'Eau, www.eaufrance.fr/comprendre/les-usages-de-l-eau-et-les/eau-et-agriculture.

We alone see our existence on Earth as a *path* endowed with meaning (and direction). An arc. A curve that takes us from birth to death. A form that unfolds in time, with a beginning, a series of adventures, and an end. In other words: *a narrative.*

'In the beginning was the Word' means only this—that the Word (action endowed with meaning) marks the beginning of our species.

Narrative gives our life a dimension of meaning utterly unknown to animals. ... Human Meaning is distinct from animal meaning in that it is built up out of narratives, stories, fictions.[1]

In her book, Huston suggests that fiction is a function created by human beings to ensure their survival. Frightened and anxious about our own deaths, we have a desperate need to create meaning, to justify our existence within the mysteries that surround us. With religions, states, and history, we constantly fabricate individual and collective stories which, when they are widely shared, become the foundations of our social and cultural constructs. Oral and pictorial traditions, followed by books, have always played a critical role is propagating these narratives. The appearance of the novel accelerated this phenomenon, to the point where it acquired the official name of "fiction." Since the 1930s, and even more since the 1950s, film has played an ever-expanding role in our ability to tell stories to millions of others. And to fashion their imaginations.

The way reality was presented in her book was something of a revelation. I can't say if this theory is exact. But it is a fiction that speaks to me. It seems to me that all the ideologies, the societal models against which we are supposed to expend so much energy, can only be effectively "battled" through fiction and through stories. In many ways, what we call the "dream of progress" is a fiction which, via its ability to inspire fantasies among much of humanity (and to convince everyone to buy into it, contributing to its viability),

1. Nancy Huston, *The Tale-Tellers: A Short Study of Humankind* (Toronto: McArthur & Co, 2008).

has changed all of humanity forever. Trying to convince all or some people to adopt a new, more ecological, more humane path, can only happen if we lay the groundwork for a new collective fiction.

In late 2010, I started to write a film with this aim in mind. It was a kind of draft, in which we would present what we already know: pioneering initiatives that are helping to reinvent agriculture, energy, urbanism, economy, democracy, and education. I wanted to see if, by placing them end to end, we could see the emergence of a story describing what the world of the future could be. And whether this fiction would be inspiring enough to motivate people to act and create, as the fiction of "progress" had done so successfully sixty years earlier. In late 2011, I met the actor and director Mélanie Laurent. In September 2012, we went to visit an extraordinary permaculture farm (see pp. 69–77). On the way back, I talked about the project that I was having such a hard time getting off the ground. She was extremely enthusiastic and we became fast friends. In February 2013, after a few setbacks with potential partners, I suggested that we direct it together. She agreed immediately, refusing other projects that would have been more lucrative and more rewarding for her on a professional level. One year later, after a great deal of work and a first test run to Réunion, we launched a crowdfunding campaign. We were aiming to get €200,000 in two months to start the actual filming. Thanks to the extraordinary enthusiasm of 10,000 people, we raised the funds in just two days. And by the end of two months, we had €450,000. The adventure could begin. Thanks to these men and women (and other partners), we were able to travel to ten countries and meet nearly fifty scientists, activists, businesspeople, and elected officials, all of whom are laying the foundations for a new world. This book and the film *Tomorrow* bear witness to this story.

We're off!

That's it, we're on our way. At least I am. I'm on the train taking me from my home to the Montparnasse station, where a taxi will drive me to the Charles-de-Gaulle airport to meet the rest of the crew: Mélanie, Alexandre, the cinematographer (who is also an old friend), his assistant Raphaël, the sound engineer Laurent, production manager Antoine, and Tiffany, who is half American and will help us out during this first two-week trip to the United States.

For days, my stomach has been hurting, my chest has been tight, the rush of anxiety that I have experienced for years overwhelms me and sets my heart racing. This is the first time I've made a film and the weeks that have just gone by have made me realize, increasingly with each passing day, just how little I know about the technical and, to a certain extent, the artistic aspects. I am afraid of being paralyzed by anxiety, of my mind being so troubled that it will be impossible to make the right decisions. Mélanie is here, of course, but it is also her first experience with a documentary and we have never really worked together. I have drawn up a bunch of lists of shots to film, questions to ask, but nothing seems to calm me down. And then I see everyone. Soon, everyone's excitement becomes infectious. Mélanie is goofing around, relaxing the atmosphere. We talk about all the amazing things we're going to see. And a sense of adventure takes over. Armed with fifteen crates, we board the flight. The first in many more to come.

Several hours later, we are flying over the Atlantic. The flight attendant has asked us to close the windows shades so that the daylight doesn't keep people awake. We are traveling at 600 mph, several miles above the ground, with absolutely no sensation of movement. The path indicated on the screen is the only thing giving us a vague idea of our progress. Our bodies are encased in rows of seats, our eyes glued to screens projecting a reality onto our brains other than the one we are actually experiencing. Like a second window we can step into, as a distraction. But I would like to explore the initial one. Slip into the night, to be able to discern what I have never seen: these immense expanses, the orcas, the dolphins, and later, the endless coastlines, the megacities thronged with cars and bodies. Traveling this way doesn't make sense. And yet, how else to do it? The film's budget only allows us to stay three or four days at each destination. Each new day means extra salaries, equipment rentals, hotels, and meals. We could, of course, have taken off on an adventure, but that would have meant leaving our families behind for many long months. And to not be paid for the time spent. Most of us have loans, rent, expenses. Trying to do it any other way would be like swimming upstream. I came to this conclusion years ago. This world is inextricable. Every step takes us in the direction the wind blows the strongest. Unless we decide to struggle against it. I tell myself that the people we are going to film have decided to make the wind blow in another direction. I like this idea.

Stanford University: Where it began

Driving up to the Stanford campus, forty minutes from San Francisco, is not the worst thing to do. Drenched in the warm orange late-afternoon light, the Mission-style ocher buildings are scattered across the immense lawns, lined with majestic pine trees. Students are everywhere, getting around on foot or by bike. A few cars wind around the small looping roads that run through the university, which is larger than many French villages. We meet Liz Hadly and Tony Barnosky, who directed the study that inspired this trip, in their lab. Liz is a biologist, which is a small word to sum up all her accomplishments. She holds degrees in anthropology and quaternary science and a PhD in integrative biology from the University of California, Berkeley. She has worked for many years in the immense American national parks, studying the evolution of the species. Tony is a paleobiologist. He holds several degrees in geology, including a PhD in geological sciences from the University of Washington. He has taught in Dublin, Pittsburgh, New York, Chile, and at Berkeley for more than twenty years. Between the two of them, they have authored an impressive number of scientific publications and earned numerous awards for their work. Along with twenty other biologists, geographers, paleontologists, geologists, biophysicians, biochemists, and environmental doctors around the world, they published "Approaching a State Shift in Earth's Biosphere" in June 2012.[1] We wanted to talk to them to get an answer to a very simple question: is the planet really on the verge of collapse?

Interview with Elizabeth Hadly and Anthony Barnosky

CYRIL: Your publication in *Nature* was a huge shock for all of us, to say the least. It's almost hard to even believe. Are there any other studies like this?

LIZ: For decades, scientists have been studying the issues we looked at: climate change, population dynamics, the loss and transformation of ecosystems, extinctions, pollution. We tried to summarize all these problems and put them in a cohesive context. And by combining them all, we saw just how much they reinforce each other.

1. Anthony D. Barnosky, Elizabeth A. Hadly, et al. "Approaching a State Shift in Earth's Biosphere," *Nature* 486 (June 2012), pp. 52–58.

TONY: We wanted to know how our biological system would react to all these upheavals, put side by side. That's how the concept of the tipping point came about.

MÉLANIE: What does that mean?

TONY: We like to think of change in terms of gradual, observable events. And that's actually how biological systems act—up to a certain point. And then suddenly, everything shifts. It's a little bit like a kettle on the stove. Nothing happens for a long time, and then from one second to the next, the water starts to boil and turns into steam. What's unique about our study is that we talk about this tipping point as something that can happen to the entire planet (and not just to isolated system), within our lifetimes.

CYRIL: Have any similar tipping points already occurred on the planet?

TONY: Yes, a certain number of them. The most recent was the shift from the Ice Age (when the northern hemisphere was nearly totally covered in ice) to the climate we have now, which allowed human civilization to develop. That was 12,000 years ago. We therefore tried to compare the speed of the climate change at that time and its speed now

MÉLANIE: And?

TONY: We are changing it ten times faster.

LIZ: The last time temperatures were at the levels that we're headed for in the next few decades was 14 million years ago. Long before the evolution of human beings. Our species has never experienced the temperatures that are likely to occur in our lifetime. Nor have most of the species now living on the planet. They have been around for two to five million years.

TONY: And that's not the only change. We can also talk about the population. We are adding people to the planet at a rate by which the population has essentially tripled in my lifetime. That's never happened before. We can also talk about the extinction of species. Right now, extinctions are as massive and rapid as during the era when the dinosaurs disappeared.

LIZ: But it takes millions of years to once again accumulate enough biodiversity so that comparable species can develop.

TONY: These changes are taking place faster than society's capacity to adapt to them. That's why problems are occurring.

CYRIL: What could happen if we reach this tipping point?

TONY: When we talk about a tipping point, many people think: "My God, we're all going to die." That's not what we're talking about. But the planet will become a far less pleasant place to live. For example, even if we limit the rise in temperature to 35.6 degrees Fahrenheit, climate change is going to cause many more natural catastrophes (storms, floods, hurricanes, typhoons, droughts), and raise water levels. We are already seeing this in the United States, where there have been many more storms in the last three years, which cost billions of dollars, than during the fifteen previous years.

CYRIL: Yet in many of the articles I read about your study, journalists tend to say that many people would not survive, perhaps due to lack of food or our inability to adapt to these changes in temperature and climate. It this possible?

LIZ: When we put together the magnitude of the changes in temperature, the speed at which it is happening, how quickly species are going extinct, and how fast the population is growing, we start to see what could happen. For example, all these people that we are adding to the planet must be fed. But at the same time, we are pursuing the widespread destruction of the biodiversity that would make it possible to do so.

MÉLANIE: So what could happen?

LIZ: When certain countries, lacking natural resources, can no longer provide their people with the goods and services they need, or can no longer import them because they have become too expensive (water, food, energy, and therefore jobs), the population will start to migrate. And in doing so, they will destabilize other countries with the risk of creating hostility among the different populations. We have already seen the beginning of this phenomenon. We have all seen the images of migrants climbing fences or drowning as they try to reach Europe and the United States.

MÉLANIE: Could this lead to conflicts?

LIZ: Probably. It will, in any case, exacerbate the tensions between those who have little and those who have a lot.

TONY: If we imagine the worst scenario, one where we don't change our economic models or reduce greenhouse gas emissions, or do nothing to limit the increasing world population, there's no doubt that the path forward will be terrifying. If we maintain the birth rate of the years 2005–2010 throughout the entire century, we will reach twenty-seven billion people by 2100. And it will be impossible to feed everyone. We already use nearly 40 percent of the landmass to produce food. We would have to raze most of the tropical forests, which would give us a little more time, but not much.

LIZ: And by razing these forests, we would cause a massive extinction of the species that live in these environments; we would destroy the ecosystems that create clean water, we would lose the trees that store carbon dioxide. Which would worsen the climate situation even more. By trying to solve one problem, we would exacerbate another one.

TONY: Looking at all these problems together, we see that this will quickly create an extremely uncomfortable world. Fortunately, these trends are easing up a bit, but we still face an enormous amount of work. We are at a time in history when we must wake up; we can see these things happening, we know most of the solutions to them. We have a good window of opportunity in the upcoming fifteen to twenty years to act, but people have to want to do it. As Jay Inslee, the governor of Washington State, said: "we are the first generation to feel the effects of climate change, and certainly that last one to be able to do anything about it."

MÉLANIE: If we work together over the next twenty years, can we still stop climate change?

LIZ: It's a bit like a car; it takes some time from the moment you brake before the car actually stops. Even if we no longer emit any greenhouse gasses, it would take a long time before the atmosphere returned to normal. So the warming will continue; that's why we have to anticipate and adapt to it, think about the seeds we'll need, about the populations.

TONY: In San Francisco, for example, most people are baseball fans. But most people don't know that by 2050, the stadium will be underwater. It's going to happen, it's not a hypothesis. The sea levels are rising and will continue to cover many of the coastlines and infrastructure, whether it's in Florida, New York, or many other places in the world. And we're only talking about an increase of 35.6 degrees Fahrenheit. If it's four or six, the problems will not only increase, but they will multiply in terms of economic cost and human lives.

LIZ: It's not only about supplies of food and water. We must now imagine the type of world we are going to live in, one in which we may lack all kinds of resources, where environments will change, where species that usually live far from each other will share the same area, as will soon be the case with the grizzly bears and polar bears in Alaska. Everything will change and we need to prepare ourselves for it.

CYRIL: What do you think we should do now? What recommendations would you make to heads of states, to companies, to citizens?

TONY: First, stabilize the world's population at around ten billion people by the end of the century. Which means that women in countries with high birth rates could have access to education (this is also true for men), birth control, and health care.

LIZ: Then lower the ecological footprint of everyone in the West. It's not just about the number of people on the planet, but also about our excessive consumption of resources. We who live in the so-called "developed" countries, consume immensely more than people who live in the so-called "developing" countries.

TONY: The goal is to lower levels of consumption in our countries, so that they can increase in India, in China, and elsewhere, while remaining sustainable. Third, no long use fossil fuels and achieve a CO_2 neutral economy as soon as possible. A certain number of studies have shown that in thirty years, we could fully replace fossil fuels with renewable energies. Our primary obstacle in reaching this goal is the logic of "business as usual." And so, fourth, we need to change our economic models. Fifth, look at how we are feeding people. Currently, our market economy encourages us to degrade the environment to produce food, then we throw away one-third of what we grow. Even though we know that techniques exist to feed ten billion people. Finally, stop the extinction of species. There are many ways to do it, like integrating nature into our economic systems and the factoring into the environmental services they contribute. We don't have a lot of time. Maybe twenty years to push things in the right direction. It's a critical time for humanity.

LIZ: Everyone thinks that someone else is going to take care of it. But we have to pursue these actions collectively.

TONY: These are obviously massive problems, but there are seven billion of us. If everyone does a little bit, this joint effort could be an immense force for change.

MÉLANIE: What did you feel when you came to all these conclusions?

LIZ: Frightened. But of course, I am confident that if we all come together as a single human community, we can change things. But I'm very afraid if we don't do it.

When we left Liz and Tony, we were totally fired up by their extraordinary energy, their integrity, their simplicity, their humanity, and at the same time, felt somewhat battered by the picture they painted of the future. Twenty years to act. My children are seven and ten years old. Mélanie's son is not yet two. Alexandre, Laurent, Raphaël all have girls and boys under the age of eight. They were going to be hit full on by the crises we were discussing. They would have to learn how to adapt, as Tony suggested. But what overwhelmed us the most was that perhaps WE were going to face this period with them. For years, we have been talking nonstop about "future generations." For years we have been lecturing about the need to act, our responsibility of leaving a viable world for our children. But in fact, this is no longer about our children, but about ourselves. And about all the human beings who are already experiencing the nightmare of global warming, of hunger, and instability in all its forms. Because ecological, social, and economic problems are all closely linked. A growing body of research exists to prove it. Many of them have established, for example, a direct link between global warming and conflict.[1] Other studies clearly show just how an unbridled exploitation of resources, combined with climate change and an ultra-liberal economy, is starving children and adults to death every day.[2] This is what Lester Brown, founder of the Worldwatch Institute and the Earth Policy Institute explains to us. Lester studies agricultural economics and was named by the *Washington Post* as "one of the world's most influential thinkers." He has spent his entire life studying the global ecological situation and, at age eighty-one, is one of the leading experts in the field.

1. "Climate change can indirectly increase risks of violent conflicts in the form of civil war and inter-group violence," IPCC Fifth Assessment Report, 2014, http://ipcc-wg2.gov/report/ar5/. *New York Times* columnist Thomas Friedman spent months researching one of the most striking examples of this statement. Four years before the war in Syria, which has already killed hundreds of thousands of people, a devastating drought gripped the country, displacing millions of people and plunging nearly two million Syrians into extreme poverty. Many of them migrated to rural areas around Damascus and Homs, where they piled into cramped, substandard housing. The government's lack of response to the distress of its people angered many farmers and fueled the flames of a much larger sense of revolt. Added to decades of political instability, religious tensions, years of dictatorship, and a context of ongoing revolutions in Arab countries, this drought contributed to the crisis in the country today. Several American studies tend to corroborate the view that climate change was a contributing factor, for example: Mark Zastrow, "Climate Change Implicated in Current Syrian Conflict," *Nature* (March 2, 2015), www.nature.com/news/climate-change-implicated-in-current-syrian-conflict-1.17027.
2. For example, Jean Ziegler's *L'Empire de la honte* (Paris: Fayard, 2007).

Interview with Lester Brown

LESTER: We cannot continue down this path much longer, for several reasons. First of all, we are cutting down trees faster than they can grow and we are overgrazing grazed lands, which are slowly turning into deserts, creating dust bowls in Africa, the Middle East, and in many other regions of the world. We're looking at soil erosion now on an unprecedented scale. To give you a concrete example: the United States has nine million sheep and goats. China has 282 million and they're destroying all the vegetation, creating a huge dust bowl in Western China.

Meanwhile, we're also overpumping the aquifers nearly everywhere. The big story with water is India, where you do not need a license to drill. There are now nearly 26 million irrigation wells in the country, operating nonstop. And they're starting to go dry. This excessive overpumping has contributed to an increase in the grain harvest in recent years, in order to feed 190 million people. In China, 120 million people depend on overpumping of the aquifer for food. But by definition, overpumping cannot be continued indefinitely. A water shortage for farming and for food has started to appear in these regions.

We're also running into another problem, which is the limit of photosynthesis. I have on my desk a folder with graphs of worldwide grain production. Rice in Japan: seventeen years ago, yields stopped rising and they've been flat ever since. In China, the world's largest rice producer by far, production has only grown by 4 percent and is going to plateau soon. In France, wheat yields have been flat for the last fifteen years, and the same it true for Germany and the UK. In the United States, it now looks as though the corn yields are starting to plateau.

A fourth trend, which is much less predictable, is climate change. We know that with a 33.8° Fahrenheit rise in temperature, we can expect a 17 percent decline in grain yields. These figures come from a large research project at Stanford University, involving six hundred counties in the United States, so this is not hypothetical. So the unfortunate reality is that the (widely optimistic) projections by international institutions of the world's production are made by agricultural economists. They just take the figures from the last twenty years and extrapolate into the future. They don't understand that we have reached certain limits.

All these factors will make it much more difficult to expand food production. Yet we will definitely need to. We're adding 80 million people to the planet a year. That means there will be 219,000 people at the dinner table tonight who weren't there last night. And at least as many again tomorrow. The other thing is that there are three billion people in the world who are moving up the food chain. In India, the annual grain consumption per person is about 400 pounds, or roughly one pound per day. When you only have one pound of grain per day, you can't convert much of it into animal protein. You consume it directly. In the United States, we consume 1.6 pounds, four times as much, about ½ pound in bread, breakfast cereals, and pastry, and the rest in the form of meat, milk, and eggs. This is the standard that the Chinese, Indians, and Africans want to achieve. But it's not going to be possible. We won't have enough resources. The indicator that tells us more about our future than any other is the world price of grain, which has doubled since 2007. And I think it's going to continue to rise. We have to do the opposite and encourage a billion people who consume the most resources to shift to a less meat-based diet. And eliminate the use of ethanol, which takes up 30 percent of our grain harvest in the United States. We're losing too much land now, either because of soil erosion and dust storms, or because of industrialization and urbanization. Added to all the other factors we have discussed, this puts us in a dramatic and unprecedented new situation. For the first time in history that I'm aware of, low-income families in Nigeria,

India, and Peru are beginning to routinely schedule foodless days. A family will get together on Sunday evening and say: "Well, this week, we will not eat on Wednesday and Saturday." Because they literally cannot afford to eat every day. If the price of grain doubles in France or the United States, it doesn't really affect us very much, but in these countries, the impact is immediate and massive.

We are talking about 24 percent of Nigerian families, 22 percent of Indian families, and 14 percent of Peruvian families. I've been tracking world agriculture for fifty years and when things got tight, people would cut down to one meal a day. But entire foodless days? This is the first time I've ever see anything like this.

CYRIL: Where is all this taking us?

LESTER: My guess is that the situation will begin to translate into political instability. And that instability itself will become disruptive.

CYRIL: You have been working with political leaders for nearly fifty years—we can see a lot of them on the photographs hanging on your walls—but why don't they react?

LESTER: The surprising thing is that most of them know and understand what's happening. What they don't know is what to do about it. We're talking about major changes to society. How do you get people to change their behaviors before they are convinced there's a problem? I prefer not to change if I can avoid it. I think most of us do. But the reality is we're going to have to change whether we want to or not. And the question is: can we change soon enough to avoid the system beginning to break down? We study earlier civilizations and more often than not, their decline was associated with a disruption in their food supply. The Sumerians, for example, 6,000 years ago: their extremely efficient, ingenious irrigation system involved digging canals to divert water from the river to the land. But over time, some of the water percolated downward and the water table rose close to the surface and starting evaporating, but the salt contained in the water accumulated on the surface and changed the soil composition. As the soil became more and more salty, the yields started to come down, without the Sumerians fully understanding what was happening. With the Mayans in Central America, it was apparently deforestation and soil erosion that caused a drop in food production. They couldn't stop it, and the area where the Mayan civilization once flourished returned to a jungle a long time ago.

The difference today is that for the first time in history, it's our global civilization that's at stake. We can't separate us from the rest of the world. The US and China are in the same boat, and we're going to have to respond to these challenges together. No country on its own can stabilize the climate. So like it or not, we're now suddenly in a situation where our future depends on working together, on a scale that we've not done before.

CYRIL: If we can see all these disasters about to happen, why aren't we doing something? It's incomprehensible.

LESTER: There's a French riddle that's used to teach schoolchildren about exponential growth: You have a lily pond that has one leaf on the first day and the number of leaves doubles each day; if you know the pond will be full on the thirtieth day, when is it half full? The answer: the twentieth day. So for twenty-nine days, we can go along feeling pretty okay, and then suddenly on the last day, everything changes. That's a metaphor for our world. We've been expanding the economy very fast over the last couple of centuries and some of us think we can continue indefinitely. But it's impossible.

CYRIL: Do you think we can achieve this in time, or are you resigned and scared about what's ahead?

LESTER: I think we should all be a little scared, but I do think we can change quickly. I remember World War II, for example. After the attack on Pearl Harbor, the United States suddenly found itself at war. We hadn't planned on it, but President Roosevelt laid out production goals: "We're going to produce sixty thousand planes, forty thousand tanks." Huge numbers! People couldn't relate to these numbers. But Roosevelt simply changed priorities. And overnight, he banned the sale of new cars in the United States. Period. The automobile companies realized that if they wanted to stay in business, they would have to convert their assembly lines to start producing tanks, or even planes. I was just in Detroit, near the former Ford plant, and I remember seeing film footage of when the bombers, the B24s and B29s, were coming off the lines. We totally restructured the US industrial economy, not in decades, not in years, but in a matter of months. If we could do that then, then certainly we can make the changes quickly enough now to keep climate change from spiraling out of control. But we need a Pearl Harbor. Will it be a drought and a huge crop failure? Will it be more destructive storms that endanger major coastal cities in the world? It's impossible to predict. The only thing we know is that we cannot continue down this same path. At some point, we will have to change direction.

Mélanie and Cyril.

1

FOOD FOR THE SURVIVAL OF THE SPECIES

Food is therefore the first problem to be solved. Overpopulation, overuse of resources, and the destruction of nature are converging in a direction that could result in the disappearance of many of us. The basic question is this: "How to feed more than ten billion people while regenerating ecosystems and stopping climate change?"

People across the board have been working on this issue for many years. And they have provided answers that fall into one of two categories: the industrial solutions, which aim to develop even more efficient and standardized technology that can be implemented rapidly over the entire planet; and more holistic solutions, which attempt to understand the mechanisms and the ways of thinking that led us to our current situation, and what new vision of the world can lead us out of it.

The industrial response generally comes from centralized institutions: governments, agribusiness, multinationals. The website of Monsanto, the world leader in the sale of genetically modified seeds and agrichemicals (pesticides, herbicides, fertilizers, and so on), states: "Increasing world population and demand for food means that agriculture will have to expand production by 70 percent by the year 2050 ... In this context, meeting the demand for food will force the world's farmers to face the following dilemma: either produce a greater yield per acre or expand the use of cultivated land ... By increasing yield per acre, genetically modified crops can help to reduce damage and even the disappearance of biodiverse zones."[1]

Reading these lines, you might think that environmental activists, scientists, and one of the world's most highly criticized multinational share the same viewpoint. What they don't share, however, are the same solutions. The website's "Products" menu,

1. Quote translated from the French site: "Les OGM nuisent à la biodiversité !" www.monsanto.com/global/fr/actualites/pages/les-ogm-nuisent-a-la-biodiversite.aspx.

which includes Roundup—a product that has just been listed as a "probable human carcinogen" by the World Health Organization (WHO)—features this text: "In a context of a growing world population and less available arable land, the strategic path is to maintain high crop yields; weed control products[1] play an essential role in farming, because without them, crop yields would fall from 60 to 80 percent (depending in the specific crop variety)."[2]

The idea goes something like this: to produce an abundant amount of cheap and supposedly healthy food (although this argument remains somewhat obscure given the strong suspicions concerning the harmful impact of numerous pesticides and herbicides like Roundup[3]), we absolutely must have improved seeds and chemical products that gain control over and fight against nature (insects, mushrooms, uncontrollable weeds). This way of looking at farming spread through the West after World War II, in the wake of massive industrialization.

Those who support a holistic response, however, believe that this type of farming is exactly what will gradually destroy our ecosystems and create the opposite result: an inability to feed all of humanity.

So, which is it? To get to the bottom of all this, we went to Brussels to meet Olivier de Schutter, United Nations Special Rapporteur on the Right to Food from 2008 to 2014. Olivier is a precise, thoughtful man, who wants to examine the overall problem, while avoiding casting blame on one side or the other. Before taking on this job, he taught international and European law at the Université de Louvain-la-Neuve in Belgium and the College

1. Pesticides, herbicides, fungicides, etc.
2. Quote translated from the French site: "Les produits de protection des cultures," www.monsanto.com/global/fr/produits/pages/les-produits-de-protection-des-cultures.aspx.
3. According to the French Institut National du Cancer, "strong suspicions exist as to the role of pesticides in the development of chronic pathologies (cancers, neurological disorders, reproductive disorders), notably for those using them in a professional capacity, which concerns one to two million people in France."

of Europe in Poland (where he continues to teach). He was also a guest professor at New York University and at Columbia University in New York. From 2002 to 2006, he coordinated the EU Network of Independent Experts on Fundamental Rights, and from 2004 to 2008, was General Secretary of the International Federation for Human Rights—not exactly the career path of a wild-eyed environmental activist.

1. Background–Interview with Olivier De Schutter

OLIVIER: Since the 1950s and 1960s, there has been a dominant narrative about farming, which goes like this: farming was struggling, amid concerns that it would be unable to meet the rising demand, unable to follow demographic growth. Production therefore had to be increased at all costs. Yet this narrative no longer applies in the twenty-first century: we now know just how much this high-yield approach contributed to rural poverty and increased pressure on resources. We see that it aggravated health problems linked to poor-quality food—because we promote quantity over quality. We must absolutely create a new narrative, taking into account the various missions that farming must fulfill and the constraints it must deal with, which are no longer those of the 1950s and 1960s.

CYRIL: What do you mean by a high-yield approach?

OLIVIER: It's a type of farming that aims to maximize the number of crops per acre, notably through the use of mechanization (tractors, harvesters, and so on), inputs (chemical fertilizers, pesticides, improved seeds), and massive irrigation. This agricultural method is the dominant model in our developed regions and is expanding to many developing countries.

CYRIL: Why do you say that we can no longer continue down this path?

OLIVIER: I believe that it is problematic for many reasons, notably environmental ones. First of all, men and women were replaced by machines, which in industrialized countries led to a major migration to cities and population decline in rural areas in the space of fifty years. And this same phenomenon is taking place at an even faster pace in developing nations.

Second, our farms produce cheap, but poor quality, calories. We have promoted rice, wheat, potatoes, soy. To achieve a more balanced, healthier food supply, we would need much more diversity.

Finally, this type of farming destroys ecosystems, by reducing biodiversity, depleting the soil through monoculture, and polluting the land and the water tables through the excessive use of chemical additives.

CYRIL: What will happen, if we continue in this direction?

OLIVIER: We have a paradoxical situation, where the fear of not producing enough to meet an increasing demand tends to encourage dead-end solutions. In the short-term, we insist on the need to increase production, even though we know that in the long-term we are destroying the ecosystems on which we depend. If we continue in this direction, we are going to have to increasingly offset the negative impact of agriculture.

CYRIL: In other words, use more and more fertilizers and pesticides so that the soil continues to produce?

OLIVIER: As we deplete the living matter from soil, we need to compensate by adding nitrogen-rich fertilizers, and even that is no longer enough to maintain productivity, which in many industrialized regions is declining. We are in a downward spiral; agriculture's dependence on gas and oil is increasing, and soils are less and less able to produce without these external inputs.

CYRIL: But oil is becoming increasingly scarce and more expensive, and it is contributing to climate change. So it can't work.

OLIVIER: This is why we have to change our course. The biggest problem is to break up the system to achieve change. What strikes me is that governments and scientists are unanimous is their recognition that the current system does not function and yet alternatives are very slow to emerge.

CYRIL: Why?

OLIVIER: There are at least four obstacles making the transition difficult. First of all, the economic barriers. The prices consumers see are false. Industrial farming does not pass on the considerable costs it incurs for the collectivity in terms of population decline in rural areas, depletion of the soil, greenhouse gas emissions, water pollution, and health costs. If it was forced to bill for these costs, food would be more expensive. And industrial farming would no longer be at all competitive.

The second barrier in sociotechnical. All the major infrastructures dealing with the transportation, storage, and transformation of raw agricultural commodities are designed for and by the agribusiness sector. To sell their products, small farmers, who practice a production model that is much more sustainable for the environment, therefore have to work with those who dominate the system. They are therefore deprived of a great deal of the value of what they produce.

CYRIL: And the third barrier?

OLIVIER: This one is cultural. We have gotten used to depending on highly processed food. People have less time to cook, to eat together as a family. Which means that our food is exactly what the industry wants to offer. This is a very difficult obstacle to overcome. To achieve a revolution in farming, we need to rethink food as an aspect of our culture and rethink our lifestyles. Spend more time cooking, preparing fresh food, maintaining a connection with producers.

And finally, the fourth obstacle is political. During my term of office, from 2008 to 2014, I was struck by the fact that many of the decisions taken by governments are not done so with the interest of their populations in mind. They are largely determined by the expectations of the agribusiness industry, because our governments are focused on their goal of increasing the Gross Domestic Product (GDP) per capita and on economic growth. Yet it is the major agro-industrial firms that receive the technological revenues and dictate to governments the policies that they must follow, whether it concerns international trade or agriculture. This is a major democratic issue. In my opinion, democracy is not defined by the fact of being able to vote every four or five years, it must be able to examine everyday life, to reinvent the systems we live by and not leave all this in the hands of the lobbies that influence politicians.

CYRIL: Who are these lobbies?

OLIVIER: The current system benefits many actors: the huge agribusinesses, the major grain producers, companies supplying inputs, agrochemical firms that are now partnered with the major seed producers to supply farmers with complete kits. All these stakeholders have a self-interest in maintaining the status quo to keep their dominant position. They have a disproportionate amount of influence among politicians.

CYRIL: What exactly happens in international negotiations? Do they propose the measures that governments should adopt?

OLIVIER: Yes, and these international negotiations are a sort of blind spot in our democratic systems. The way they take place, often behind closed doors, hidden from public view, deprives citizens of their ability to influence the decision-making process, and also means that elected officials do not have to be accountable to their populations. When a treaty is finally concluded after months or even years of negotiations, the parliaments basically have no other choice than to approve it; otherwise, the years of work accomplished by the negotiators would have been useless.

CYRIL: What is the way forward, what were the recommendations in the report you submitted at the end of your term in office?

OLIVIER: There is a new story to write about farming, and it requires first and foremost a relocalization of food-producing systems. Policies should be less sector-based (policies concerning labor, agriculture, education) and more oriented around territories. This means creating stronger connections among producers and consumers, having greater diversity within each region, so that territories can, as much as possible, meet their own needs. This improves resilience to external events and helps local populations take control of the food-producing systems on which they depend. Farming has been pushed in the opposite direction for the last fifty years. Supply chains are growing longer and longer, international markets remain the overriding obsession for governments, companies have grown larger and more concentrated. We should move toward a decentralization and relocalization of agriculture.

CYRIL: Why is it so important for territories to produce their own food?

OLIVIER: Regions that depend on food imports and exports as a source of revenue are vulnerable to external events: climate change, greater volatility in response to the price of energy or raw materials on financial markets, geopolitical upheavals that are hard to predict. Resilience requires a greater capacity to meet one's own needs. This obviously does not mean total self-sufficiency. But it does mean this: reducing dependency on international markets and prioritizing local and regional markets. It's also important for agronomical reasons. In regions that produce only a single crop (as with soy, for example, in Argentina and Brazil), the soils are becoming depleted, they are not regenerating or at least much less than where polyculture and crop rotation are practiced.

CYRIL: Do we also have to return to more natural methods of farming, as you discuss? We have been told for years that stopping the use of chemical fertilizers and pesticides would lead straight to famine.

OLIVIER: We have to separate the transition costs from the long-term solutions. We are now highly dependent on inputs. In the short-term, breaking this dependence on gas and oil would indeed be difficult; a transition would take several years. But in the long term, with peak oil and gas, along with climate change, we don't have a choice. Solutions exist, but they have not been sufficiently explained to farmers, nor are they sufficiently understood by the public at large. They involve replacing pesticides by planting companion crops that repel insect pests, or fertilizing the soil by growing beans, which capture nitrogen from the air and fix it in the ground, or through agroforestry.

CYRIL: If we used these solutions, would we be able to feed all of humanity?

OLIVIER: We are absolutely able to feed everyone using agroecological techniques, which are not—and I have to stress this point—a return to traditional farming. This does not mean shifting from a high-yield system with extensive use of input to a low-yield system. We are not talking about refusing technical progress. Agroecology is the farming of the future, of the twenty-first century. It is a conscious approach to farming, which we must achieve for a more efficient use of resources—land, water, biomass—and which aims to provide a buffer against increased volatility in the price of fossil fuels.

CYRIL: Do statistical studies exist in support of this?

OLIVIER: There are different ways of calculating productivity: studies measuring productivity very often look at it in terms of a single commodity, for example, the tons of corn, wheat, or rice grown per acre. And from this viewpoint, agroecology loses out because it does not produce only corn or rice on an acre, but incorporates a diversity of combined crops. If we factor in this different way of calculating yield, we see the agroecological systems can be extremely productive.

CYRIL: Is this the message you communicated during your term in office?

OLIVIER: Yes, I wanted to answer a very simple question: Can agroecology feed the world? And my answer came in the form of a report to the UN Human Rights Council in March 2011. And my answer was clearly positive. We have a very large number of studies, conducted in many different countries, which show that wherever agroecology has been implemented, wherever farmers have received adequate training and adopted good practices, they can double their yields per acre. Of course, what works in one region will not work in another one, as agroecology is a science that depends on local resources. It cannot be imposed from the outside by technocrats; it is shared from one person to another, laterally. Multiple studies show that small plots of land incorporating diversified farming practices are more productive per acre than large monocropped areas—which are extremely impressive because they provide huge volumes, but are not, in fact, the best way to use the rare resources that we have.

CYRIL: Does this mean that small farmers are better able to feed humanity?

OLIVIER: In the world today, on the one hand, we have a small number of farmers who cultivate huge surface areas using sophisticated, mechanized production tools: these are the most visible farmers, because they supply the international markets and agribusinesses. And one the other, there is a huge mass of small farmers who have five to seven acres in West Africa, twenty-five to fifty acres in Brazil, essentially for local markets, without being concerned about changes in the world markets, which they don't depend on. Agriculture as practiced by small farmers is important for the development of rural areas, for the reduction of poverty in these areas, so the local populations can have access to diversified food production, and to maintain ecosystems, as these farmers generally practice a type of agriculture that does not deplete the soil as much—it does not require massive irrigation, for example, which can destroy environments. It is a type of farming that deserves our support, but which is threatened, because the industrial farmers are more competitive and control the markets; they bring prices down and put small farmers out of business. This then results in a mass migration to cities. The tragedy of farming is that we have not recognized this plurality and that public authorities have overwhelmingly supported the industrial farmers, while neglecting the small farmers.

CYRIL: What is the proportion between the two?

OLIVIER: We generally estimate about 10 percent of farms practice industrial farming, on 250 acres or more. And the remaining 90 percent grow their crops on much smaller plots. This second type of farming includes 1.1 billion people around the world. According to some higher figures, up to two billion people may depend on family-run farms.

CYRIL: But can we really say that the bulk of food in the world is produced by small farmers?

OLIVIER: A large share of the volume produced by small farmers is never included in national figures, because they are goods that people produce and consume themselves or that they produce for their village or community. Nevertheless, we estimate that 70 to 75 percent of our food comes from them. They supply a very large share of what we eat. The intensive farmers can produce large volumes of raw commodities, but only a part of it concerns food. The rest is often used to feed livestock (notably most of the soy grown throughout the world) or is increasingly used as agroenergy, notably as biofuel.

CYRIL: That's interesting. So the farmers who produce the least amount of food receive most of the subsidies, while those who produce 75 percent of what we eat receive the least?

OLIVIER: These small farmers are generally the neglected by public policies. This is because they are less able to create economies of scale than large farmers and sell products at a low cost on the markets. What do governments want? Governments want to keep social peace by ensuring that households spend as little as possible on food. In the EU, for example, families spend an average of 12 to 13 percent of their budget on food. Tomorrow, if families had to pay the actual cost of the food they eat, forcing them to pay the social, environmental, and public health costs of the current industrial farming system, we'd have to raise that budget to 25 or 30 percent to feed ourselves. And that would be politically intolerable.

CYRIL: What's the solution?

OLIVIER: After working for six years, traveling around the world, and drawing up reports on the right to food, I have come to realize that the transition must start at the bottom. For too long, we have counted on public policies, on governments to effect change. What will drive change is the social innovations brought by individuals, where small farmers partner with consumers and local authorities to invent new ways of producing and consuming. The role of governments must be to support this transition, without imposing it from the top down. It's important to have adequate economic incentives and regulations, but it must be up to the citizens to decide what kind of food-production system they want to have. I believe that this is where our hope lies. This is why I am extremely interested in the transition movements, which call for us to develop another concept of democracy. True democracy involves a decentralization of solutions, rewarding inventiveness at the local level. This is the direction we must take to reconstruct our food-producing systems.

2. Relocalizing production:
The urban farming adventure

Detroit

The city was as deserted as people had described to us. Around Detroit's downtown area, a few buildings overlooked roads twice as wide as any boulevard in France, with no more than a few dozen cars on them. The most modern of them were still brand new. The headquarters of General Motors looked liked Fort Knox in the middle of an abandoned cityscape. As we explored the city further, other more beautiful buildings appeared, dating from the golden age of American architecture. Each small square of golden light from the windows gave them a reassuring look. Others were hopelessly dark. As we got closer, we noticed that the facades were cracked, bleak, completely dark. The hundreds of broken windows looked like black holes, creating a disturbing picture, a ghastly and compelling vision of diminished splendor. A few people wandered around the squares below them, sometimes joined by a handful of "disaster tourists," dragging along their wheeled suitcases. On the outskirts, what was once a typical American suburb, with long stretches of lawn and lovely homes surrounded by hundred-year-old trees, was now nothing more than a field of rubble in places. Every other house had been abandoned, vandalized, and sometimes even burned to the ground. On Halloween, a few adolescents had started lighting fires for fun in the empty homes, most of which were built of wood. Sometimes they didn't even wait for the inhabitants to leave, setting fires in the middle of the night, while everyone was sleeping, forcing those who had been their neighbors to leave this devastated place for good—and where they didn't even have any work anymore—packing up their belongings in old cars, purchased during Detroit's gilded age. Some owners took it upon themselves to deliberately set fire to their homes,

in the hopes of getting some money, however little, from insurance. Here and there, neighborhood buildings were regularly collapsing. Inside the community church looked like it had been hit by a hurricane: benches overturned, walls destroyed, prayer books abandoned in the midst of rubble, and old VHS cassettes. The magnificent, imposing train station, built in 1913, which stood in the middle of an absurd no-man's land, along with the hospital, school, and theater whose stage had collapsed, had all suffered the same fate. Half-horrified, half-fascinated, we wandered through the city, stopping from time to time to film inside a few buildings. We sometimes tried to talk with neighborhood residents who were willing to open up to us, while we were ashamed to be gawking at them like animals at a county fair, our brand-new equipment in hand, our huge rental pickup truck parked on the street corner.

People had told us about the gardens, about the men and women who were working to bring Detroit back to life through farming. But so far, we hadn't see any of it. We had a few addresses to check out, we could have looked them up, but some part of us was waiting for a eureka moment about the spectacular revolution we thought was happening. A fantasy waiting to happen. This scenario was repeated with every trip, but not once did we experience this Hollywood moment. We always had to be patient, meet people, explore, scratch below the surface before we could discover the power of the people and the places.

In Detroit, we first had to meet Tepfirah Rushdan, who we called Tepper for a long time, while her friends knew her simply as T. She met us in a small park, Lafayette Greens, on Lafayette Street. Tepper is the Director of Urban Agriculture for The Greening of Detroit. When she joined the non-profit, she wanted to learn how to grow vegetables, but most of all, she saw it as an extraordinary way to reconstruct communities, so that all the residents—who were mostly poor and African-American (83 percent of the population)—could be proud of producing something with their own hands and help reconstruct the city. From 1950 to the present, the former automobile capital of the world has lost more than half of its residents. The population dropped from two million to around seven hundred thousand. Several events contributed to Detroit's decline: the riots in the 1960s that triggered a first exodus, but most of all the collapse of what was essentially an economic and industrial monoculture. The entire population depended on a single industry for jobs and prosperity. When the global market developed, free trade meant that vehicles from abroad could be imported to American; they were often more reliable and less expensive, with the result that multiple factories were forced to close. The white middle class left the downtown area for the suburbs, then the suburbs for other towns. Tax revenue fell dramatically, while the city's maintenance needs remained the same. Spiraling debt and mismanagement finally toppled the city into bankruptcy. And, as Trish Hubbel, Community and Public Relations Director at The Greening of Detroit, told us, it became almost impossible for people to find fresh produce. The combination of a vanishing purchasing power and shuttered supermarkets left residents with few solutions other than junk food. And while hunger threatens nearly one billion people in the world, the debilitating effects of obesity affect nearly 1.5 billion. In the United States, where 34 percent of the population is obese, the health system spends 160 billion dollars annually to treat the multiple health issues linked to excess weight; it is now the cause of death for hundreds of thousands of people (2.8 million men and women in the world).[1] So Trish, Tepper, and the dozens of staff members of Greening of Detroit set up a program to promote urban agriculture in three places throughout the city, an education program in dozens of schools, and an ambitious tree-planting project. Since 1998, 14,000 children have learned how to grow fruits and vegetables, to eat healthy fresh food, and to take care of the land that provides them

1. http://www.who.int/features/factfiles/obesity/facts/en/index1.html. See also "Obesity and Overweight: Fact Sheet," World Health Organization, June 2016, http://www.who.int/mediacentre/factsheets/fs311/en.

with food. The young people of Detroit contributed 450,000 hours of community service, 89,000 trees were planted, 618 adults have been retrained to work in farming or "green" businesses, and 1,518 gardens (primarily in schools) were created or supported. The goal is to create a new culture in which everyone participates, to construct a healthy and resilient food-production system for all. At the Detroit Market Garden where we met Trish, in 2015 alone, almost seven tons of vegetables were grown in the four greenhouses and then sold to local markets and restaurants; 7,315 pounds of food were distributed to local organizations, and five adults received hands-on training in farm gardening. At the same time, since 2004, the organization has been coordinating the restoration of the 26-acre Romanowski Park, working with other community associations and neighborhood residents; the farm garden and orchard (apples and pears) produce food for the community.[1]

"After the bankruptcy and devastation of the city, we hit rock bottom. Today we are rising from our ashes, which really represents the unique spirit in Detroit. It's a resilient town," Trish tell us before we head out.

Waiting for us a few miles away is Shane Bernardo, a mainstay of Earthworks Urban Farm, a project supported by Capuchin friars. The son of Filipino parents, he was born in Detroit. He has been running this outreach program for several years. On 2.5 acres, the 6.5 tons of food produced is extremely diverse: fruits and vegetables (most of them unknown to most Americans), aromatic and medicinal herbs, and edible flowers. It is sold by the Grown in Detroit cooperative, used in the Capuchin Soup Kitchen that serves 2,000 meals a day to unemployed members of the community (Earthworks also has an agricultural training program), marketed in small

1. www.greeningofdetroit.com

One of the Keep Growing Detroit farms, in downtown Detroit.

farmers' markets and some health centers, and is processed and sold as jam to support the project. Like the Greening of Detroit and in most of the gardens we visited, everything is grown organically, which is particularly important to Shane: "One of my goals is to increase the amount of healthy food in our community, and to teach young people how to grow their food. I lost my father in 2010 due to his poor health: diabetes, obesity, heart condition. This is what inspired me to do this work. We are totally dependent on an industrialized system of food production that does not promote health or well-being. We must stop all this. Today, we need to starve the system that is starving us by doing without all these multinationals. In Detroit, we decided to reclaim the land, like a declaration of political independence, and to meet our essential needs by ourselves. The problem is not simply to make food available; we need to reclaim control over our food, over our social and political system, to become resilient and self-sufficient. Detroit is something of a Ground Zero of the global economic crisis. The devastation is similar to what New Orleans experienced with Hurricane Katrina. We endured it for many years. Today, we have had enough of waiting for someone to come take care of us. We can't just resist and react; we have to be creative if we want to build a world we want to live in. Because no one is going to come save us."

According to members of the urban agriculture movements, there are now nearly 1,600 farms and gardens in the city.[1] And 1,400 of them are maintained by the 20,000 volunteers of Keep Growing Detroit. Co-director Ashley Atkinson tells us that their mission is "to create a city with real food sovereignty, where most of the fruit and vegetables that citizens consume are grown within the city limits by Detroiters for Detroiters." More specifically, they aim to achieve a rate of 51 percent within ten years. Which means

1. This figure is hard to determine. Adding up the data from the various organizations, we actually came up with more than 3,000 farms and gardens.

a ten-fold increase over current production. But Ashley remains optimistic: "The hardest part is the initial 5 to 10 percent. We have more than forty square miles of vacant lots that we could cultivate. Studies were conducted to determine whether our goals were achievable, and they are!" To reach them, Keep Growing Detroit depends on everyone's willingness to create kitchen gardens or urban farms in individual gardens, schools, and parks. They provide the seeds, plants, and compost, and teach people how to farm. During these training sessions, they identify potential leaders, who are encouraged to participate actively in their own neighborhoods. They organize events to involve even more people and to create partnerships with local markets to make food available to everyone.

Eastern Market is the primary hub where producers and consumers meet up. The largest historic public market in a country where most of the markets have disappeared, it covers over five acres and has more than one hundred and fifty food-sellers. Paralleling the urban agriculture movement is a community of food entrepreneurs that transforms and sells what the farms produce. Among them, the Food Lab, with 147 businesses[1] that embrace the triple-bottom-line model. Instead of pursuing profits only, they operate their companies to meet three criteria: profit, people, planet. They all want to help revive independent businesses which, in addition to creating jobs, provide a sustainable and essential service to Detroiters. They include Devita, who helps set up commercial kitchens and teaches the basics of family cooking; Chloé, a young Frenchwoman who produces and distributes lava cakes; the Sisters on a Roll, who move around the city with their truck, bringing quality food (cooked on site) to the most isolated and disadvantage neighborhoods; Noam, with his Fresh Corner Café; and Tanya and her pancakes, biscuits, and vegan products. The philosophy, which promotes entrepreneurship as one of the most powerful models of social and ecological

1. July 3, 2015. There were only 84 when we visited one year earlier.

transformation, was inspired by BALLE, or the Business Alliance for Local Living Economies (see pp. 192–195). Jess, Director of Food Lab, is a member, as is Malik Yakini, Executive Director of D-Town Farm, a 7-acre organic urban farm in Rouge Park. He believes that the urban agriculture movement offers a tremendous potential for revitalizing the city and reconstructing communities (particularly by emancipating the African-American community, still subjugated by a white economic elite), but it will be not enough to feed Detroit. "Urban agriculture is the new sexy thing, but the way people look at it is often detached from the reality of the work that agriculture requires. I often tell people that urban farming sounds great on a PowerPoint presentation. But it won't replace rural agriculture. Urban and peri-urban areas and rural areas all need to be producing food. In the United States, food travels about 1,500 miles on average, from the place it's grown to where it's consumed. The impact on the environment is tremendous. We have to grow food closer to where people live and return to an earlier concept of the city, which can't be just a cluster of buildings, sidewalks, and shopping centers."

Hundreds of cities in North America are following Detroit's example by reintroducing agriculture among their buildings: New York with its 800 farms and gardens, Los Angeles, San Francisco, Washington, Saint Louis, Chicago, Boston, Seattle, Philadelphia, as well as Toronto, Ottawa, Montreal, and Vancouver. In all, nearly 20,000 community-run plots are maintained, along with the 43 million Americans who say they grow some of their own food.[1] Europe is not far behind, as we shall soon see.

We have left Detroit. This is our third airplane in just a few days. Since we left France, I feel as if I've spent my life in airport terminals. Our days are organized around cars, buses, subways, and airplanes. Constantly driven by an energy that is external to us. Right

1. Bénédicte Manier, *Un million de révolutions tranquilles* (Paris: Éditions Les Liens qui Libèrent, 2012), p. 118.

now we are flying over Lake Michigan, and I realize the we have seen virtually nothing of the place we just visited. Guided by our smartphones and our GPS devices, not once did we unfold a map that would have given us an idea of where we were in a larger context. If so many Americans live this way, how will it be possible to get across any type of message on the fragility of our ecosystems? I look at the businesspeople around me, glued to their computers. One of them pulls down the shade that lets the sun stream in. They take airplanes like we would catch a train. Flying at an altitude of 16,000 feet is no big deal anymore. Yet 80 percent of the people in the world have never set foot in an airplane. And perhaps never will. Here, the space is virtualized; we have removed ourselves from a natural environment to travel from air-conditioned box to air-conditioned box, in an orgy of prepackaged, over-sweetened, over-salted food, packed into clean, smooth shelves. Below us, a fleecy-looking ocean stretches as far as the eye can see. Billions of water molecules bound together to form one of the most poetic forms in existence. We will soon land and repeat our loading and unloading maneuvers; we will march down new sterile-looking corridors in new airports. I miss walking, I miss nature. And I wonder how much longer it will take before this feeling weakens, dissipates, perhaps even disappears.

Todmorden

Todmorden is a town in Yorkshire that, despite its small size (population: 14,000), has much in common with Detroit. Like it's larger sister, it is a single-industry city: textiles. It, too, was hit hard by deindustrialization. Unemployment is nearly double the national average (although it doesn't come close to Detroit, which posts nearly 40 percent unemployment), and as in Detroit, food was at the heart of a movement that transformed the town.

It all began with an initiative by two local women, "ordinary folks" as they like to call themselves: Pam and Mary. Pam Warhust is thin, with short dark bobbed hair, a bit blunt. She wears jeans, contemporary glasses, speaks with a clear, strong voice. And a thick accent. She is articulate and seems to be at ease speaking in public. She appears to be very well read, like those kids of middle-class teachers who have instilled in them the idea that knowledge is the greatest source of wealth. I imagine her parents were like that. Later, we would learn that they were working-class, activists, and that they grew up with the stories of the major union battles from the early twentieth century. She now runs their—cooperative—establishment, the Bear Café. And is in the process of handing over everyday operations to her daughter. Mary Clear is nearly her opposite, at least from our first impression. A bit stout, graying, decked out in flowery shirts, headbands, and baggy jeans, perfect for gardening. Her eyes are the color of the sea, steeped in an impressive humanity. Pam shakes your hand, while Marie wraps you up in a huge hug the first time you meet. Pam discusses, Marie gets carried away, laughs, nods her approval, moves you to tears—and waits until Pam, who seems to consider herself the smarter of the two finishes speaking, to put in her two cents, ready to offer a completely different opinion. They are both in their fifties and spend a good part of the conversation joking around. They have great senses of humor, and it's a lot of fun. Sitting in the Bear Café, they tell us how it all began.

"About seven years ago," starts Pam, "I was at a conference, and people were talking about the state of the planet, climate change, how we were overusing resources, and I thought, I've heard people talk about this for a long time, but I've never heard about anyone doing anything about it."

This conference took place in London and brought together representatives from boroughs around the country. Pam came from the borough of Calderdale, which includes Todmorden. She would later say that it was two sentences by Tim Land, professor of food policy at

City University, that triggered everything. The man was droning on about climate change and she felt crushed by the figures, the challenges. She couldn't concentrate on what he was saying. It was all horribly abstract, as usual. Until Tom explained that he had started out as a cattle-breeder and began to tell the audience that this type of livestock raising absolutely had to be stopped. A few minutes later, he added: "Stop growing flowers; grow vegetables instead."

Pam went home feeling ebullient, thinking that the time had come to act, that she could no longer wait, listening to men in suits natter on at conferences. There had to be something simple, powerful, within everyone's reach. She had an idea, which she immediately shared with Mary, a community coordinator for the town, and "the best networker in the entire world." In just a few days they drew up what would become an international movement: Incredible Edibles.

Their idea was simple: to encourage neighborhood residents to plant fruit and vegetables all over town, to work together and share the harvest, free of charge. As Pam explained: "Food is something that concerns all of us, we talk about it, we buy it, we like it, or don't like it. It is one of the rare things you can have a conversation about with a perfect stranger."

The second principle of what would become the Incredible Edible spirit was the idea that they would not wait for anyone's authorization before starting to act: "I had been in politics and I had had enough of all the reports suggesting ideas, committees, votes that triggered new reports, strategy documents, and so on and so forth. All that is just hot air. If we are really concerned about our children, we have to act differently. And no longer wait for other people to do things for us."

Pam and Mary decided to invite anyone who was interested to the Bear Café, to discuss a couple questions: "Do you want to have a great future for your kids, do you want to think about food?" They thought that if five people came, it would be a success. But sixty local residents showed up that evening, crowding into the upstairs room.

"We told them about our idea," said Pam. "When we stopped, there was a two-second silence and then the room erupted. Everyone started talking at once. People had come with photographs from World War II, when the city was full of fruit trees and gardens. There's nothing unique about what we were proposing, we weren't trying to show off. We simply asked them: 'Do you remember what we are capable of doing? Of all that we have done in the past and that we can draw on for the future?' Then every one of the sixty people started talking, telling their own stories, everywhere. Because what we know how to do best is to tell stories. That's what touches people, what makes a difference."

A few days later, a first experiment took place in Mary's garden, which runs along a small road at the base of a hill. They tore down the wall and transformed it into a public area. Mary and her husband pulled up the roses, planted kale, mint, lettuce, fennel, and the now-famous sign: "Help yourself." People passing by stopped, intrigued, and a few months later, a few finally dared to picked a few things, a raspberry or two.

"What was interesting was to take over the side of a very busy road that had become a dump, that nobody respected, without paying for it or asking permission. Mary had more seeds than she needed for a lifetime, and we planted them with the help of volunteers. Within one year, the town council had installed a public bench there so that people could enjoy the garden. And we didn't even ask them to do it. It's often better not to ask, especially of those in charge, because they usually think they have to say no. When in fact they feel so much better when they can decide on their own to get involved with something that moves them," says Pam with a smile.

The team of volunteers grew month after month, expanding and colonizing the town. "We selected certain places, smack in middle of streets, so that people could really see us," says Mary. The strategy was to create propaganda gardens, places where people would strike up conversations. These small, localized plots gradually transformed into garden streets, where entire sections became "edible landscapes." Nick Green, a PhD in biochemistry, is a former entrepreneur and current farmer; he is one of the architects behind the movement's success. Small, round, and sporting a full bushy beard, he speaks with a soft, nasal voice. With his hat, he looks like he could have stepped out of a Tolkien novel. But his most striking feature is the happiness that seems to radiate from within. A profound satisfaction that he is where he is supposed to be, doing what he's supposedly to be doing.

"At first I didn't go to the meetings. But someone said that I was 'the best gardener,' because I used to buy small fruit trees at the supermarket and wondered, where do I plant this? Someone told me that if I kept doing it, they would support me. So I kept doing it. Later, they told me that the group needed someone to organize the fund-raising activities. I was treasurer for four years; I went looking for money and the project grew. It turns out that it was the right thing to do at that time, the place to invest energy. This experience changed something in my mind. Today, I don't worry, I'm no longer concerned with the state of the world, with young people who don't know anything or with waste. Because I'm doing something positive. And all I do is think about the next positive thing to be done."

Under Nick's guidance, the residents started planting everywhere, in schoolyards, the gardens of the town hall, in front of the station, at the hospital (where a medicinal garden grows next to a line of red currents, which is next to the parking lot surrounded by cherry trees), the police station (with corn, zucchini, and artichokes), and even at an unemployment agency, where those looking for work can carry off tomatoes, zucchini, beets, apples, and onions. In seven years, more than one thousand fruit trees have been planted all throughout the town.

"Today, we use the trees to grow new ones: every year we get five to six hundred new trees from cuttings we take from the older ones. We give some away, sell others. In all, we have grown three to four thousand trees and planted one thousand. It's a tremendous investment for the future. And now that the trees are big, we have fruit for everyone. This summer I was able to walk from the hospital to the police station, eating cherries all the way."

Nick continued: "When we started, we didn't really know what we were doing, but three or four years down the road, we thought we needed to get serious about training young people, about producing food, and getting people involved in the land again."

The small crew knocked on a lot of doors and finally found a swampy plot of land ten minutes from the city center. Nick was enthusiastic about the project and started Incredible Farm, a social enterprise that teaches school kids and young adults how to farm, and novice farmers how to become more experienced; it is also a nursery for plants and provides food for the town's restaurants. In just a few years, Nick learned the principles of permaculture, boosted productivity, and trained hundreds of people. Like Malik in Detroit, the founders of Incredible Edibles believe that we must now create closer links between urban and rural spaces.

"The type of agriculture that we have today involves a minimum number of people and a maximum number of machines. Here we want the opposite: more jobs, more farms. The bulk of the world's food comes from tiny farmers and they are much more productive, they produce most of the world's food. While big industrial farmers are good at producing money. But it's not money that we need in the future, and it's not money that will keep us alive, it's food. And for that we have to let people own and farm the land," says Nick.

Incredible Farm produces the equivalent of 6.2 tons of food per acre, and Nick thinks they can do much better. Even so, they have managed to prove that even under difficult conditions, it's possible to harvest large quantities of food by using techniques adapted to a site's specific topographical and climate conditions, land that people

---

Nick Green on his Incredible Farm.

said was unsuitable for market gardening. Indeed, as an aside, most of the land around Todmorden is waterlogged. In July, when we were walking through the small streets of the town after two straight days of sunshine, I pulled Mary over to show her some plant looking a bit dried out and suggested that "it might be a good idea to water them." I was obviously thinking about the film and how the vegetables would look. She looked at me like she couldn't understand what I was saying. After pondering whether my question was for real or if perhaps she hadn't understood my rusty English, I ventured to say: "You never water?" This time, she smiled broadly: "No. It rains every day."

Hundreds of people have been trained at the Incredible Farm in just a few years and multiple networks formed. Butchers, bakers, and kitchen gardeners are once again offering local products for sale in the main square and the public marketplace. The town's restaurants have added them to their menus. Thanks to the propaganda gardens, and Pam and Mary's energy, the entire town now has a new story to tell, that of a small city in West Yorkshire that has reclaimed ownership of its food-producing system. The vegetable beds do not provide the bulk of the produce, far from it, but they were the trigger for a much large revitalization. Now, 83 percent of residents say they buy some of their food locally, in a country that produces less than 50 percent of what it consumes. But the most incredible was still to come.

While the small group had decided to move forward without consulting local authorities, it was then the officials who, as Pam had predicted, were contacting the residents. After the initial surprise, they began to talk with these oddballs who were colonizing the sidewalks. "We told them: 'We don't want your money, but later, if we need to, can we come and ask for your help?' And they agreed. Several years later, we were looking for farmland. We had taken small bits of land and street corners here and there, but we needed more. We wanted to show 15,000 people how they could feed themselves, think for themselves." The gardening fever swept through the administration. Robin Tuddenham, Director of Communities and Service Support for Calderdale, which includes Todmorden, took on the project and became an enthusiastic supporter. In a few weeks, all the vacant land and property zoned as unconstructible in the region of 200,000 inhabitants was inventoried in a database and put online. Any resident can get access to a plot of land for farming; they just have to provide a photo, submit a request, and pay a symbolic fee. The borough of Calderdale is so proud of this program that it is now trying to export it to other English regions. "This is not government land; it belongs to the people," insists Robin. "And we have to ensure that the population reclaims it. If local authorities don't get involved, we will always be facing the same situations: groups of activists doing their best, fighting and knocking on doors. Local governments need to talk to each other and convince the central government that this is the way of the future. Here, we work with an organization called Locality to promote this program around the entire country. Public services can no longer make all the decisions as they have done for the last forty years, with experts telling people what is best for them. We no longer have enough resources, enough time; the population is changing and people are living longer, wanting more, want to have more control over their lives. And they can do it! So why not see this as a solution rather than always as a problem?"

As Pam says, the Incredible Edibles movement "is a story that people seem to love, which speaks to their hearts and their minds." They love it so much that they are reproducing this model back in their own homes. Starting with England, where more than eighty towns have followed Todmorden's example. Then in France, where under the impetus of François Rouillay and Jean-Michel Herbillon, initiatives have been launched in more than four hundred towns and

Estelle and policeman Greg, in front of the precinct's planters.

villages. Niger, Australia, Russia, Argentina, Mexico, South Africa, Philippines—in all, more than eight hundred sites have adopted the model of shared food. Some are in the very early stages, but the seeds have been planted and the story is spreading, inevitably. Some call it Incredible Edibles, others don't, but according to Mary: "It makes absolutely no difference; the concept is not about making money, there is no empire to construct. Ordinary people want to do it, get together, learn new skills, and that's all that matters. We don't have the power or money of governments, but we have the power of good things on our side!"

Week after week, Estelle Brown, the tireless and charming guide for the town, hosts groups that come from around the world: India, Korea, United States, Morocco, Argentina. This year, three groups of Japanese came and have started "edible canals" modeled after the "edible green routes" in Yorkshire. According to Estelle: "It's not about growing food. Everyone can do that; it's easy. It's about building a community. Because when problems come, it's your ability to face them together, to share, and take care of each other that makes the difference."

And this is what happened in Todmorden, where the local food system has grown, where "garden tourism" has literally skyrocketed, and vandalism and aggressive acts of all kinds have dropped by 18 percent since the vegetable beds were set up. Which fills Pam with pride and hope for the future: "We had lost the ability to believe that we could change things. We sometimes seem to have forgotten that we actually created the system, the economy, finance, the social model. It is we who developed it all, believing that it was the best way to go. Today, we can see that our system is broken. Okay then, we'll construct another one! We have raised a generation of victims, people who feel that they have nothing to give, who don't know where to start so that their world becomes a better place. But if you start with the smallest things, food, they're not afraid. When people plant seeds in the garden behind their house or in middle of a street, and then this small act is added to all those of an entire community, so that people can come together and share, then confidence returns. And all these people start believing in themselves again. Feeling that they are capable of doing anything."

The Todmorden experiment seemed somewhat charmingly marginal when we visited this small town for the first time. But we had overlooked the power of the narrative, as discussed by Nancy Huston, and that of food. A power that had already proven itself in the past with the Victory Gardens, when in 1943 more than twenty million Americans produced 30 to 40 percent of the country's vegetables. In France, during a time of peace and abundance, individuals grow an estimated 7 percent. We were beginning to see the story of the twenty-first century that Olivier had discussed, that of a self-sufficient agriculture that regenerates ecosystems, which implies a reappropriation of the land by a large number of people. We still had to confirm the glowing promises of productivity discussed in the UN report and by Nick. For that, we traveled to Normandy to visit one of the most promising market gardening farms in the world.

3. Producing differently: The miracles of permaculture

If you wonder what farms of the future could look like, you should go see Charles and Perrine Hervé-Gruyer.[1] Visiting them is a transformative experience for anyone familiar with traditional market gardens. This is where I took Mélanie in September 2012, when she wanted to see what the society of tomorrow could look like. And it is without a doubt one of the places that most inspired us to

1. Dates and times of tours, events and courses available at www.fermedubec.com. See Perrine and Charles Hervé-Gruyer, *Miraculous Abundance* (White River Junction, Chelsea Green Publishing, 2016)

make this film. At first sight, Bec-Hellouin looks more like a garden than a farm. The various farmed areas are arranged in a multitude of shapes and colors, some in rows, others in circles, with ponds interspersed with meadows, mandala gardens, a greenhouse, and a small patch of forest. Nothing seems to be organized according to the practices of conventional agriculture. And yet each inch of growing space seems designed to perfection.

Like Nick (and Rob Hopkins, who you will hear from later), Charles and Perrine practice permaculture. Permaculture (short for "permanent cultures") is "a design system for human installations that are inspired from nature," in the words of Charles. It aims to recreate the extensive diversity and interdependence that exists in ecosystems. Each element is beneficial to the others and is nurtured by the overall environment. It is a circular model, which produces no waste. Permaculture can be applied to multiple sectors: cities (notably transitioning cities), companies, the economy, energy. Applied to agriculture, these principles incorporate the best practices developed by farmers over centuries from all over the planet (growing in raised beds and in layers, composting, the importance of trees, companion planting, animal traction) and all that the life sciences have taught us over the last fifty years. The goal is to reproduce the way nature works; it has persisted for millions of years, without oil, without tilling, without mechanization, while producing an abundance of life, in environments that are sometimes nutrient poor. By creating a very close relationship among the biotope, the plants, the insects, and the animals, permaculture will recreate profusion where once there was deficiency. As Charles says, "the results of permaculture means that we can imagine the future of human societies with an abundance of essential goods (but not gadgets), while excluding waste."

Over the years, farmers using permaculture techniques have tried to establish theories about this imitation of nature by formulating general principles, which they then constantly test out and expand. "One of the first operating principles of an ecosystem is diversity," explains Charles. So that in the densest areas of the farm, nearly one thousand different varieties are grown on just over two acres (the total surface area of the farm is slightly more than ten acres). Which is the exact opposite of the industrial approach, for which greater variety is an obstacle to the process of optimization. In addition, the land is never left bare, so that it can't be dried out by the sun or eroded by rain. The crops are therefore planted densely and the soil is always mulched (covered with straw, wood chips, or reeds, which retain water, protect the ground, and enrich it as they decompose). What permaculture farmers have also noticed is the incredible fertility of the soil in certain natural environments. To reproduce it, they implement several strategies. First of all, they help the soil recover an intense microbiological life (with lots of earthworms, bacteria, insects, all kinds of mushrooms that aerate the ground, giving it vitality, like the bacteria in our guts). To do so, they add compost and organic material (straw residue, for example), but they also use cover crops as green manure (for example, plants that help store nitrogen in the ground, like legumes) and trees. As Charles says, "practically all the arable land on the planet was created by forests. Tree roots provide organic matter to the subsoil, an environment for populations of mycorrhiza—small fungi that, in a symbiotic association with the roots, are important agents of fertility." Crops are therefore frequently grown among fruit trees, which can be arranged to provide shade and cooler temperatures for the plants below them. Charles and Perrine also pay special attention to the soil, which for them is "the foundation of all farming." And which modern agriculture tends to neglect, viewing it too often as a substrate on which to pour synthetic products. One of the most widely used techniques at Bec-Hellouin are raised beds—particularly rounded or "permanent" beds that are about three feet across and a dozen feet long. Most of the raised beds at Bec-Hellouin are also curved, forming magnificent mandala or circular shapes.

"It's a system as old as the world, used for thousands of years in China, Greece, by the Incans and the Mayans," explains Charles. "Once again, the idea is to imitate nature, where the soil is never tilled and never bare. We create a large mound of arable soil that we then avoid tilling. The bed is permanent. We obtain a highly fertile, very loose, deep soil, and we don't disturb the microorganisms. We plant our crops and protect them with a mulch that decomposes year after rich, enriching the soil." This means no more tilling, far less weeding (thanks to the mulch and because the seeds of the weeds buried deep are not brought to the surface), no erosion, less irrigation (the soil retains water better), soil that heats up faster, a surface that is never walked on and in which we can plant more densely, and therefore, achieve much higher productivity. "In the United States, the productivity of raised beds has been studied for forty-five years, notably by John Jeavons. The figures are spectacular: by improving the soil and planting more densely, farmers can produce six, seven, or eight times more on the same surface area. Up to thirty times more for certain crops. With the techniques that we are developing at Bec-Hellouin, where we incorporate different practices, we produce, on average, ten times more, taking into account all the crops."

Simple, ingenious hand tools are used for these different practices. Among them, the precision seeder, designed by one of the masters of permaculture: Eliot Coleman. It is used on flat beds, 32 inches wide, and can seed up to twenty-six rows of vegetables, where a tractor could only plant three. With intercropping. "We grow the way Paris market gardeners did in the nineteenth century: two, three, or four crops together. Which means we regularly have up to eight rotations, or eight crops per years in the same bed—while the average for organic farmers is something like 1.2 rotations. We aim for the maximum return on a very small space. If you think of 10 square feet where you will grow eight crops, that comes out to be the same as having 80 square feet. We have merely concentrated our work, the compost, irrigation, weeding. And ultimately, it's more efficient!"

Thanks to their incomparable expertise, the market gardeners had made Paris, with close to 1.8 million residents, self-sufficient in vegetables throughout the entire second half of the nineteenth century, and they were even able to export their products to England. The cultivated plots were about one acre, on average, with one worker per quarter acre and up to eight crop rotations per year—as opposed to one worker for multiple acres today, and far fewer rotations. In all, 1,500 acres were required to achieve this impressive level of production. To grow year-round, or nearly, they used another trick that Charles and Perrine soon adopted as well: hot beds. "It's an old technique that involves using the heat from fresh manure as it decomposes. You make a big square mound of manure, 20 to 24 inches high, and as early as the month of January, you have soil at 77 to 83° F degrees, naturally. This heat lasts about six weeks and is even better for starting plants. With a hot bed made early January, by the end of the month, we are already harvesting from it. On this one, we are now on our fifth or sixth crop of the year. And ultimately, what you have left is compost for the following season."

All these techniques are obviously linked together for optimal results, as in the greenhouse we visit with Perrine. "Here is a hot bed, but in the middle of summer. It's very humid, dense, rich, full of earthworms. My crops that ripen very early were able to use the heat from the decomposing manure in the middle of winter; and in spring, I have lots of organic material that retains moisture. So that the crops also never need to be watered. It's an exceptional technique. In this bed, we have one example of intercropping for summer crops: basil at the base of tomatoes. As tomatoes are creepers, they catch light from above. Basil is very happy in the shade. And neither one needs much water. Plus, since basil has such

---

Charles and Perrine, with crops from the vegetable beds.

a strong scent, it keeps away any pests that might latch on to the tomatoes. If we don't cut the basil and let it go to seed, we use it as a mulch; in other words, we cover the soil with it to hold in moisture and to create a permanent decomposition of organic material. The grape vine over the tomatoes forms a kind of screen, releasing humidity, which is good for the vegetables below, especially during a hot summer like this one. And the icing on the cake: we get grapes. So they all produce, but the purpose of each plant is not just to produce, it is also to play a role in the ecosystem. They all have several functions; that's what's great about permaculture."

A few dozen yards from the greenhouses, Charles takes us into the forest garden, "an imitation of a natural forest, but where all the plants are edible." As in a wild forest, the vegetation grows at several different layers, with the fruit trees at the top, and the berries and small fruit closer to the ground. "It's an environment that requires zero work, no fuel, no watering, no fertilizer. It's extremely economical! It produces a plethora of good fruit, and plus, it's a small oasis of biodiversity, totally autonomous, which stores carbon and creates soil. It always flourishes, every year, in good weather and bad, whether it's sunny or rainy."

The role of trees is crucial at Bec-Hellouin, for the reasons previously discussed, but also in terms of food security. For Charles, humanity made a mistake by basing its diet on annual plants (those that must be reseeded every year): "Currently, humans eat about twenty crops, and 60 percent of our diet is based on wheat, corn, and rice, which are all annual grains. Over the course of evolution, prehistoric humans thrived in nature, eating mostly fruit, berries, leaves, and roots: all perennial plants. Our organism is designed for this type of food. Our diet, which relies on grains, meat, and dairy products, isn't very good for our health or for the planet. Our range of food is decreasing, and this loss of diversity is extremely detrimental. Building a sustainable society requires greater use of fruit than of annual crops. Trees are sustainable: a plum, apple, or pear tree can live for fifty, seventy, maybe a hundred years. Once it's been planted, it will continue to bear fruit year after year."

By implementing all these practices and techniques, the small Bec-Hellouin farm achieves extraordinary yields without using a single drop of fuel or any agrochemical products.

To confirm the validity of these practices, Charles and Perrine initiated a three-year study in conjunction with the INRA[1] and AgroParis-Tech.[2] The results were made public in the spring of 2015; they confirm that it is possible to create a sustainable activity producing a decent income on a quarter of an acre. During the third year of the study, the farm achieved annual sales of €56,000, with a net monthly salary of approximately €2,000 (and even €2,500 in the upper range). These figures are similar to those obtained by our colleagues farming 2.5 acres, sometimes more. It demonstrates that by working entirely by hand on a small surface area, we can produce as much as with a tractor on an area ten times larger." This "performance" has launched a new approach to farming that Charles, Perrine, and many other permaculture farmers around the world are starting to see take hold. According to Charles: "We can imagine a society with micro-farms everywhere, in the city, at the edge of cities, which ensure real food security, which produce for local communities and which beautify the countryside. People who have small gardens of a few dozen square feet can become part-time farmers, at home, requiring virtually zero investment. It's a type of agriculture that is both economically profitable, offering market gardeners a better quality of life (people are working in the middle of a large garden), producing the high-quality products that are sought after by consumers and starred chefs, and helping to heal the Earth. Because it re-creates soil, it protects biodiversity and stores carbon. What's interesting about this approach is not just the idea

1. Institut National de la Recherche Agronomique.
2. École d'Agronomie de la Région Parisienne.

of miniaturizing everything. We have observed that by concentrating vegetable crops in a very small area, we can redesign territories. By producing on a quarter acre what is usually grown mechanically on 2.5 acres, we free up about 2.2 acres where it becomes possible to plant a few hundred trees, have animals, create a forest garden, beehives, a pond, and construct a house. A micro-farm can be created on 2.5 acres; it would be incredibly rich, a genuine micro-farm with a gratifying lifestyle, with enormous biodiversity. The farm produces its own fertility, as biomass is everywhere: in the trees, the hedges, the ponds, animal manure. It is a truly autonomous and resilient system. Currently, it takes 10 to 12 calories of fossil fuel to produce one calorie of food that reaches our plate. It's a total aberration; we know that tomorrow or soon down the line, fuel will be much more scarce and much more expensive, that we will no longer be able to transport food in the same way, that we will have even more climate disruptions. Yet I'm pretty sure that we'll all still need to eat. Inventing ways to feed ourselves without using fuel, and growing crops entirely manually is not a hare-brained dilettante idea. It's a vital necessity if we are to feed humanity in the future. Besides, when we look at the planet today, the immense majority of farmers work without any kind of mechanization at all; they work with their hands. Permaculture farming that takes full advantage of an ecosystemic approach, of what nature provides, can make enormous sense for feeding all local populations."

4. A new story about farming

In addition to the Bec-Hellouin example and Olivier De Schutter's report, multiple studies have confirmed the productivity of what is generically called "organic farming" and its ability to feed the planet.

In the words of researcher and agronomist Jacques Caplat: "Every single international study that has examined the actual yields on real farms covering millions of acres (and not just the experimental yields of reductionist agronomists) has reached the same conclusion, without exception. In countries with non-temperate climates, which correspond to three-quarters of the planet and nearly all of humanity, yields from organic farming[1] are now greater than those from conventional agriculture. The only regions of the world where organic yields are lower than conventional farming are in Canada and Europe. Is it any wonder? Farmers in Europe and North America cannot obtain the varieties that are best adapted to their environments (prevented by regulations concerning seeds); they do not have knowledge about companion planting and agroforestry (some pioneers are currently working on this, but much remains to be done); and they cannot develop labor-intensive systems (because the tax system was constructed to discourage jobs in favor of mechanization, creating terribly unfair competition against these labor-intensive farming)."[2]

And even this last statement may not be entirely true, given the results at Bec-Hellouin, which correspond more or less to the necessary conditions described by Jacques Caplat (although granted, it requires an enormous amount of work).

We now know that it is possible to feed ten billion people, while regenerating ecosystems, storing CO_2 in the earth and trees, and creating millions of jobs in the West—provided we change our outlook on agriculture, that we change the laws to facilitate the development of agroecological and permaculture farms. And to eat drastically less meat.

---

1. A term that includes practices like agroecology and permaculture.
2. Jacques Caplat, "La bio peut-elle vraiment nourrir le monde ?," Changeons d'agriculture, November 29, 2014, www.changeonsdagriculture.fr/la-bio-peut-elle-vraiment-nourrir-le-monde-a113788336 (in French). See also his book, *L'Agriculture biologique pour nourrir l'humanité* (Arles: Actes Sud, 2012).

But for the time being, as Olivier De Schutter explains, we support ways to pursue short-term economic growth and the good health of a few agribusiness and agrochemical multinationals. We have given them control of immense centralized food systems, even though common sense and ethics call for the creation of autonomous and organic systems in each and every region. It is, in fact, an entirely new model of society that must be invented if we are to achieve this. And above all, this societal model must be able to function without fossil fuels before it's too late.

2

SUCCESSFUL ENERGY TRANSITION

Numerous research studies exist about energy transition, paralleled by an equal number of furious debates. It's enough to confuse anybody—from the climate skeptics and lobbyists for the American oil industry who are quick to say that "fossil fuels are essential to making this planet a better place to live";[1] to those who, like Claude Allègre in France, claim that "there are no climate refugees at present, it doesn't exist,"[2] suggesting that the urgency of shifting to other energy sources may be overestimated; along with others who state that "there are sufficient traditional oil and gas reserves to last through the end of the century.[3] We decided to pursue all these subjects further with energy engineer Thierry Salomon, member of a panel of experts on the issue of energy transition organized by the French government in 2013 and co-founder of the association négaWatt. Thierry is an amiable man, with a wry sense of humor; he is obsessed by the idea that change can only come from methods that have already proved to be effective. He has been working with a collective of some thirty engineers for more than ten years to develop an energy transition scenario for France, detailed nearly hour by hour, through 2050. More than one million Excel cells have been collated to calculate as precisely as possible what we could do and how. Off the record, he admits just how disconcerted he was with the rudimentary quality of the models used by the ministries as a basis for their decision-making, when civil society scientists must produce research a hundred times more

1. Alex Epstein debating Bill McKibben, "McKibben vs. Epstein Debate on Fossil Fuels — Full Audio," YouTube video, 1:38:04, November 8, 2012, https://www.youtube. com/watch?v=o_a9RPoJ7PA.
2. "Claude Allègre 'climatosceptique,'" dailymotion video, 13:32, December 7, 2009, www.dailymotion.com/video/xbeml4_claude-allegre-climatosceptique-07_news. According to UN figures from 2012, one person moves their home every second due to climate change, which represents 32 million climate refugees per year in 82 countries. A figure that is expected to reach 200 million annually by around 2050.
3. Guennadi Chmal, president of the Union of Oil and Gas Producers of Russia, quoted in "Quand la fin du pétrole aura-t-elle lieu ?" *Sputnik*, October 21, 2013, http://sptnkne.ws/b22e.

thorough before anyone will even listen to them. But more and more people are now paying attention to him and his colleagues.

1. Background–Interview with Thierry Salomon

CYRIL: We have just spent part of our trip learning how to change the agricultural model, and this brings us to the issue of oil, which is everywhere in our lives.

THIERRY: Everything in our world is organized around so-called fossil energies. Oil, of course, but also coal and gas. They are omnipresent in our everyday lives and on a geopolitical level. Oil, for example, is used for 98 percent of our transportation. And the agrofood industry is essentially totally dependent on it.

CYRIL: How would you sum up the main problems of fossil energies?

THIERRY: They pose four basic problems. Pollution and climate change, obviously. From extraction to emissions, with the emission of particles, greenhouse gases; all this is extremely well known. Then the problem of limited resources, which will lead to higher prices. And this price hike may be considerable, particularly for oil, which is an essentially speculative resource. Third, they create geopolitical tension. As they exist in a very limited number of countries, appropriation is a major issue. Fossil energies, notably oil, are involved in everything that is happening in the Ukraine, Iraq, and Syria. And finally, the false impression that these resources are abundant precludes support for renewable energies. Fossil fuels are concentrated, efficient, easy to use; they are readily available and make money for the dominant class. Fighting against them is extremely difficult.

CYRIL: Can we do without them altogether?

THIERRY: We started to work on these questions in the early 2000s, and the farther we go with our research, the more we think that yes, we can. Furthermore, we recognize the immense benefits to us in shifting to sources of flow energy. Not only in terms of energy, but also for the organization of the society in general, for governance, and for the world we want to create for the future.

For France, we drew up a scenario demonstrating the possibility of shifting entirely to renewable energy sources by 2050: the negaWatt plan. It covers all our needs for heat, electricity, transportation. It was an enormous ten-year research project, developed by some twenty specialists.

CYRIL: What are the conclusions?

THIERRY: In one or two generations, we can achieve this goal, provided we work diligently on reducing our energy consumption. This is the meaning of the term "negaWatt." It is the energy that we do not consume and therefore is not produced, all while maintaining an acceptable standard of living. We cannot constantly think in terms of megawatts, of "more and more." The largest potential source of energy in the future will be the energy that we save.

CYRIL: What does this source represent?

THIERRY: From 50 to 60 percent of global energy consumption. All the serious studies on this issue have reached the same conclusion. And our research in France confirms it: we waste half of the energy we produce. The problem is that these negaWatts are a little like the sea of plastic: we don't see them. Yet they are all around us. Does it make sense, for example, to drive around town in a 1.2- to 1.6-ton car to transport a guy who only weights 155 pounds? Does it really make sense to have video screens in our subway systems that use an amount of energy that is equivalent—for a single one of these screens—to that used by two families? Yet there are apparently a million of them. A few years ago, calculations showed that on a European level, six to seven nuclear reactors were required merely to keep appliances in standby mode, including two in France. And the list goes on. There is something very wrong with all this. And we have gotten used to not seeing it.

CYRIL: How can we save all this energy?

THIERRY: We need to think in terms of needs, this is the basic principle of the negaWatt concept. And rate them according to a grid that goes from the essential to the harmful, and includes what is necessary and what is superfluous. And this grid should be put into law.

CYRIL: Individual actions aren't enough?

THIERRY: No. If everyone saved energy, it wouldn't be enough. It's essential that they do so, but what's important is the offer they have available. When with just a few clicks you can fly halfway across the world at a price lower than the taxi fare that takes you to the airport, something is not right. You will have emitted two to three tons of CO_2 into the atmosphere without any impact on your wallet. We can, of course, say: "I'm not going halfway across the world," but it doesn't work like that; there are family connections, desires. What we have to do is integrate the external aspects and the consequences of our energy use into all of our actions. And we need global regulations to cover these issues. They cannot be decreed at a country level. It's the only way to truly change our use. We need collective intelligence, as for other societal issues. We have written a certain number of incentives, regulations, and proposals into our highway code indicating what we can and cannot do. There are rules. This means that I can take my car and say: "I can survive this, it's not the law of the jungle." At négaWatt, we believe that we must now work on a collective set of rules for energy. We have accepted extremely strict regulations concerning vehicles, for example, that have had a remarkable impact. Dropping from twenty thousand deaths a year to four thousand is no small achievement. Same thing for tobacco. Society accepted it perfectly well, even though initially everyone thought the opposite. And beyond regulations, we must say stop, or place a very high tax on extravagant energy use.

CYRIL: Where should we be saving energy primarily?

THIERRY: In France, we often talk about energy by considering it as electricity, but electricity (household appliances like refrigerators and computers, and lighting) accounts for only 20 percent of our usage. The largest energy use is due to heat and air conditioning (and calories in a wider sense: hot water, heating, industrial heating, air conditioning, cold chain) and mobility (transportation of people and goods). Those two alone represent 80 percent of the energy we use. Yet in France, electricity occupies 99 percent of the debate, notably in terms of nuclear power, which would supposedly ensure our energy independence. The reality is more stark.[1] In 2011, we imported €71 billion worth of oil and gas, a budget that exceeds those of the Health, Education, Youth, and Culture ministries combined.

1. France has an energy independence rate of just 9 percent, according to Global Chance, if we include the uranium imported by Areva: www.lemonde.fr/les-decodeurs/article/2014/10/02/transition-energetique-10-chiffrespour-comprendre-le-debat_4498694_4355770.html#EgZMtC2xoWetgH9z.99.

CYRIL: What is the first step?

THIERRY: First of all, look at buildings. We now know how to construct zero-energy buildings, which produce as much energy as they use (via solar panels). They must become more widespread. But it's not enough. New construction accounts for only 1 percent of the total buildings globally. With new constructions, it would take one to two hundred years to change the energy mix. We must therefore take on existing buildings. For the time being, we are living in a very strange situation where, for the same usage, some people will need four times as much energy as others for heat. We wouldn't accept that some vehicles on the roads consume 1.3 gallons per 60 miles, while others burn over five gallons for the same distance. It would be absurd. Yet this is what's happening in the building industry. We urgently need a massive and efficient overhaul. Even if it may seem hard initially, the benefits are threefold: for the future occupants (their health and their wallets); for the economy and employment (renovating building entails local jobs, not outsourced ones, for some thirty years); and for the planet, with three to four times less energy used and with sustainable energies replacing fossil fuels. Economically, this is not just an intellectual exercise. A 2011 study published by a German public investment bank showed that a building renovation program launched in 2008 had cost €4.7 billion, but had generated €8.8 billion in tax revenue from these new activities. Furthermore, hundreds of thousands of new jobs then saved the government €4 billion in social security and unemployment benefits. The return was therefore three times larger than the investment.

CYRIL: And for mobility? I'm guessing that it's not enough to change fuels for vehicles; we must reorganize territories.

THIERRY: We need both. Instead of starting with the object (the vehicle), it's more important to think about what we need: do I really need to travel? What kind of travel is for pleasure, for work? Then develop strategies to meet them. And there are multiple possibilities, from public transportation to car-sharing schemes.

CYRIL: Once we have achieved energy savings, can we produce enough from renewable energy sources?

THIERRY: Yes, and that's the entire purpose of our methodology. First of all, to develop approaches to energy efficiency and restraint (which in France would reduce our needs by 60 percent), then look at what we still need to produce. And for that, we have an extraordinary nuclear power plant, located 93 million miles away that can provide all the energy we need on Earth: our reliable Sun. Every year, it sends us ten thousand times the total quantity of energy used by all of humanity. The problem is how to harness and transform it.

CYRIL: What would renewable energy production look like in a country like France?

THIERRY: France is fortunate to have multiple options. The country does not use them much, but it has every possible renewable energy source, with the second largest wind-power source in Europe, large solar resources from north to south, geothermal underground, biomass (not only with wood, but with all the by-products), lots of hydroelectric resources, marine energy. To produce the 40 percent we need (once we have saved the 60 percent), we will use a mix of all this, with a predominance of biomass.

What's interesting is to link energy to food, therefore agriculture. To do so, we are working on other research with another scenario called "Afterres," developed by Solagro,[1] to provide a global vision

1. A group of French agronomists.

of the entire country. And to answer these questions: What should be on our plates in the future? What type of culture will we have? How to plan it region by region? Which renewable energy sources to use? The answer is to match production to consumption. One thing is sure: we need to eat less meat, as it is extremely energy-intensive and requires a great deal of space.

CYRIL: Is this energy transition already underway in any other country?

THIERRY: Germany, Denmark, and Austria have strongly committed to this. Sweden is already at 51 percent of renewable energies (as opposed to France, at 11 percent), notably through an extremely high carbon tax, €100 per ton—which does not interfere with its strong growth. Overall, it appears that on an economic level, countries that have moved toward energy transition are doing better than others. Long-range planning conducted in Germany in the 1980s led to the development of highly detailed scenarios. All this contributed to creating a remarkably strong consensus among the population that crossed party lines and mobilized industries. Two highly ambitious projects were launched: one for renewables, a sector where considerable progress has been made; and another one concerning energy efficiency, with a strongly committed industry that is laying the groundwork for future markets. At certain times of the day in Germany, more than half of the electrical energy consumption is already provided by renewable energies.

CYRIL: What is the difference between these countries and France?

THIERRY: Maybe a less centralized approach. France is an extremely centralized country, which looks to its leader, to an omnipotent and omniscient president; a country where it seems that everything happens at a ministerial level among senior government officials.

Programs that have been tested are often imposed at a national level, which can end up being catastrophic. I think that transition can work, provided we look at it differently. The word "transition" is interesting. It is not a model, it's an approach. We start with a certain number of small local experiments, which grow in the gaps left unfilled by institutions, which are then replicated when they work; and if they are successful, we create a standard to promote it. This movement is interesting because it starts at the grass-roots level and then receives support from higher up to make it more widespread.

CYRIL: There is an environmental movement[1] that states we cannot get by without nuclear power if we are to reduce CO_2. That we have too little time. What does négaWatt think?

THIERRY: Our opinion on nuclear is very simple: when you look at the entire sector, from start to finish, from the uranium mined in Niger to the waste buried for some eternity underground—and really, how pretentious to think we control eternity—you see that this entire industry has immense weaknesses that could lead to tragic events. A report by the Institut de Radioprotection et de Sûreté Nucléaire (IRSN, the French Institute for Radiological Protection and Nuclear Safety) estimates a cost ranging from €300 million to €1.5 billion in the event of a simple nuclear accident. And this does not even factor in the human, ecological, and psychological costs. These figures do not come from anti-nuclear environmental activists, but from the industry itself. We are taking a completely crazy risk in maintaining this industry (nothing less than the economic collapse of the country), by arguing that the risks are statistically very low. But statistics cloud our judgment. For a turkey that is to be eaten on Christmas, the statistical risks are absolutely miniscule.

1. See also statements by James Lovelock on this issue.

From January 1 to December 23 everything is fine, it is well fed. But December 24 arrives, and with it, a serious problem. But there were no signs, statistically, of what was about to happen because it had just spent its entire life without anything going wrong. Because nothing has yet happened, nothing will happen in the future. It's the same with nuclear. The fact of having fifty-eight aging reactors in France increases the potential for a major accident. Given the current technology, we believe we should stop using nuclear. It's a dangerous dead end. And it's a goal that's entirely possible to achieve within twenty years, if we use the extremely high investments required to modernize and renovate these old plants. We could redirect this considerable sum of money to renewable energies. The same holds true for jobs; we will not replace the people who have retired, but rather create jobs in the renewables sector, while maintaining the staff necessary for dismantling the plants and for security.

CYRIL: What impact would the negaWatt scenario have on jobs in France?

THIERRY: A net balance of around 600,000 to 700,000 jobs over fifteen years, factoring in job loss and creation. The bulk of the new jobs would be in building renovation, in the development of renewable energies, and in the relocalization of our energy system. The bulk of the losses would be in the nuclear and automobile industries.

CYRIL: Where do these figures come from?

THIERRY: From a study conducted by the CIRED,[1] which is part of the Centre National de la Recherche Scientifique (CNRS, French National Center for Scientific Research). Other macroeconomic

1. Centre International de Recherche sur l'Environnement et le Développement.

studies have been done on the negaWatt scenario. Not only does France not collapse, but they show that the GDP increases.

CYRIL: So energy transition creates jobs, it is good for the planet, for our health, yet we still are not doing it. It's bizarre.

THIERRY: I feel that humankind can react massively to something that is visible: an earthquake, a war. But the end of oil, climate change? We don't believe it. If the CO_2 molecules changed color in the atmosphere, maybe we would react. Yet we should be very frightened with what they're telling us. When the GIEC makes catastrophic projections for the years 2050 or 2100, it doesn't stop there. The temperature will continue to go and will rise 14 to 27° F. It is human life itself that is at risk. It is essential for psychologists, artists, and marketing professionals to think about the reasons for the collective denial and to come up with solutions.

CYRIL: And politicians? You have participated in many governmental studies concerning energy transition in France; what prevents them from changing?

THIERRY: I see that they are very afraid of change. Which is strange because what frightens me is not changing. Most of the conversations during elections turn around this idea of change, but when it's time to actually implement it, nothing works, everything is stuck—often because of institutional reasons that are layered over the interests of certain individuals, companies, and lobbies. All this creates a block of conservative thought, of people who want to make sure that nothing changes, who don't see farther than just a couple years down the line. But the problem of time is a major one. What the nega-Watt scenario offers is a direction for the next thirty-five years. It's a very long timeframe, and at the same time very short in terms of humanity. Unfortunately, a politician measures time in terms of five or six years; an industrialist, two years; and a financial advisor, a nanosecond.[1] We should think about the driving forces so that we can once again shift to a proper time frame, where we are not merely looking at what will happen the day after tomorrow. Many families are still thinking in terms of their children, transmitting property and cultures from one generation to the next. These ideas of heritage may seem conservative to a certain number of environmentalists, but they are deeply rooted motivations on which we can develop initiatives and foster debate.

CYRIL: Another powerful force for change we are exploring is that of the story. How would you describe the world of energy in future?

THIERRY: If we are to offer a story that's not science fiction (which we don't allow ourselves to do in our research), it would look something like this: in 2050, a normal family will live in a collective building that has several shared elements (space, equipment, garden). It will have been renovated or be new, but in any case, it will use hardly any energy for heating, even less for hot water, and all the electrical appliances will consume very low amounts of energy. It will produce as much energy as it uses, primarily through solar panels. Families can fully monitor its energy use in real time, appliance by appliance, via smart meters. They will use public transportation, but not exclusively (it won't exist everywhere, as this would be too expensive). In urban areas, they will use a small 550-pound electrical vehicle, which will be either shared or co-owned. To go see their elderly aunt in the middle of the Corrèze region, they will rent a hybrid sedan that is primarily powered by electricity in urban centers and renewable methane gas the rest of the time. This gas will be delivered via a network of stations modeled after our current gas stations. This family will use far less electricity, but will

1. An allusion to high-frequency trading.

still have the mobility that we enjoy today and will be able to travel the same number of miles. But people will travel more for social reasons and less out of necessity (notably for professional reasons). The family will live in a country where virtually all the electricity is renewable, thanks to a mix of solar, wind, and biomass. Storage problems will have been solved, notably using gas, which can store through a "power to gas" process.[1] This energy production will be decentralized and run by collectives, companies, and consumer groups (on a cooperative model). Wind parks will belong to all these stakeholders, and the income they produce will be used to insulate the last remaining buildings that require it. Ultimately, the collectivity will use less money to purchase energy from charming leaders like Mr. Putin and the Gulf countries. This €70 billion per year, which will not be outsourced, will be reinvested in the local economy to create useful companies and jobs.

CYRIL: Will we still have large energy companies or will the production be entirely delocalized?

THIERRY: We will still have a few energy mastodons to run the large installations, such as wind power at sea (which we will definitely need). This involves setting up extremely expensive offshore oil technology (and in fact, this could be a good way to recycle the oil industry on the one hand, and shipyards, on the other). But there will also be many companies more closely associated to local regions. The trick is to have them work alongside one another, so that small- and medium-sized companies are not devoured by these large structures. Here again, the German example is interesting;

---

1. Power-to-gas, or P2G, consists in transforming electricity into methane. Electricity is transformed into hydrogen gas by water electrolysis. This hydrogen can then be converted into methane via a reaction with carbon dioxide known as the Sabatier reaction. This is then easily stored or injected into the natural gas grid (https://en.wikipedia.org/wiki/Power_to_gas).

the large companies have major partnerships with the small- and medium-sized companies that are more territorially based.

2. Renewable islands

We were motivated when we left the small Paris offices of néga-Watt. Since studies and scenarios now showed the real possibilities of freeing ourselves from fossil energies, we set out to find cities and countries that were already on this path. As with all the subjects we looked into, we wanted to see, in situ, if it all really worked. And in the places we visited, overall we found all the elements Thierry Salomon had discussed: an energy mix with diverse renewable sources, parallel efforts to reduce consumption and increase the production of renewable energies, along with an urgent sense that it was time to act. A handful of key concepts gradually became clear as we went along: diversity, autonomy, resilience, cooperation.

We were also able to see that the regions spearheading energy transition are often islands (Iceland, Cape Verde, Réunion), semi-islands (Denmark), or peninsulas (Sweden). An island is a restricted environment, where the sense of fragility is possibly stronger than elsewhere and the need to foster autonomy is even stronger. Because of these inherent constraints, many islands have therefore become laboratories of what continents should implement in the future.

Iceland: Geothermal and hydroelectric power

The sun doesn't set in Iceland in the month of June, or perhaps for just an hour or so. Taking a break in my hotel room, still amazed at the lunar landscape that we had just visited, I try to block the windows with the curtains, as best as I can. It is 11:00 p.m.

and still broad daylight outside. When I open my eyes again, at 4:00 a.m., the light seems exactly the same. Time doesn't pass the same way here, it seems to expand, multiply. Nature is everywhere. Reykjavik may be a world-famous capital city, but it is still fairly small (120,000 residents), sitting atop a rough, unspoiled world, where people have to create their own conditions to survive and prosper. The country's energy policy seems linked to a feeling we can't ignore: when you're in Iceland, you're in the middle of nowhere. Which is why, with the oil crisis of 1973, the island's government decided to become self-sufficient. Oil was going to become more expensive, supply problems would only worsen, and they therefore had to put an end to this dependency. Even if the situation did not exactly pan out as predicted in the subsequent two decades (the price of oil was once again relatively low in the 1980s and 1990s, after the huge hike of 1979), it's fair to say that the Icelanders saw the way the wind was blowing thirty-five years before anyone else.

Their concerns at the time are now those of transitioners all around the world. To achieve their goal, the authorities decided to draw on the island's natural resources, two of which were predominant. Iceland is a volcanic island (with two hundred volcanoes), and its hot springs are hugely popular among locals as well as tourists, who come visit them from all over the world. It had to be possible to harness this heat. The country also has many impressive waterfalls and glaciers, among the largest in Europe, covering one-tenth of the surface area. They are located at altitudes up to several thousand feet, and multiple high-flow glacial rivers start from them. The strong flow, combined with the vertical drop, constitutes an exceptional potential energy source. Because of the infrastructure developed in these two sectors, in just two decades, this small country of 330,000 inhabitants now posts a phenomenal score of 87 percent

---

Geothermal power plant near Reykjavik.

of renewable energies.[1] The overall mix is 69 percent geothermal, 18 percent hydroelectric, 11 percent oil, and 2 percent coal. More specifically, geothermal provides 90 percent of the island's (collective) heat, from power plants that supply the cities via immense pipelines (the longest one is 49 miles long), and 27 percent of the electricity. Hydroelectricity covers the remaining 10 percent of the heating needs and 73 percent of electricity. The 13 percent use of oil and coal essentially goes for operating the fishing boats and vehicles. Mobility therefore remains a crucial issue to solve in the Icelandic energy transition, as described by Guðni Jóhannesson, CEO of Orkustofnun, Iceland's National Energy Authority: "It is one of our next goals. We are working to produce fuel from our renewable energies. We already have electrical cars, cars that operate on methane gas produced from waste. We constructed a plant that captures CO_2 from the air and, with hydrogen, produces the methanol that we can mix with oil. We also have a fleet of hydrogen-powered cars and a few buses that operate in Reykjavík. All these technologies are already operational, but are still relatively expensive. They need to be improved and promoted. We think that within ten to twenty years, we will be able to put them into widespread use to construct a future without fossil fuels."

Iceland produces far more energy than it needs. It has therefore attracted many companies who see these energy sources as an opportunity to expand their operations. One, in particular: currently, 73 percent of its electricity is absorbed by the aluminum industry, a particularly energy-intensive (and not very ecological) sector. And the country thinks it can produce even more by improving its technology. At present, Iceland has become a sort of global consultant, to help other regions in the world used geothermal to replace fossil fuels.

1. "Energy Recovery," Statistics Iceland, http://www.statice.is/statistics/business-sectors/energy/energy-recovery/.

"There is a huge potential in developing countries," continues Guðni. "In the African Rift Valley, we could produce about 15 GW of thermoelectricity in countries like Kenya and Ethiopia (the equivalent of about twenty nuclear reactors). Today, 40 percent of the world's oil is used for essential needs like heating water and homes. We could easily replace this in all the countries that have geothermal resources, like Switzerland, Germany, France, and Italy. Combining it with other renewable energies could reduce the use of fossil fuels to levels that would not endanger the climate."

Réunion: Sun and Agrinergie

The specific problems concerning the autonomy of islands are somewhat similar in Réunion, but the country is not as far along. For now, the island's global energy mix comprises 35 percent renewable energies and 65 percent fossil fuels. The country is still significantly oil-dependent: diesel fuel accounts for half of the energy needs. A strike or a hitch in supply can bring the island's economy to its knees in just a few days. "Today, a single company holds a monopoly over the supply, giving it considerable power. Our work is to break this monopoly and diversify our production sources," explains regional president Didier Robert. "Our goal is to achieve energy self-sufficiency, through renewables, by 2025 or 2030." But Réunion faces other challenges. While the density in Iceland is just over three inhabitants per square mile, the population on this small tropical island is skyrocketing. The coasts offer the only places that are easily habitable, due to the volcano and protected natural parks; nearly nine hundred thousand people already live in this area, a figure that is expected to reach one million by 2030. Solutions need to be found to build homes, grow food, and produce renewable energy on a constantly decreasing amount of land. In addition, it is essential to solve the issue of the intermittent supply of renewables (as sunlight and wind are variable, production is not constant), which prevents the mix from exceeding 35 percent for the moment.

A small SME French company, Akuo Energy, began to address this problem in 2007. It develops renewable energy sources all over the planet, which it calls Agrinergie. It's a simple idea: since it makes no sense to choose between producing food and producing energy, why not do both at once in the same place? The first experience alternated solar panels, interspersed with rows of crops that benefitted from the shade of the photovoltaic installations. These were aromatic herbs. Although the trial was encouraging, the space was too small to grow significant amounts of food. A second experiment was conducted with market garden greenhouses; it proved to be far more successful.

The ground is used for farming, and half of the roofs for electricity production (the other half is left open to let light in). Farmers were reticent at first, as they only saw the problems involved in the process—demonstrating that it's crucial to factor in cultural practices. But once solutions were found, the process was extremely beneficial in several ways. The greenhouses protect the crops from the orangutans and extreme weather (which occurs regularly in these tropical regions), harvest rain water, and make the sites self-sufficient in terms of water—and all of this for free. Akuo makes them available to the farmers for a symbolic cost of one euro, in exchange for the right to use the roofs.

For Jean-Bernard Gonthier, an organic farmer and president of the Chamber of Agriculture, the twelve greenhouses provide food for six hundred households, or more than two thousand people, on the island. And they did not move an inch when Cyclone Bejisa hit in 2014, while many other farms were devastated, with the destruction of nearly all the crops. But the system can also let farmers work even when they do not have the possibility of purchasing land. In this case, Akuo lets them use the land for the same symbolic cost of one euro for a term of twenty to forty years. "We make the company's financial capacity available to farmers," says Éric Scotto, founder and president CEO of Akuo. "We have two massive challenges in the upcoming decades: make territories self-sufficient in terms of food and of energy. And the financial cost is a major obstacle for both. By creating partnerships between these two sectors, we hope to achieve it."

The concept is so promising that Akuo is trying to replicate it on much of the unused land. At the Port Prison, the island's primary detention center, thanks to a partnership with the prefecture and the prison administration, the company has transformed the abandoned industrial zone around the prison into a food-production and reintegration site. Market garden greenhouses with solar panels on the roofs now stand alongside an arboretum, fourteen beehives, and a solar power plant. This new space not only offers a more appealing landscape for the prisoners, it also improves their lives. Several dozen of them work there regularly and can attend job training sessions with a view of their futures: organic gardening, beekeeping, solar-panel production. "One step outside the fence is already something," says Patrick, who has been in detention for three years and has a history of recidivism over the last twenty years. "When you go to prison, you have a family, sometimes a job, a house; and most of the time you get out with nothing. So it's important to have a skill." For now, the jobs are limited to the most motivated and to those considered to have the best chance for reinsertion. Patrick's son, also incarcerated, has not yet been able to participate. Since 2009, thirty-seven prisoners have been trained, and eight have found jobs in this sector once they had served their time. The goal is for 240 prisoners to re-enter working life in the next twenty years.

Akuo also wanted to use this new experimental site to tackle the problem of storage, which is crucial in energy transition. The 9 megawatts of panels were therefore connected to 9 megawatts of batteries. With the nine cubes that look like small sheet-metal construction shacks, housing racks of rechargeable batteries, and surrounded by panels, the plant can supply continuous electricity to one-third of the city of Port (36,000 inhabitants). When constructed, it was the most powerful installation of its kind in the world. As Anne Lemonier, who runs the project, explained: "Many islands have managed to add a large percentage of renewable energies to their mix, but most of the energies, like wind and solar, are intermittent. On Réunion, once the renewable production exceeds 30 percent, the electricity company disconnects a certain number of our plants so that they don't destabilize the grid. If we want to exceed this percentage, it is crucial to be able to store energy." Given that storage is most often linked to the grid, the Akuo team conducted an experiment, which had never been done before: directly couple the plant to the batteries, locally. When clouds block the sun, the storage system instantly takes over to ensure a stable and constant energy supply. "To achieve a 100 percent renewable energy mix," says Anne, "we must have 50 percent of continuous energies that provide a stable supply, like biomass, hydroelectricity, geothermal, and marine energy, and 50 percent of intermittent energies, like solar and wind, coupled to a storage system." As Thierry Salomon told us, several storage solutions exist. The one Akuo chose consists of lithium-ion batteries, which are usually used for electrical vehicles. "The batteries contain recyclable manganese, magnesium, nickel, and carbon electrodes. And very little lithium-ion. In this type of power plant, the life span of a battery corresponds to 80 percent of the initial capacity. They are then used in other sectors that are less demanding in terms of performance (electric vehicles, for example). Suppliers then collect them for dismantling and recycling." This concept has attracted interest from the French government, which is now ready to support it on other islands and in mainland France, but also other tropical regions facing the same energy issues.

These greenhouses near Tampon provide power to 515 homes.

It could be argued that Iceland and Réunion are areas with relatively small populations, yet we began to see a different scale in Denmark and Sweden, with 5.6 and 10 million inhabitants, respectively. These two Scandinavian countries have officially stated a goal of achieving 100 percent renewable energy by 2050. Sweden had already reached 51 percent in 2013, and Denmark, 36 percent. But even more impressive are the goals set forth by a certain number of cities in these two countries. Located just a few miles apart, Copenhagen and Malmö were our next stops, with target dates for becoming entirely CO_2 neutral by 2025 and 2030, respectively.

We still have more four hours left to go in our flight. I am reviewing our eighteen days of filming, trying to pull out the most salient points. Everything went by so quickly. We were only able to superficially share the lives of all the people we met. Even so, I'm sad to leave them behind. As if the intensity of what we had experienced was far greater than the actual time we spent together. Once we land in Réunion, we are stopping for a weeklong break before I travel alone to Copenhagen, where the rest of the crew will join me the following day. Hunkered down in my seat, I look around. Everyone is glued to their screens—either the one on the seat in front of them, or their tablet, telephone, or computer. Take the subway and you'll see the same thing. Rows of heads bowed down, shoulders hunched, totally absorbed, ignoring everyone around them. This need for a screen that never seems to be satisfied. The permanent screen, a permanent focus of our eyes and hands, permeating every corner of our existences, abolishing daydreaming, observation, even boredom. It's madness. No time, no space, no limits: spending hours and hours mechanically immersed in a sea of interactions, knowledge, nonstop words. Every day, I, too, deal with mountains of emails, texts, and voicemail that land on this bit of metal and glass. They have speeded up my life, eliminating any breathing room between meetings, encounters, work. And given the workaholic that I am, they have provided me with a portable office, a space that is perpetually open for work and communication of all kinds. Smartphones have replaced silence. I find the magnetic appeal of the screen nearly unbearable. It pulls me in, isolates me from people, objects, scents, and sounds, and dulls my judgment while it hotwires my nervous system. When I'm in front of a screen, I feel as if I don't even belong to my own life, that I'm not dealing with my own issues. The images are overwhelming, distracting my mind without focusing it in a specific direction. My willpower weakens, I don't want to do anything but stay right where I am, scrolling through different content, jumping from site to site. I become a receptacle for symbols, ideas, trends. I sometimes think I could spend my entire life in this parallel reality, watching films and videos, reading articles nonstop. And look at my real life as if it was a series of transitions between successive screen displays. If I was also hooked on online video games, with the tangible possibility of living other lives, I could very well be totally lost. I sometimes feel that my days disappear in a virtual world that terrifies me. So I try to find a way to be more real, by cooking, gardening, fixing things.

Another aspect of these moments of disconnection and acuity terrifies me: if I am so dependent and fascinated by these screens, there is a strong probability that others are as well. Indeed, the statistics are alarming: with smartphones, tablets, computers, and televisions, the average French person spends nearly four hours a day on these devices for pleasure (which, with the widespread use of smartphones, seems a low estimate) and several hours more for professional use. A few years ago, I played around with a few calculations: a person who spends seven hours a day in front of a screen for work and some four hours for leisure would pass more than twenty years of their life in front of a thin layer of backlit glass. With an eight-hour night, they would sleep for twenty-five years. For a total of forty-five years either in bed or in front of a screen. Which barely leaves forty years for all the rest: running errands, washing clothes, vacuuming, cooking, transportation, paying bills, repairing the car. And how much time is left for dreaming, walking in the open air, reading poetry, feeling the wind blow, making love, creating, extraordinary encounters? It seems as if an increasing share of our attention and our energy is diverted from political, educational, and environmental concerns, finding comfort in the entertaining and colorful bosom of our screens. Should we perhaps be giving this more thought?

3. Copenhagen:
The first carbon-neutral capital

In Copenhagen, a country with two million residents (including 570,000 within the city limits), the municipal government has invested nearly €1 billion to install one hundred wind turbines and is working hard to eliminate all use of oil and coal in its heating, air conditioning, and energy production systems. To get the population to accept these turbines, despite the "not in my back yard" (NIMBY) syndrome, the city deployed a typically Danish response: cooperative wind turbines. In the late 1980s, a small group of individuals decided to raise awareness among the population about the need to produce renewable energy. They organized public meetings and contacted the national utility company, DONG energy. A project for an offshore cooperative wind farm was proposed in 1996, called Middelgrunden. It was launched in 2000, with twenty turbines, ten of which belonged to 8,700 individuals and ten to DONG. At the time, this was the world's largest offshore wind farm, producing 4 percent of the city's electricity. Hans Sørensen was part of this small group; today he runs the farm. "If we were to have a chance

---

The Middelgrunden Wind Turbine Cooperative.

of getting the population to accept the wind turbines, they had to be involved with the project from the start and earn the profits generated by the production of electricity. The profits and governance had to remain local." In practice, when the members of the cooperative invest their money to purchase the turbines, they receive an annual return of 6 to 7 percent, which is far more than most investments. The law now requires that each new project developed in Denmark have a minimum of 20 percent local and citizen shareholders, thereby also ensuring success for the entrepreneurs and the city, and a democratic process for residents. In 2025, with one hundred new turbines, wind will supply virtually all the city's electricity. And it will soon be possible to store it using natural gas and electric vehicle batteries. Because on windy days, Denmark already produces more than it uses, as in a few days in July 2014 when the wind farms met 140 percent of the country's needs.[1] At present, the surplus is exported to Germany, Sweden, and Norway, where it can be stored using hydroelectric systems. When the wind drops and Denmark needs power, it can import hydroelectricity from Norway. For Hans, this interregional cooperation, based on the diversity of renewable energies within each country, is key to the future. At the same time, the municipality is putting pressure on the energy companies to transform their coal and fuel plants into green power plants, as described by Jørgen Abildgaard, Executive Project Director for the Copenhagen Climate Plan 2025: "We decided to shift to renewables, so companies don't have a choice, they have to give us what we want. Most are replacing coal with biomass. One of the city's largest power plants has already totally reconverted. The second will have completed the process within four or five years." And when Jørgen talks about a "large factory," he means *really* large. We went to one of them, Avedøre, just opposite the Middelgrunden wind farm, and we were stunned by the

1. Arthur Nelson, "Wind Power Generates 140% of Denmark's Electricity Demand," *The Guardian*, July 10, 2015, https://www.theguardian.com/environment/2015/jul/10/denmark-wind-windfarm-power-exceed-electricity-demand.

figures. By burning forestry biomass from nearby European countries, used palettes and dry straw delivered by local farmers after the harvests, it produces electricity for 1.3 million households and heating for 200,000 families. The plant is one of the most efficient in the world: 94 percent of the materials burned is transformed into energy, whereas this rate is usually closer to 50 percent.

More broadly, it's the city's entire heating system that is gradually changing, to eliminate fossil fuels. In the short term, a hybrid system that burns biomass and plastic-free waste has already reduced the use of fossil fuels by 58 percent. In the medium- and long-term, geothermal will replace coal and fuel. But, as Thierry Salomon stressed, it is also essential to save energy, particularly for an energy-intensive sector like heating, and even more so in a cold country like Denmark.

For Morten Kabell, deputy mayor of Technical and Environmental Affairs, this involves costly but essential investments. "In Copenhagen, we have thermally renovated many of our buildings and developed a collective heating system. For me, as a city resident, the result has been a significant drop in my heating bill. For a 1,100-square-foot apartment in the city center, I pay just €60 per month.[1] One of my German colleagues visited last month and didn't believe me. I explained that all this required substantial expenditure, but that the money came back. The cost-benefit analysis is largely in our favor." In any case, this approach is essential to achieving the goals set by Copenhagen: 40 percent of greenhouse gas emissions in Denmark come from buildings. Alongside this major undertaking, many eco-neighborhoods have been constructed (as in the old port) or are about to break ground. Everything has been designed to be as ecological as possible: maximum insulation, green roofs, solar panels, waste management.

1. In France, the cost for the same surface area is €175.

Else on Queen Louise's Bridge, with bike paths.

Transportation is the other major source of emissions, and here again, Copenhagen has a plan. The city is already extremely bike friendly, with 27 miles of bike paths, highways for bikes, and bridges for bikes only. As Else Kloppenborg, special advisor to the Smart City program, explains, four out of five people have a bike at home (as opposed to one in five with a car), and 41 percent of the city residents use them every day as transportation—nearly one-half of Copenhagen's residents. Figures that give us, Parisians, food for thought. Nothing seems to discourage them, whether it's riding to work, running errands, taking kids to school, rain, wind, or snow. Cargo bikes, with cabins in the front, are great for carrying kids and large objects; small canvas-covered trailers transport groceries; while others with carry cots or tandems are also great for kids (who, by age six, are already riding their own bikes). When we ask Else if people ride less in bad weather, she just laughs. Everyone carries a rain jacket and rain pants in case of showers. And if it's cold, "we put on a coat," she adds, with a smile. In the last few years, after a snowfall, the city has been clearing the bikes paths first, and people are still out and about, as attested by multiple photos online. For Else, as for everyone else we talked to, it's perfectly normal. Bikes are usually faster (you're not stuck in traffic and you don't have to find a parking spot), better for your health, less expensive, and friendlier to use. Economic studies conducted by the city also confirm our personal impressions: a savings of €230 million in health costs every year because people are riding bikes, and every kilometer ridden by a cyclist brings a net social gain of 16 centimes to the municipality, compared to the same distance traveled by car. As for travel time, all the studies conducted in different towns in different countries confirm that the average biking time is essentially the same or faster than cars, for distances under 3 miles.[1]

1. See Olivier Razemon, *Le Pouvoir de la pédale* (Paris: Rue de l'Échiquier, 2014).

On a broader scale, the city has created an interconnected network of green transportation. The trains, metro, buses, boats, and bike systems are designed to function together so that residents can travel within a radius of 50 miles without using a car. When we tested this out with Else, we understood that the bike is the basic axiom that links the various other motorized transportation methods. Rails and ramps have been installed to make it easier to get up and down the staircases in the stations and onto the water buses. Bike racks are installed in the trains and special areas in the metro cars. If you want to take a dip at the city's beach, you can take your bike to the metro, ride seven or eight stops, then pedal a good five minutes and you're there. "With this system, we can construct stations somewhat farther apart, avoiding larger and more expensive infrastructure. This way, we can optimize each method of transportation," explains Else. The result: cars account for only 33 percent of the transportation in the city. But Copenhagen wants to go further and bring this figure down to 25 percent by 2025. And, like Morten, she doesn't mince her words: "Of course, I have lots of people who are lobbying, saying that we can't get rid of cars. But we can and we will. Because we have to do it. Not only for the environment, but also for the congestion. If everyone decided to travel in vehicles, we simply could no longer get around Copenhagen." The city has calculated that with the same amount of time and space, a car carries one person; while a bus carries four to five; and bikes, six. Even today in the greater Copenhagen area, 190,000 cumulative hours are lost every day in traffic jams—a figure that would be even higher without the current system. Even if 25 percent of trips continue to be made by car, the goal is also to change the fuel they use.

The city already has some forty electric vehicles and fifty hydrogen-powered ones, proof that these techniques are efficient. It is motivating manufacturers to develop cheaper technologies and make them more available. At the same time, it is setting up a network of stations, still in the early stages, that will ultimately let people travel around the entire country. For Jørgen, it is a "global agenda" that must involve all stakeholders: "All these measures represent massive expenditures. We cannot do it alone. We have therefore set up an investment plan that brings together entrepreneurs, investors, and individuals." When we asked him how they achieved this, Jørgen gave us an answer that may surprise ecologists: "We created solid, attractive economic models, and we gave them good business stories. When you take on environmental issues, you need to prove that you have a good business plan, because ultimately, that is what the financial sector, the banks, and the investors look at. We worked extremely hard to prove that our models are solid, and they are. To do so, we mobilized the country's best and brightest minds, and created partnerships with the universities and business schools." With the result that an American study ranked Copenhagen as the city that is most resilient to climate change.[1]

According to Morten, the city's transformation was fast-tracked by the trauma linked to the failure of the negotiations at the Copenhagen climate summit. "The 2009 summit was an absolute disaster for the climate and the environment. It showed that political leaders didn't have the power, because they didn't have the will. They didn't want to truly transform society. For me, it was above all a question of political courage and cooperation. Here in Copenhagen, we want to move in this direction, and we are encouraged to do so by the population. Many of the recent changes, like shifting from cars to bikes, came from residents, not from the city. They demonstrated, they came to talk to us, they launched their own projects, and we followed. In other cases, we were behind the initiatives. You can't expect elected officials to do everything; if we want to change, it will happen together." For him, as for many other people we met, a city or regional level is a particularly propitious place to begin the

1. Boyd Cohen, "Global Ranking of Top 10 Resilient Cities," *Triple Pundit*, June 28, 2011, www.triplepundit.com/2011/06/top-10-globally-resilient-cities/.

transition. "In many countries, the governments are not doing much in terms of climate change, but cities are strongly involved. This is especially true in the United States and Canada, for example. I see cities as the new world leaders: where nations have failed, they must take over. We don't have any other choice. When people ask me: How can you allow yourselves to make all these investments to become carbon neutral? I tell them: How can you allow yourselves not to? Look at the world around us; there is no other alternative."

4. Malmö: The eco-district of the future

This same conclusion motivated Copenhagen's neighbors in Malmö, on the other side of the large bridge linking the two cities. We headed to the Bo01 eco-district, one of top destinations for architects, elected officials, and ecologists the world over. In 2001, on the industrial wasteland of the harbor of Västra Hamnen,[1] the city decided to construct several thousand housing units to demonstrate that it is possible to live comfortably while saving natural resources and reducing energy consumption. The goal, set forth in the planning stages, was to be 100 percent self-sufficient through the use of renewable energies. The first one thousand buildings were designed in 2001 with an energy use of 100 kilowatt hours per square meter per year, which represents a 40 percent reduction over the average building in Sweden. The most recent ones (as the district is still expanding), use only 50 kilowatt hours. The buildings have green roofs, along with solar water heaters. Electricity comes from a wind turbine that meets the needs of one thousand apartments, and the homes are heated via a centralized system that draws heat from the warm water contained in the limestone rocks 300 feet underground.

1. Western Harbor.

Some buildings are collective; others are individual, but they are all different. And, as opposed to many modern neighborhoods, Boo1 has small streets because, as explained by Daniel Skog, who has been involved in the eco-district for fifteen years and is the city's director of communications: "The architect, Klas Tham, took his inspiration from medieval European cities. He wondered what made them so appealing, and from there, he developed his own theory. In this small network of little streets, you never knew who you'd come across, an old friend who may appear around a corner. The city was a place of unexpected encounters. He wanted to recreate this same feeling." The overall layout of the district stresses diversity and functionality. Everything was designed so that residents can live without cars. The city center is a fifteen-minute walk away, just five minutes by bike (the district has 5 miles of bike paths), and biogas-powered buses run every ten minutes. A few storefront businesses have opened: cafés, restaurants, gyms, hairdressers, and a small organic supermarket, one of the most beautiful we've ever seen. The few parking lots are on the outskirts, equipped by electrical chargers powered by solar panels.

Lots of parks were created around the buildings, along with canals fed by rainwater. "Experiencing the seasons, seeing trees and water is essential for the city of tomorrow," says Daniel. "Studies by Swedish hospitals have shown that people get better faster when they are in contact with nature."

Inside the buildings, smart meters inform residents of their water and electricity use, and offer solutions for reducing them. Water-saving devices are installed on the taps and toilets, along with plugs that reduce electric bills. All the waste is collected and sorted into recyclable items and food waste, which goes to produce biogas.

Cord Siegel and Maria Larsson are architects. They have been living in the district for eleven years, and have constructed three buildings here, including the one in which they live. For this first project, Cord received the Kasper Salin Prize from the Swedish

Society of Architecture, one of the country's most prestigious awards. "When we started this project, we were about thirty years old, an age when most people move out to a house in the suburbs. Our idea was to bring our single-family home into the city." The couple and their young daughter live in an apartment, on the top floor of a five-story building. A small elevator opens straight into the living room. The floor is polished concrete; huge windows face the ocean. The minimalist decoration adds to the sense of space. From the balcony, a New-York-style fire-escape staircase leads to the small rooftop garden. From here, we can film the breathtaking view over the entire Western Harbor. "We use less energy here than in a single-family home, it's easier to live a sustainable lifestyle. We don't have a car; we share one with other residents when we need one. We take the train a lot, as we can take our bikes along. You get a better sense of distance with a bike, and it's great exercise!" As if to prove his point, Cord pulls out his folding bike, opens it with a snap and starts riding around the apartment. He then shoves it into the elevator and invites us to follow him to his second project, where Nicolaï, Ova, and their two children live.

The neighborhood is a bit drab, and the buildings are not as beautiful as in the center of Boo1. The second section of the district is more homogenous, and the buildings look a bit like all the others in modern cities. But they are less expensive, and the city can thus encourage a more diverse population. Cord explains that half of the residents are owners, and the other half, renters. The rent is about €900 a month for a 700-square-foot, three-room apartment. It's not outrageous, but not cheap either—on the high-end of the average cost for Sweden. You can't miss Ova and Nicolaï's small house in the middle of all these cubes. Not only is it shorter, but it stands next to a transparent tower, filled with inexplicable pipework, with a small turbine on the roof—the "educational tower,"

Cord, an architect, and his folding bike in the heart of Boo1.

as Cord call it. "We display energy instead of hiding it. On the walls, on rooftops, on the meters. It's a way to make it more real, so that residents pay attention." The electricity comes from the turbine and a few solar panels on the roof; heat from the collective system described above; and the plant waste (from the small garden behind and food scraps) goes to a mixer that produces biogas. People can fill their car tanks from the small blue pump on the corner of the building. And perhaps in the future, their electric bikes. In any case, that's Cord's dream. An electric car is parked behind the garage door, plugged snugly into the wall socket. Other batteries (in addition to the car battery) are built into the wall; they store the energy surplus produced by the panels and the mini-turbine. Nicolaï tells us that his lifelong dream has been to build his own home and make it 100 percent self-sufficient (a dream shared by many others, to judge by the number of magazines and TV shows on this subject). He is therefore happy to show us around. "When people talk about an ecological lifestyle, you imagine dank holes where it's about 60° F and where you can never take off your thick sweater. Myself, I don't believe that. Here, we have huge glass windows that insulate better than walls, a swimming pool heated by solar water heaters in which we can swim at least six months a year, a thermostat that maintains a constant temperature, with a minimal use of energy." Ova clearly agrees: "Why waste energy when you don't have to? Many of our friends moved to the suburbs when they had kids, but I didn't feel ready to do that. Here, we are next to the sea, there are parks, and we can walk to the city center. We have everything we want, and it's sustainable." When we ask Cord if the pool is really a reasonable choice for an environmental architect, he doesn't take offense at all, and explains his pet project: to make people feel so great at home that they stop flying all over the world for their vacations. It might not work for everyone, but it's worth a try.

During our trip to Copenhagen and Malmö, I was thinking about all the environmentalists I know, like my friend Yvan[1] and even Pierre Rabhi, for whom the (big) city is a heresy, a sprawling, relentless monster that is creating artificial landscapes; absorbing labor and resources (and in the process fueling a rural population decline); and dehumanizing relationships among people, who remain anonymous, eager for distraction, increasingly disconnected from the nature on which they depend for survival, but which they no longer understand. I can hear their voices, anticipate their criticism of the film; they had demonstrated that it's possible to build light, self-sufficient homes as close as possible to nature, trees, and fields. The twenty-two homes in the Hameau des Buis,[2] with their wood-frame structures and bricks made of local earth and straw, are never below 60° F in the middle of the winter (which can be harsh in the Ardèches Cevennes region), without any heat at all. Stoves that burn wood from the nearby forests provide extra heat in winter, and solar panels help with electricity use. A kitchen garden supplies the vegetables for the eighty residents; a baker makes the bread; there's a school for the children. According to Pierre and Yvan, these structures are far less fragile than cities, which depend on dense, complex networks and supplies trucked in daily. They offer a solution that is much better adapted to the crises forecast for the future. And their environmental footprint is minimal. The buildings are made entirely of natural materials, taken from the biotype; they will most likely return to it, without leaving a trace.

In Copenhagen, we had the opportunity to discuss these subjects (and many others) with architect and urban planner Jan Gehl, known as the father of what is now commonly called the "Copenhagenization" of cities: returning them to pedestrians and cyclists. He is the

1. Yvan Saint-Jours, with whom I co-founded the magazine *Kaizen* and who created the magazine *La Maison écologique*, popular with advocates of ecoconstruction.
2. The ecovillage founded by Pierre's daughter Sophie and her partner, Laurent Bouquet.

author of *Cities for People*. He is also responsible for returning Times Square and a neighborhood in Moscow to pedestrians, and was the inspiration for Copenhagen's urban planning. Like any self-respecting architect, he only wears black, and has a sparkle in his eye and a sharp wit. He stopped by the barber shop the day before filming to "look his best." Suffice it to say that we had a wonderful time, perched atop a bridge over a canal that had been recently cleaned up and rehabilitated. People can now swim and row in it; as well as picnic, bike, and skateboard along the banks. In short, just enjoy it.

5. Interview with Jan Gehl

CYRIL: There's a trend, especially in environmental movements, that says maybe we shouldn't live in cities, that they are not sustainable, and that we should return to the land, to the countryside. What do you think about that?

JAN: Personally, I don't think we have the choice. The world's population is expanding rapidly. There are already seven billion of us, and it will soon grow to nine. The most rational and economical way to house all these human beings in a sustainable way is to live in well-designed cities, rather than scattered around the countryside or in suburbs. But we need to make them better than these junky places we inherited from the twentieth century.

CYRIL: But shouldn't we limit the number of residents? When you see twenty million people packed together ...

JAN: Sometimes even thirty million.

CYRIL: ... it poses considerable challenges involving supplies, pollution, a disconnect with nature, anonymity.

JAN: Yes, we see that in countries like China, India, Brazil, where cities are growing very quickly. For me, the key lies in subdivisions. It's crucial to have autonomous neighborhoods in which residents can find all the services they need; where they have access to culture, education, health care; where they can get around on foot or by bike most of the time; where heat, water, and electricity can be optimized, rather that heating individual homes; where shared equipment (cars, objects, appliances) is possible. We need to reintroduce into these neighborhoods places where people can meet, converse, and play, and nature.

CYRIL: Why do we live in cities? Is it just a question of efficiency?

JAN: Human beings got together and built cities to better interact with one another, and together, to develop cultures. Cities have played a major role in the growth of civilizations, and I think this will continue. It's an effervescent place, a concentration of ideas, exchange, and differences. Of course, you could say that today, with all the available digital technologies, we can communicate without needing to see one another. But the physical and interpersonal possibilities offered by real-time encounters are fundamental to the development of our societies. Indirect communication will never be able to replace face-to-face communication, via dialogue.

CYRIL: Do you want to return cities to people, as the title of your book, *Cities for People*, suggests?

JAN: Absolutely. There were two major movements in the second half of the twentieth century that destroyed the life of the inner cities. On the one hand, a massive increase in the use of cars, which filled all the empty spaces and pushed residents onto sidewalks. And on the other, large-scale urban and architectural modernism, according to which, instead of building streets and squares, we constructed suburbs filled with single-family homes, after the American model. Everything was designed around the car. A countermovement to reconquer cities has been growing over the last twenty years. We don't build cities that are adapted to the needs of cars and urban planners; we need to make sure that citizens can live fulfilled lives in them.

CYRIL: How?

JAN: First of all, by returning public spaces to the residents. My firm has worked for many cities in Australia and New Zealand, but also in Moscow, London, and Malmö. They all want to become more attractive, more livable, more sustainable. For years, we conducted numerous research studies with the University of Copenhagen on the best strategies to adopt; we are now publishing them. In New York, we transformed part of Times Square, around Broadway, into a pedestrian area. The day that cars stopped driving through, Times Square filled up with people! In New York today, there are some fifty squares that have been taken back from automobiles and returned to the city's residents. And they are all very popular, because we need these places of exchange and encounter in our modern societies.

CYRIL: As an architect and urban planner, how do you design a city made for people?

JAN: I'm going to share a little revelation. We now know, from research conducted over the past fifty years, that if we build more roads, we will have more traffic. Amazing, right? So if we build more bike paths and infrastructure for bikes (parking lots, rails on staircases, racks in trains, etc.), the streets, squares, and canal and river banks will become more public places, and people will reclaim the streets, as in New York. We have a choice in city planning: will we bring more cars into the streets or more people?

CYRIL: That's definitely a revelation!

JAN: And that's not all. We are also starting to realize that modern urban design is very harmful to our health. Spending your life sitting in a chair in front of a computer, a television, or in a car can cause all kinds of pathologies. Even major health institutions are recommending that cities be designed so that people walk or bike as much as possible.

CYRIL: And it obviously costs less to get people to walk or bike than to pay for medical treatment.

JAN: There's nothing less expensive for a city than to create infrastructure for pedestrians and bicyclists. Infrastructure for subways, trams, buses, and cars is much more expensive. The more bikes and pedestrians there are, the less it costs. Furthermore, we know that for social inclusiveness and to give us a sense of security it is important that we can get know one another, have interactions, rather than remain hidden away in our houses, afraid of our neighbors. Living at home, watching films on TV, phone constantly in hand, is not enough. In cities, we can stay connected to diversity, use our senses, be close to things, learn from one another. The collateral benefits of this type of urban planning are considerable. It creates a more vibrant, more sustainable, more secure, more healthy city. So what are we waiting for?

CYRIL: Is Copenhagen a good example of a city that has been handed back to its residents?

JAN: Yes, certainly. What's remarkable is that it started so early. As far back as 1962, Copenhagen began to get cars off the main streets. Everyone said that it would never work, that we were not Italians, and would never use public spaces. Yet the city held firm, and the

---

A section of Boo1, with diverse styles of housing.

following year, we had all become Italians, sitting on café terraces and strolling around the city. Other streets soon opted to become car free, and gradually, Copenhagen was transformed. More and more residents realized that their daily lives had improved immensely, and we started to love our city even more. We were at peace with the traffic, the noise, the pollution.

CYRIL: Do you think that this could work around the world? In every culture?

JAN: I would say that the less a culture is developed [in terms of economic industrialization], the more it seems obvious that people living in cities need to be taken care of, that policies should be developed to provide more mobility to poor people. They cannot have cars in the short term, but they can have good public transportation, good sidewalks, and good bike paths linked to the train stations.

CYRIL: But how to do this in countries like China, where the number of cars are skyrocketing?

JAN: There are some interesting things happening in China. In recent decades, with the economic growth, bikes were banned from Shanghai and Beijing because city planners thought they interfered with progress. And cars totally overwhelmed the cities, with the results that we now see. But the trend is reversing now, and bikes are making a comeback. With my company, we are involved in redesigning the downtown area of Shanghai, where the city wants to recreate beautiful public places, small narrow streets, and bike paths.

CYRIL: Is this a change in the way we view progress?

JAN: In the past, progress was equated with cars and giant buildings. Today, we are looking more in terms of happiness, health. It's about replacing quantity with quality. Once immediate needs are taken care of, people start to ask themselves what the "good life" would be. And when you look at what past models gave us in cities like Miami and Los Angeles, with all the car traffic, it's hard not to wonder: "Is this really the best that humanity can do?"

CYRIL: In the rankings of cities where people say they are happiest to live, Copenhagen comes in first, with Vancouver. It looks like your strategy works.

JAN: Yes, it's been a fantastic feeling to get up every day, for the last fifty years, with the impression that the city is getting better every day, that my children will live in a nicer city than I did. There are so many cities where the opposite is true.

CYRIL: Is that why you have been so invested in these projects? For the future of your children and the people who live here?

JAN: Of course; I'm an architect. It's clear to me that architects exist to improve the world. First of all, we model buildings, cities, then it is these structures that model us. What we construct influences our everyday lives; it's a serious responsibility. Look at the impact of those concrete slabs that went up all over the suburbs in the 1960s, '70s, and '80s. If you build cities where you can't exist without a car, as in many places in America, everyone will use them, it's inevitable. If a city is clogged with cars, noise, pollution, then people will be more aggressive. On the other hand, if you build operas on every street corner, more people will go listen to music; it you create parks, everyone will fill them up; and on it goes. We should ask ourselves what kind of environment we would like our children and grandchildren to grow up in.

It's one in the morning. I'm just back from a full day of filming, and our dinner went on late into the evening. Once again, we (or at least some of us) couldn't resist the temptation to throw back a few beers while we talked about solving the world's problems. We'll pay for it tomorrow. I step into my standardized hotel room, with its standardized bed, insert my magnetic card into the slot next to the door to activate the electricity that suddenly lights up six or seven bulbs: on the ceiling, the bedside tables, the bathroom, the small desk. I collapse on the bed, throw my shoes in a corner, and open my computer to check my messages. We had decided to leave, nearly on a whim, in April 2014, when we learned that our crowd-funding could work, and that in certain countries, we had to film in the summer of that year. We wanted to release the film in late 2015, during the COP21 climate summer in Paris; and farmlands in November are not all that impressive on film. All throughout the filming, I spent most of my evening preparing for upcoming trips: identifying places, preparing meetings, drawing up rough itineraries, creating day-by-day schedules with our local contacts. At the same time, I was posting photographs taken during the day on the film's Facebook page, to keep our backers up to date on our journeys. That evening, as I read the news, I came across a 2008 article in *The Guardian* on James Lovelock (an environmental guru, prophet of climate change, father of the Gaia theory, according to which the planet is a living entity with an immune system, just like our own), posted by one of my friends in San Francisco.

I start to scan it, then began to read more carefully. The old warrior (born in 1919, ninety years old when the article was published) had given up. It went on to say that we had irreversibly reached the tipping point of climate change. It's too late, there isn't anything we can do. Extreme climate conditions will be widespread by 2020. By 2040, Europe's climate will be unlivable. Parts of England will be underwater, and the situation will be worse in the southern hemisphere. We will have to provide shelter for millions of climate refugees. Building wind turbines serves no purpose; we should prepare for our survival. The contrast with the day we had just spent was immense, with ordinary men and women rolling up their sleeves to improve the fate of the planet, without realizing that their efforts are all in vain. Lovelock is not, of course, an oracle. He has even come up with a few dumb statements (in my opinion) with his defense of nuclear energy as critical to stopping global warming in time. But looking back at his predictions made in the 1970s (most of which have come to pass), it's impossible to overlook what he has to say and not conclude that he's right about certain points. Despite our good will, we are prisoners of our comforts and our habits. I can even see it among people who are the most "committed," the presidents of environmental nonprofits who travel to scuba dive and fish in New Zealand, the most determined activists who regularly chow down a good steak (or a burger, as we had done many times while filming, before I definitively became a vegetarian), the friends who nearly apologize after purchasing the latest iPhone the minute it's released (because they think that if you're an environmentalist, it's good form to apologize). I have often bought Levi jeans and Apple computers, while criticizing the imperialism of multinationals, finding good reasons to spend money on useful clothes manufactured halfway across the globe. And take my car to go just a few miles when my bike would have worked just as well. Everything is too easy, too tempting. So flashy we can't resist. A few years ago, I read a fantastic book by Bertrand Méheust, *La Politique de l'oxymore*,[1] which reached the same conclusion: our primary obstacle, which we may never manage to overcome, is our drive for comfort.

I decide to turn off my computer for the night, to settle deep into my decidedly comfortable double bed in my lifeless room, and take up these issues in the light of day, with help from our next luminaries.

---

1. Bertrand Méheust, *La Politique de l'oxymore* (Paris: La Découverte, 2009).

6. A zero-waste city:
The story of San Francisco

San Francisco was like a kid's dream for most of the crew. Everyone had their own myths to explore: film masterpieces like *Vertigo*, *Bullitt*, or *The Lady from Shanghai*; the Beat Generation and the famous City Lights bookshop; the Sentinel Building; Castro and Harvey Milk's social battles; the music of Jefferson Airplane and Sly and the Family Stone.

But San Francisco is also famous on another level. In just a few years, the city has vaulted to the forefront of recycling with their Zero Waste scheme, which, as Julie Bryant, the city's senior coordinator for the project, consists in reducing, reusing, and recycling all the waste produced by the city. It's obviously an essential approach in a world where 10 million tons of waste are thrown away every day.[1] Landfills, rivers, forests, and oceans are filled with garbage from Western society. In Africa, entire towns are depositories for the old computers, televisions, and vehicles that we no longer use, polluting the water and earth, and poisoning the children. At the same time, one-third of the food we produce ends up in the garbage. Not only does it not feed the people who need it, but it piles up in landfills, or is simply incinerated. In an attempt to solve this problem, San Francisco set up one of the world's most ambitious plans: the goal is to achieve 100 percent of composed or recycled waste by 2020. In 2014, the city had already reached the impressive landfill diversion rate of 80 percent, which includes residential material, material generated by commercial businesses, and construction and demolition debris.[2]

---

1. Planetscope: www.planetoscope.com/dechets/363-production-de-dechets-dans-le-monde.html.
2. Meanwhile, a 2015 study by the French consumer group UFC Que Choisir (What to choose) revealed that 75 percent of waste is not recycled: Armelle Bohineust, "Les Trois quarts des déchets ne sont pas recycles," *Le Figaro.fr*, April 23, 2015, http://www.lefigaro.fr/societes/2015/04/23/20005-20150423ARTFIG00086-les-trois-quarts-des-dechets-ne-sont-pas-recycles.php.

The strategy was clear: to make the process easy and mandatory. Easy through the installation of three bins: green for compostables, blue for recyclables, and black for landfill-bound material. Each household has small containers for inside, which are then emptied into the large bins of corresponding colors. The same goes for all restaurants, gas stations, and public property. You wash your hands after a trip to the bathroom? Your recycled paper towel goes in the green bin. Eat a banana on the street? Same thing. And on it goes. Mandatory, says Julie, because "technically, people can be fined $100 for not recycling or composting properly." Recycle and compost, it's the law here. In practice, the city relies more on financial incentives. Trash collection is billed by weight, and the more you put in your black bin (landfill material), the more you pay. The more you recycle and compost, on the other hand, the lower your bill. The local Hilton Hotel saves more than $250,000 annually by managing its waste materials.

The government institutions with which Julie works have saved the tidy little sum of $3 million since the program was launched. To reduce waste at the source, particularly the plastic that covers the beaches and ends up part of the Great Pacific Garbage Patch,[1] San Francisco banned the sale of plastic bags in 2007 and asked businesses to have customers pay for biodegradable starch or paper bags. In practice, a quick trip around one of the city's shopping malls reveals that even though most of the shops are playing along, not all of them are following the guidelines. Julie regrets this, but points out how hard it is to follow up on everyone all the time. The new challenge is a ban of plastic bottles on public property,

1. An immense stretch of plastic debris, with pieces measuring less than 0.2 inches, floating in suspension on the surface or up to a depth of 98 feet, located in the North Pacific Ocean and measuring one-third the surface area of the United States or six times the size of France.

Robert (fourth from the left), with a few colleagues at Recology.

which took effect as of February 2015. "We don't need plastic bottles," says Julie. "Tap water is good and healthy; you just have to have a water bottle of your own and fill it up at home or from one of the drinking fountains around town."

When used plastic is thrown away in the right bin, it is transported to the Recology plant, the cooperative that takes care of the city's waste. Here, dozens of employees hand sort the material, before it is sorted a second time, by machine. Ayanna Banks works there. Like her colleagues she is paid $22 an hour, as opposed to the $7.25 that is the average hourly rate in the United States. She doesn't tell us that sorting garbage is her dream job, but she says that it does have a certain meaning. "It's changed the way my family sees things. We are now aware just how important the environment is. I had never thought about how all the stuff we throw away will pollute the land where we'll grow our food, the water that we'll drink, but it makes sense, when you think about it." And when we tell her that in France we only recycle bottles,[1] but not other types of plastic, she looks amazed and yells, "Whaaat?!" Then bursts out laughing. "Here, we recycle all kinds of hard plastic—it's not possible to recycle plastic film or bags," explains Robert, spokesperson for Recology. "To sort them, we use an optical scanner. Come see where it was made." We step closer and Robert is amused to show us where it came from: the Netherlands. In practice, the waste rolls along a belt and, depending on whether the object is transparent or colored, and its level of density, the scanner releases small bursts of air that separate the objects into the different sorting areas. A simple idea, someone just had to think of it. And Robert drives his point home: "Recycling and composting create ten times more jobs than

1. In fact, three of seven types of plastic are recycled in France: PET (1), PEHD (2), and PP (5), but this is what the Éco Emballage recycling guide still advises: "Unless you are participating in the expanded sorting program, only plastic bottles and containers are recycled. When in doubt, throw the rest away with your household waste (tubs, bags, small trays, film made of plastic)."

landfills or incineration. It's huge. It is a significant source of local ecological jobs for countries with high unemployment, like Spain or Greece. In the United States, if every city recycled 75 percent of its waste, which is less than the current rate in San Francisco, we would create 1.5 million new jobs. In California, it would mean 125,000 permanent and local new jobs."

Calculating roughly in my head (and using my telephone), I tried to add up jobs created by relocalizing food as explained by Charles, by energy transition as discussed by Thierry, and adding those generated by recycling. I came up with a figure somewhere around 1.5 million,[1] in a country like France, where more than 3.5 million people are unemployed. Seeing as this issue is always a priority among those running for office, as well as among French people surveyed, it seems that there a few areas yet to be pursued. "All cities are trying to attract business," continues Robert, "and recycling and composting represent an opportunity to create new jobs from local resources. It's a radical new perspective. Here, when we see waste, we don't see garbage, but cardboard, glass, plastic compost. We see resources."

Local farmers immediately took note. While the blue bins end up in the plant in San Francisco's harbor, the contents of the green bins are sent outside the city, where organic and green waste (grass cuttings, branches, and so on) are transformed into compost, Robert's favorite material. Throughout the eleven-step process, food and garden waste are treated separately. A tractor loads it onto conveyor belts leading to a centrifuge that separate large and small objects. The smaller ones fall through large holes into a pile, while the larger ones continue along the belt, where Recology employees remove plastic

1. A study conducted by Terre de Liens Normandie estimated that 600,000 jobs would be created by relocating agriculture; A CNRS study for négaWatt estimates 684,000 through energy transition; and a ration of jobs created in California applied to France would amount to 215,000 new jobs in the recycling sector in France (as opposed to barely 30,000 at present. Philippe Collet, "Recyclage: des pistes pour créer plus d'emplois en France," *ActuEnvironment.com*, January 2, 20014, www.actu-environne-ment.com/ae/news/soutien-emploi-recyclage-france-rapport-cgeiet-cgedd-20332.php4).

bags, cans, sneakers and anything else that doesn't belong there. That biggest pieces (branches, for example), go through a noisy shredder that spits out wood chips, not far from the piles of smaller waste. During the next step, all the piles of waste are mixed up, sprayed with water, and arranged in mounds some 150 feet long. Machines aerate and turn over the spongy material. Several other steps follow. In the middle of the process, the piles that have started to look like compost are lined up in rows, and the gas they emit is filtered through wood that absorbs the CO_2, which would otherwise be released into the atmosphere. Then this wood itself is composted. The next step involves screening the material, to obtain smaller and smaller material. "This is what the plants want," insists Roberts, "pieces so small that the nutrients can be absorbed by the roots." Other rows are once again turned over and watered regularly for several weeks. At this stage, the temperature of the compost is around 160° F. This fermentation kills harmful bacteria and encourages the growth of beneficial ones. Robert is kneeling on the compost, running his hands through it; it's hot, and he digs down even deeper, his hands disappearing in to the black material, as fine as sand. He smells a handful. "It smells like a farm. In this small section [indicating a circle maybe two feet across] there are more microbes than there are people on the planet. It keeps the soil alive."

By the end of the process, Recology has obtained high-quality compost, which is sold to local farmers. To make it even better fertilizer, it can be mixed, with minerals on request. Farmers and vineyards get their soil analyzed to determined what they need to add. Recology can then prepare custom blends using nine amendments (gypsum, rock phosphate, lime, sulfate, etc.). "The microbial activity of compost releases minerals, so that they can be absorbed by the roots of plants," explains Robert. And the revenue from the sale helps pay for this operation. "We sell it for $9 the cubic yard, and we can't make enough; there's a tremendous demand. It's the best thing you can do with your scraps. Compost returns nutrients to the soil, saves water (a humus-rich soil can hold twice its weight in water, which translates into far less irrigation), and helps grow cover crops that pull carbon out of the atmosphere." Robert showed us a study stating that if one-fourth of the farmland was covered with compost, the soil could absorb three-quarters of the state's CO_2 emissions.[1] "We are combining the ancient practice of composting with something very new: waste recycling. This is how we need to build the future. We need to stop burning and burying food, it's absurd. We need to make compost.

Dave Vella, manager of the Chateau Montelena Winery in Napa Valley, agrees. We followed Robert and the compost truck to the vineyards, where he had nothing but praise for the project: "Soil is like a bank. Every time you harvest a crop, you withdraw minerals, organic material, bacteria from it. And you cannot keep taking elements out indefinitely, sometimes you need to make deposits. Adding nitrates, potassium[2] is not enough. That's what I used to do thirty years ago, and my yield was decreasing. I had to keep adding more and more. I then started using compost fifteen years ago, and Recology's compost for the last ten years. With compost, we are recreating humus, the blood of the soil. The earth is more balanced, the plants are healthy and rarely sick, and the yields are constant. You have to learn from your mistakes to improve." When we ask him if he thinks this model can be replicated, his answer is categorical: "All the major metropolitan areas should be composting their table scraps and yard waste. Why fill up the landfills with this stuff, when farmers want it for their land? I'm a farmer; I want compost." It's a question of leaving behind a system in which we produce stuff to throw away. A system that infuriates Robert: "It's totally crazy to spend money and energy to pump oil from the ground (oil that has taken millions of years to develop), and make plastic objects that we throw away after using once or twice, then bury them all in landfills or destroy them completely by incinerating them. By reusing and recycling, we will

1. See also studies by the Rodale Institute.
2. The ubiquitous NPK (nitrogen, potassium, phosphorus) chemical fertilizers.

decrease our dependence on oil, our costs, our environmental footprints. The same goes for other materials. An aluminum container can be recycled nearly indefinitely, while extracting aluminum from mountains destroys nature and uses an incredible amount of energy. We also need to find alternatives to plastic as a packing material; use our purchasing power and stop buying them. Industrialists would then have to find sustainable solutions."

Morten's prediction that cities could become future world leaders seems to be supported in San Francisco, whose approach has been contagious. More than one thousand universities and three hundred cities in the United States have duplicated this composting program. Some 118 jurisdictions have adopted ordinances prohibiting plastic bags. Every day, the city gets calls from around the world, from Europe to South America. Robert recently traveled to Lyon and Nantes in France: "In Nantes, they started by telling me they were strong environmentalists, then they sent me to visit their incinerators. Afterward, I had lunch with six city officials. A couple next to us was eating crab. I asked them where the shells went. To the incinerator, of course. I told them than when I was a kid, there was a drawing in my schoolbook showing a Native American digging a hole in the ground, burying fish bones, covering them, and then planting seeds of corn. They knew that the bones were beneficial to the corn. We haven't invented anything in San Francisco; we are just trying to remember lessons from the past."

Achieving energy transition therefore means saving energy and raw materials, and producing what we really need, using recycling and diverse renewable energies. As with agriculture, the stakeholders we met felt that a partial decentralization of production methods and distribution networks was necessary so that territories could achieve more autonomy.

We were starting to see the outlines of a world in which producing and consuming much of our food and energy locally was crucial to dealing with the crises of the upcoming decades.

But a new subject of investigation was starting to emerge. Economics and finance had become omnipresent in our conversations. They were essential tools for Morten in Copenhagen, Éric in Réunion, and Julie in San Francisco. But others view them as major obstacles to any transformation of our societies. First, energy transition is expensive, and many governments claim they don't have enough funds to finance it. And second, as Thierry and Olivier explained to us, the power of multinationals and lobbies is always overwhelming in terms of maintaining an extremely lucrative system (as least for the handful of people who control it). The example of Canada is now sadly infamous. The discovery of oil in the Alberta tar sands (a mixture of clay, water, and crude oil) held out the prospect of 1.8 trillion barrels, including 170 billion that could be extracted immediately with the current state of technology. It was ranked as the world's third largest reserve, a considerable windfall that could bring hundreds of billions to the government, and which had already required nearly 400 billion in investment from the oil companies on site. Not only has it been a total environmental disaster, but the increase in greenhouse gases in Canada since 1990 (nearly 18 percent) has been caused nearly entirely by the mining site.[1] Worse, multiple scenarios predict that if Canada mines all these deposits, any hope of remaining below the 35.6° F global temperature increase evaporates. For both these reasons, Canada withdrew from the Kyoto Protocol and systematically opposes measures recommended at worldwide climate summits. Regardless of whether the entire planet will suffer the dramatic consequences of climate change, regardless of whether nature will be devastated, 150,000 jobs were created and there is a huge pile of money to be made.

1. Greenhouse Gas Emissions, Environment and Climate Change Canada, http:// www.ec.gc.ca/indicateurs-indicators/default.asp?lang=En&n=FBF8455E-1.

3

AN ECONOMY FOR THE FUTURE

Economics is now the sector used to justify political and business decisions. As if the economy transcends everything else. Understanding it has therefore become essential, more now than at any other time. Curiously, however, no one really talks about economics. Ask anyone (other than an economist) to talk to you about the trade balance, the mechanism for monetary creation, inflation, or growth levers—most likely the conversation will gently ease toward a softer topic: literature, film, science, health, sports, gardening, cooking, or even the weather. Unfortunately, none of these subjects impact the course of our world as economy can. When the entire crew sighed collectively, thinking that this section would be the most boring and least cinematic, I took everyone to see my friend Pierre Rabhi.[1] He is the most charming and gentle of men, unmoved by shallow theories, but with a tenacious habit of bringing everything down to the basics. The small troupe was delighted. It was truly exhilarating to discuss the global economy with this Algerian-born farmer decked out in his faithful suspenders, who stands barely five feet tall, and was, as always, in sandals.

1. Background–Interview with Pierre Rabhi

CYRIL: Why do you think we aren't able to implement the changes we will need so that humanity can survive future crises?

PIERRE: I think that we have confused our abilities, which are enormous, with intelligence. The human brain is a highly perfected tool;

1. Pierre Rabhi is an Algerian-born French farmer, author, and philosopher. A pioneer in the field of agroecology, he has contributed significantly to food security in the Sahel. He has written over a dozen well-received books that have influenced activists such as Nicolas Hulot and Fabrice Nicolino, CEOs including François Lemarchand and Tristan Lecomte, and actresses like Juliette Binoche and Marion Cotillard.

it can create tremendous machines, like the one you are using to film. But overall, these accomplishments do not produce an intelligent system, because we are destroying the very foundations of what we need to stay alive: water, soil, trees. I have always said that if extraterrestrials were studying us, they'd be tearing their hair out, they wouldn't understand a thing: "How is it that they know how to do so many things, yet they are so dumb? Why have they turned this magnificent planet into a battlefield of slaughter and destruction?"

CYRIL: That's a good question. Why are we doing this?

PIERRE: For me, one of the aberrations of the global system is this much-vaunted endless economic growth, which is constantly touted as the solution to all our problems (unemployment, poverty, and so on), even though it is our primary problem. The idea of never-ending growth has turned us into an insatiable species which, instead of looking at the planet as a true miracle, a marvelous oasis floating in the middle of a vast sidereal desert, a magnificent place to live, views it instead as a source of raw materials that has to be drained down to the last fish and last tree. If we compared the history of the planet to a twenty-four-hour clock, human beings would only have existed the last two minutes. When we see the extent of our impact over this tiny period, the absurdity of our actions and the responsibility incumbent on humanity are even more obvious. Yet for the time being, it seems as if we are in the dark ages.

CYRIL: We started this trip with the understanding of the enormous impact stories have on us. Is this story of endless growth another one? A kind of myth to which we have adhered, that is leading us in this direction?

PIERRE: It's obviously a myth based on an aberration. Logically speaking, it's not possible to have a system of endless growth in a finite reality. If we had other planets, we could say that once this one has been depleted, we would go somewhere else. But we don't.

CYRIL: How would you describe this myth?

PIERRE: The Promethean myth; man as demiurge who wants to become God. Human beings, with their technology and science, have set themselves up as supreme creatures, able to overcome nature, dominate it, use it. For me, this break with the natural world has been decisive and has brought us to the situation we now know. But we have forgotten one small detail: does the human species need nature? Yes. Does nature need the human species? No. This is where we should start. A few days ago, somebody came by to interview me about the problems of water. I told her: "You are made of water and I am made of water; you are not doing a story on something that is external to us, but is one of the main elements of our reality." Too often, we look at nature as something external; we call it the "environment," but we are nature! We are mammals, whether we like it or not. Human beings are of course unique; we are thinking creatures, with a sense of time and space, and an understanding that we will die, that this planet is temporary. It's a difficult reality to come to terms with, one that is certainly at the root of all our turmoil. And it leads us on a desperate quest for security—through religion, dominance over women and children, the arm's race, homeland defense, wars, and also, accumulation.

CYRIL: Consumerism?

PIERRE: Endlessly producing and consuming. This is a purely human activity! The difference between animal behavior and human behavior is that the lion only attacks the antelope when it is hungry; it doesn't attack to destroy it, collect it, and sell it to friends. It doesn't have any warehouses so it can say: "I can make it so you don't have to hunt; I have antelopes." The predatory behavior of human beings involves accumulation, with a single goal: to make money. In so-called evolved societies, money has taken over as the essential element, like a kind of energy that holds everything together. Acquiring it increases our sense of security and our power. It has become the primary tool of domination.

CYRIL: With what impact?

PIERRE: Predatory behavior as a way of existence has become so widespread that it is not only destroying nature, but is also creating enormous inequalities. The ratio that economists generally quote is that one-fifth of humanity consumes four-fifths of the planet's resources. On the one hand, we have populations that are indeed rich, but which consume large quantities of anti-anxiety medications to compensate for their malaise; on the other, entire populations that are neglected. Furthermore, this unbridled quest for profit has made our world homogenous. This paradigm began in Europe, and Europe is its first victim. In the sixteenth, seventeenth centuries, it still encompassed different ethnic groups, people who had their own ways of dressing and eating, their own stories and traditions, multiple languages. We overlaid a monoculture atop this multitude of diverse cultures—which was largely exported via colonization. Europe would never have been able to survive if it had remained within its own borders. This model requires so many resources that land, raw materials, and labor had to be taken from around the world. The only thing is that this excess is unsustainable. You often hear that if everyone lived like Americans, we would need seven planets;[1] but we only have one.

1. According to the environmental footprint determined by the WWF.

CYRIL: So it is not merely a demographics problem?

PIERRE: Of course not. I get angry, for example, when people say that world hunger is caused by demographics. You can't accuse people who have nothing to eat that they are themselves responsible for famine! We know that one-third of the food produced on the planet ends up in the garbage, and that a great deal of arable land is used to produce biofuel. I am not necessarily in favor of having more people on the planet, but we have to be somewhat responsible and get away from these myths that are so well scripted that some people view them as absolute truths.

CYRIL: You say that in the West, even though we have accumulated wealth, we are not necessarily happier.

PIERRE: How could we be? The West has made money the measure of time, with the oft quoted: "Time is money," which is a particularly odious statement. Once we accept that time is money, the die is cast. We can no longer "waste time"; we have to "save" it. This creates a kind of frenzy, which has expanded ever further with current tools of productivity, like computers.

CYRIL: What are we to do?

PIERRE: Return to the eternal, natural rhythms. This is why I am a firm believer in the kitchen garden. I return to a real sense of time there. I can yell at my tomato plant, but it's not going to give me back anything until the tomatoes are ripe. A single tomato seed holds the potential for several tons of food. A single kernel of wheat, when multiplied, can feed all of humanity. It's absolutely magical! The power of life can be concentrated in a seed, but it is indexed to time. It has to ripen. In our over-active society, we have created tools to handle the frenzy, rather than challenge the situation itself.

We are totally out of sync with the laws of nature, particularly in cities, where people no longer have a relationship with nature that fosters patience and these eternal rhythms. When we live like this, we not only sacrifice materials and resources, we also sacrifice our ability to rejoice in the beauty of nature. Not only do we pollute and degrade it, but we also get rid of the very things that bring us joy. For me, the environment is joy. I love this little story that perfectly expresses this idea of frenzy and "always more." It's about a fisherman who has just finished working; his boat is tied up next to him on the beach, his net is stretched, and he is resting. A serious man walks by, looks at the boat as says: "Sir, you should be at sea at this time of the day." "Why?" he asks. "Well, to earn a living; you'll never amount to anything just napping that way. It that boat yours?" "Yes." "But it's small." "Yes, it is." "You could have a bigger one." "And then?" "Well, then, you could catch a lot more fish." "And then?" "You'd have so much money that you could buy an even bigger boat." "And then?" "You could hire people to work so you don't have to." "And then?" "You could rest!" "Well, that's exactly what I'm doing right now."

This insatiability is widely maintained by the work that advertisers have done on the collective human psyche. They work on a subliminal level, not on tangible reality. Because in reality, once I have enough to eat, I have clothes, I have a roof over my head, and I am healthy, I have everything I need. After that, everything else is superfluous. What is destroying the planet today? It's not the essentials, all that everyone needs to survive. It's this out-of-control, permanent fantasy world of desire that fuels the pseudo-economic machine. In reality, this doesn't have anything to do with economy.

CYRIL: Why is that?

PIERRE: Etymologically, "economy" has nothing to do with this wasteful system. *Oikos nomos,* means "household manager."[1] Waste is contradictory to economy, even in its definition. If I am being wasteful, I am not being economical. When you know that a good share of the creativity of wealthy countries is put to use to create waste, I can't imagine that you can call that an economy. Economy should be based on Lavoisier's law of conservation: "Nothing is lost, nothing is created, everything is transformed." Everything is recycled. In a forest, energy, instead of being dissipated, is returned to the ground, where the waste decomposes and becomes food for other organisms, in a nearly infinite cycle.

CYRIL: In short, consume less and better.

PIERRE: Rediscover the power of moderation, autonomy, intelligence. I wrote a book called *Vers la sobriété heureuse,*[2] in which I discussed our experience, with my wife, Michelle. There is something liberating about the idea of restraint. The time I save working for my survival is time I can devote to my inner growth. Ivan Illich calculated that when the time spent working to buy and pay all the expenses of a car are factored into the time actually spent driving a car, the speed of a car would average out at just 3.7 mph. About the same pace as walking. After a while, it is our possessions that possess us. We become slaves to them.

CYRIL: Like the story about Thoreau, who picked up three stones in the river and put them on his desk because he thought they were pretty, until he realized that he would have to dust them off every day—so he put them back in the river.

1. According to Webster's: From the Greek term, *oikos,* "house," and *nomos,* "to manage."
2. Pierre Rabhi, *Vers la sobriété heureuse* (Arles: Actes Sud, [2010] 2013).

PIERRE: I think we are alienated. In lectures, people laugh when I say: "You know, the path of a human being in modern times is to be locked into *bahut* ("chest" in French, but also slang for "school) from preschool to university, with the hope of one day working in a *boîte* (literally "box," also means "company"), large or small, to earn money so that at night, you can go dance in another *boîte* (nightclub), drive there in your "crate," before ending up in an old folks' home and then the final "box." If that's the path to liberation, then I don't know anything about freedom. Moderation and autonomy mobilizes communities, wherever they are, to meet their needs and achieve greater freedom. This is why I say that growing your own food is an act of dissidence. Either I take the position of "Someone feeds me," and I am dependent on a food production system that does what it likes; or I try to find a more liberating situation. In France, 80 percent of the food produced is forced to go through one of the five purchasing centers (Carrefour, Leclerc, Auchan, etc.). They determine the price paid to producers and the sales price for consumers. Which determines, directly or indirectly, the farming methods, the size of fruits and vegetables, the production conditions for their products, and the way the people in the factories are paid and treated. They hold all the power. In our world, a handful of multinationals (Monsanto, Bayer, Syngenta) control virtually all of the seeds that we need to feed ourselves. So of course I cannot meet all my needs, but all the needs I can meet, I do. I am then in a counterinsurgency situation against a totalitarian system, which makes all human beings dependent. We cannot always bemoan our fate, looking for scapegoats or ways to shirk our responsibility. We cannot wait for the government to offer us an ideal society, or for multinationals to change from the inside. We have to do our share, like the hummingbird in the story. We don't want multinationals anymore? Then go buy elsewhere. We don't want a chemical agriculture? Cultivate your own garden or buy from a CSA?[1] These actions may seem insignificant, but they are huge. And if there are a lot of us in open dissent, we have the power to profoundly modify things and shift the direction of society toward more positive goals.

For the last dozen years or so, awareness that the entire economy is dominated by finance has spread throughout society. There have been many TV documentaries on the subject,[2] along with the publication of multiples books[3] and articles, while a candidate for the French presidential elections (who won) targeted finance as "the adversary against which we have to do battle."[4] According to many journalists, economists, and activists, the financialization of the economy always pushes for immediate profits, at the expense of employees and ecosystems. As Muhammad Yunus, Bengali entrepreneur, economist, and winner of the Nobel Peace Prize in 2006, told us: "One of the most disturbing signs that our economy is moving in the wrong direction is the figure that was made public this year concerning income disparity. Right now, the 85 richest people in the world own as much as the 3.5 billion poorest. It's appalling. It shows us just how much our capitalist system is a bloodsucking machine. It draws resources to the top, concentrating them at the top. It is absolutely unsustainable in the long term. At the same time, we are also destroying the planet, which is making our situation even worse." The figure discussed by Yunus comes from a report published by Oxfam on January 20, 2014, just before the

1. Community-supported agriculture network, a system of support among growers and consumers, by which the grower supplies weekly baskets of produce (often organic) that have been prepaid by members.
2. Including the excellent film, *Goldman Sachs: The Bank that Rules the World*.
3. Including Naomi Klein's remarkable book, *The Shock Doctrine* (New York: Henry Holt & Co, 2007).
4. "My true adversary does not have a name, a face, a party; it will never stand for election; will never hold office; and yet it governs. This adversary is the world of finance." François Hollande, January 22, 2012, in a speech given at Le Bourget, during the French presidential election campaign.

Davos Summit.[1] It then listed a few others that are staggering in terms of inequality across the planet. Culminating with: "Almost half of the world's wealth is now owned by just 1 percent of the population. The wealth of the 1 percent richest people in the world amounts to $110 trillion. That's sixty-five times the total wealth of the bottom half of the world's population. Seven out of ten people live in countries where economic inequality has increased in the last thirty years. The richest 1 percent increased their share of income in twenty-four out of twenty-six countries for which we have data between 1980 and 2012. In the United States the wealthiest 1 percent captured 95 percent of the post-financial crisis growth since 2009, while the bottom 90 percent became poorer."

Extraordinary wealth has been accumulated by an ever-smaller number of people, while poverty and famine continue unabated. One child dies of hunger every seven seconds; two billion people now live on less than $2 per day[2] (which would not necessarily be a problem in societies where money is not predominant, but becomes difficult in societies that have been forced to adopt our global, financial-oriented system); and unemployment in increasing to dangerous levels in a number of countries, including in Europe where it exceeds 10 percent in France, 12 percent in Italy, and is around 25 percent in Spain and Greece.

When you realize that approximately €20 trillion are not included in the redistributive mechanisms of taxes, because they have been placed in tax havens, and that just 1 percent of this amount would be enough to solve the problems of hunger, health, and education for the entire planet, it's enough to fuel discontent.[3] In the words

1. See Working for the Few, www.oxfam.org/en/research/working-few.
2. Inequality Watch, www.inegalites.fr/spip.php?article381.
3. In 2012, a study by the Tax Justice Network, directed by a former chief economist for the consultant firm McKinsey, estimated at approximately €20 trillion the amount of money hidden in secret tax havens, while according to calculations by Lester Brown and the Earth Policy Institute, it would cost less than €200 billion

of Louis Brandeis, a judge on the US Supreme Court: "We may have democracy, or we may have wealth concentrated in the hands of the few, but we cannot have both."[1]

In November 2013, the World Economic Forum made no mistake when, in its Outlook on the Global Agenda 2014 report, it ranked increasing income disparity as the second biggest risk for the near future. This report underscored just how inequality affects the social stability of countries and threatens global security. According to a study co-financed by one of the NASA laboratories in 2014 and published by the *Guardian*,[2] two essential factors can trigger the collapse of a society when they converge: "The stretching of resources due to the strain placed on the ecological carrying capacity" and "the economic stratification of society into elites (the rich) and masses (commoners, or the poor)." For researchers, the convergence of these two phenomena "has played a central role in the character or in the process of the collapse over the last five thousand years." It very much looks as if we are now facing this exact situation.

Indeed, everyone is getting poorer. And has to fight to keep their heads above water. If I look at my personal situation, the conclusion is clear. A couple, middle class, two children, a house in one of the poorest towns in France, 50 miles from Paris. Food budget: €800 per month. Insurance, plus complementary insurance: €400. Mortgage: €1,500 per month for another twenty-three years. Car loan: €250. School cafeteria and other fees: €300. Electricity, gas, and water bills: €250. Music conservatory, music and dance classes, basketball, and tennis fees: €150 per month—all without factoring in

per year to stabilize population, eradicate poverty, and restore ecosystems—in other terms, what this money would produce in taxes, or merely one-eighth of worldwide annual military spending. See Lester R. Brown, *World on the Edge: How to Prevent Environmental and Economic Collapse* (New York: W. W. Norton, 2011), p. 17.

1. Quoted in "Working for the Few," Oxfam International, January 20, 2014, http://www.ipu.org/splz-e/unga14/oxfam.pdf, p. 10.

2. Nafeez Ahmed, "Nasa-Funded Study: Industrial Civilisation Headed for 'Irreversible Collapse,'" *The Guardian*, March 14, 2014, http://www.theguardian.com/environment/earth-insight/2014/mar/14/nasa-civilisation-irreversible-collapse-study-scientists.

clothes, books, going out. To stay afloat in our contemporary consumer society, we need the tidy sum of €4,500 every month. And every month, each little everyday expense is skyrocketing. Squeezed by prizes that keep going up, the SMEs, VSBs,[1] and other independent workers inflate their prices to be able to survive, crushing the working classes, whose salaries are not in sync with the alarming rates driven by the market. At the same time, consumerist pressures are increasing. Advertisers, whose overbilled activity must support the national effort to "increase consumption" with the outright goal of "boosting growth," inundate us with a flow of images and messages meant to feed our endless hunger for objects, clothes, and gadgets. Our house is filled with them. Although we are not among the keenest consumers, we definitely ensure a respectable contribution to the national effort. Our closets are overflowing with a thousand things that seemed utterly essential when they were purchased and which are now stored on forgotten shelves. With every move, they are transported in boxes that will never be opened or else end up in the garbage without us ever questioning whether they were worthwhile or not. Children's toy gather dust, their rooms are filled with gifts, compulsive and useless purchases, fueled by a desire for things that we have transmitted to them, even against our own principles. When we will stop? Even though we know by heart where all this accumulation leads? What will other people do? All those who are bored with and indifferent to these issues? I have no idea. I think that right now, I don't even want to know. I have to pack my bags, close my Excel sheet. We're leaving tomorrow for northern France, then Belgium and Switzerland, to plunge into the world of business, banks, and currencies. Will I find some answers that I can actually use in this life?

1. Very Small Businesses.

2. Pocheco: Producing in an environmentally friendly way is more cost-effective

So, this incessant goal of growth that Pierre discusses and which will soon ruin me, runs counter to the need to save, as stressed by Thierry, Robert, and all the other stakeholders in energy transition. It is a double bind: to move toward renewable energy sources, we have to consume less, but to keep the economy up and running, we have to consume more. It's enough to make you crazy.

Our question is now this: is it possible to organize an economic system where companies can create wealth, jobs, and meet our needs, without destroying the planet and without infinite growth? Could we imagine that some of them would abide by the principles of thermodynamics discussed by Pierre and display a certain sense of restraint?

The answer was right under our noses, or nearly—exactly 142 miles from Paris. Pocheco has 114 employees and is located in Forest-sur-Marque, near Lille in northern France. It produces two billion envelopes every year. I had visited it several times and become friends with its CEO, Emmanuel Druon. I knew he could answer a good number of our questions.

But the crew was dragging their feet (again) when I brought up the site (an envelope factory in northern France). A suburb of Lille was clearly not as exciting as Detroit or San Francisco. But when our minibus finally left the factory, nearly all of us thought that this sequence had been the most striking of our entire journey.

Nearly twenty years ago, when Emmanuel Druon became manager of Pocheco, he discovered a catastrophic situation: sexual harassment and bullying, barrels of toxic material buried in the courtyard, embezzlement, and a company on the verge of bankruptcy.

Part of the Pocheco staff; the site operates 24/7.

The ambiance among employees was highly charged; even more so between the administrators and the unions. The initial meetings were hostile, and for several months Emmanuel was hesitant to leave his office. He then became friends with Yazid Bousselaoui, who rapidly became his right-hand man. He knew the employees, they trusted him, and he told Emmanuel which ones would be willing to re-engage in dialogue. A small core group was formed. The quasi-desperate situation freed them up, motivating everyone to come up with a dream for the company, even though they were fully aware it wouldn't be easy. As Emmanuel likes to say: "This region has the highest rate of unemployment, the highest rates of cancer, and records the most votes for the right-wing Front National party."

Emmanuel had worked in the "traditional" company model for ten years, as an executive with L'Oréal where, in his own words, he endured "the brutality, management by terror," market shares to be conquered, and shareholders to pay. He hated that world. Here, he wanted to do things differently. Having the power to create something new was both exciting and terrifying, but his passion took over, and after several months, then several years, a sense of trust was forged among the employees. Gradually, the entire playing field changed.

The small management team set up a "flat" organizational structure, as they like to call it, which gives a maximum amount of autonomy to each employee. This freedom came with a condition: not to betray a colleague's trust, remain transparent, work together, and do one's best to keep the company afloat. In exchange, two innovative measures were instituted: an income disparity of one to four (as opposed to an average of one to one hundred in French companies), and profits that are systematically reinvested in the company. The shareholders (primarily Emmanuel) do not receive dividends. He explained: "In recent decades, the economy has been literally addicted to profits—which go to an ever-smaller number of people. The problem is that if you take 10 to 15 percent of the profits from what you produce for a few shareholders, it's money that you can't use to modernize the company. You can't invest, or not enough. So you tend to think along short-term lines, try to find the lowest prices, even if your raw materials travel three times around the planet before they get to you, that they have destroyed ecosystems where people work in deplorable conditions to extract them." For the first few months there were no funds to invest. All his energy went toward turning the company around. But gradually, as the employees started to feel calm and more ambitious, the situation shifted, particularly in terms of the purchasing policy. "We decided that we were too poor to buy crap," said Emmanuel, glancing over at his colleagues. "So we only buy very high-quality raw materials." For an envelope manufacturer, raw material is paper. The steering committee (there is no manager at Pocheco, or board of administration) started to look for a supplier who could provide quality in an ethical way. They decided on UPM, a particularly ethical Finnish company. "Every time they cut down a tree, they replant four others, respecting the biodiversity of the species. A tree captures the most CO_2 in the first ten years of its growth, so the activity's footprint is actually positive. In addition, most of the wood we use comes from thinning cuts,[1] or for certain envelopes we have created recently, like our Oxymore model, made from sawmill waste.[2] In this way, the forest is exploited in an optimal way, they cut the fewest possible trees, and nothing is wasted (the large trunks are used for furniture and construction, while the branches and waste go for paper), and they replant more than they cut." Before selecting UPM, Emmanuel traveled to Finland to take a look for himself. He was also able to see that the machines cutting down the trees are on legs rather than tracks so that they don't crush the small trees; that they use fuel from paper pulp and hardly emit any CO_2; that

1. A technique of clearing plants around main trees that are left to grow for several decades.
2. Sawdust and wood chips.

the factory reprocesses all the water, releasing totally pure water into the environment; that it has lowered its use of water resources by 50 percent over fifteen years; and that the paper is transported by ship and then train, considered to be less polluting than truck transport. But, continued Emmanuel, "We choose the best solution in light of our current knowledge and progress. As soon as we can do better, we'll change!" Research is also underway to reduce the paperweight of the envelopes: "If we decrease their weight by a few grams, we can save a lot of resources," explained Yazid. Paper and cardboard waste is collected, then resold and recycled. It is then used to make new boxes, which is the least energy-intensive way to recycle, according to Yazid and Emmanuel, as it only requires bleaching the paper pulp with chlorine. Other improvements were made to the envelopes, like water-based glues and a paper transparent window (rather than plastic), which makes it easier to recycle the envelopes.

Improvements were then made at the printing stage, where the team began to look at the inks. They quickly decided to move toward water-based compositions and natural pigments—which wasn't necessarily an easy step. It took more than one year of research to find, in 1998, the right mix, which is irreproachable both in terms of quality and environmental impact. They went through several failed attempts, with ink trays that filled up with strangely colorful foam. "When we were still using toxic inks, made from solvents and alcohol, employees in the shop had to wear masks and gloves that went up past their elbows. It was impossible to breathe in there. Once we shifted to water-based products, we removed all that stuff and it doesn't smell," said Mélodie, who works in production. Water-based inks also mean that trays of primary colors can been used, with color mixes made on site (before, they had to use one tray for each color). Fewer trays, less transport, reduced wastage—and what does remain is remixed and used to print the gray color inside the envelope. "It doesn't look like much, but the fact of recycling the unused products has reduced our ink use by 25 percent. Even if they aren't toxic, we can still be frugal," said Emmanuel.

Pocheco now uses rainwater, harvested from the roof, and Marseille soap to clean the tools and machines. "This dirty, but not toxic water, is piped to the bamboo grove, where the root systems of the trees activate the bacteria, decompose the dirt, derive nourishment; the only biomass generated is the bamboo stalks. We grow, cut, and dry it, and use it for our heating system," he continued. According to studies conducted by the team, bamboo has a higher heating capacity than oak. This is not the only material used in the recently installed wood furnace: it also burns pallets in chip form. It is used as supplementary heat, because most of the heating comes from another source. Pocheco had powerful ventilators to capture all the paper dust that fills the air, which would otherwise clog the machines and be a respiratory irritant for the staff, which filtered and released the air outside—until the staff realized that these machines were not only incredible noisy, but they also produced a lot of heat. They then decided to place them all in a single room, insulated to decrease the noise levels, and harness all this energy to heat the buildings. With this step, Pocheco was able to completely give up gas and diesel. It is cheaper and also safer, because there are no more inflammable and explosive materials in the shops. Pocheco's ingenious employees are thinking about how they can harness the air released by the pumps during the summer (when they don't need heat), to power turbines that would produce electricity. Because, as Emmanuel said, "it's a shame to waste it."

Pocheco soon stood out from its competitors for its efficiency, but also for its ingenuity and the unique products it was offering its customers—like its packaging, for example. Before, to ship the hundreds of millions of envelopes required by banks, and telephone and insurance companies, which have to send bills and statements, Pocheco used thousands of cardboard boxes, which were thrown away as soon as the envelopes were unpacked. Emmanuel and his colleagues designed an innovative system: a huge spool around which 38,000 envelopes are rolled and the carefully banded by a machine. On arrival, the final users have an unspooler to unpack their products, and then send to spool back to Pocheco.

Not only are there no more boxes, but the envelopes are easier to transport, handling them is easy for both employees and customers, and it's faster. "With this technique, we have reduced our use of cardboard boxes by one-third, and have increased productivity," said Emmanuel. By inventing this system, Pocheco was also able to capture a market for 500 million envelopes—not the least of the benefits.

From deficit results, the company was able to balance its books, then start to make a profit, which raised the question of how to manage it. Emmanuel told us a great story: "This site was created in 1848. It had a traditional factory roof, covered with the original tiles. It had never been kept up, and the roof had been leaking for several years. We used to put buckets all around inside the shop to catch the rainwater. Nobody complained; we were used to it. But one day, after reinvesting the company revenue, we started to accumulate some reserves. So we said, 'What if we insulated the roof? We wouldn't have to heat as much, and it would be dry.' We had a few estimates done for several different options. The first, to seal and insulate it, would cost €800,000 for 27,000 square feet. We talked it over with Élodie, the staff, and the Pocheco engineering team (which had been formed in the meantime to calculate the company's environmental impact as precisely as possible), and we wondered if we couldn't do better than to simply repair it. It was a factory roof; we could make it more productive. We could install solar panels to produce energy; plants to recover rainwater and store it for future use;[1] install an adiabatic cooling system, whereby hot

1. These are sedums, selected on the advice of the Bailleul botanical conservatory, which have the added advantage of capturing fine particles emitted by diesel engines, therefore reducing air pollution.

air taken from the shop in the summer runs through water-moistened boxes, losing calories and lowering the inside temperature by about 7° F (in summer, of course); insulate more thoroughly; and install large windows to bring in natural light (which reduces electricity use). We priced this project, which came to €2 million for 2,000 square meters (21,500 square feet)—a difference of €1.2 million. We weren't rich; this represented a huge investment. Except that when we factored in a more long-term view, it would have taken twenty years to recoup our investment of €800,000 by saving €40,000 in gas costs annually. With the €2 million option, we could sell €200,000 of electricity per year. Both options saved money in terms of our gas bill, but the second one would be profitable in just over eight years. Our roof has therefore become productive. This is what eco-economics is all about!" The staff even went further, by collecting the tiles on the old roof and crushing them to make the substrate for the green roof and installing thirteen beehives that produce 442 pounds of honey every year. "We know that bees are endangered because of the use of pesticides. Wherever possible, we have to install beehives and take care of them," concluded Emmanuel. Today, the Pocheco team is dreaming of an industry that doesn't destroy the environment, but contributes to its regeneration.

In 2011, a fire damaged part of the buildings, destroying nearly 30 percent of the factory's inventory. The company barely avoided bankruptcy. But instead of giving up, the entire staff pitched in. Within hours after the fire started, a good number of employees were already on the site, helping the firemen—who told Emmanuel that they had never seen workers so concerned about protecting and repairing their production tools. A new building went up, with wood paneling to make it more attractive to the neighbors, and a conservatory orchard was planted all around it, including rare species, "but also a pilfering garden," explained Emmanuel, "so that the local kids can come steal fruit from time to time." They planted apple and pear trees, raspberries, figs, and grapes. The new building includes large glass windows so that employees can see nature, sky, and trees while they work. "In the summer, whenever you go outside to take a break, you can pick some fruit, watch the flowers grow, and see the bees at work everywhere." The insurance company required Pocheco to install a water tank in case of any future fires. It only took a few weeks before they decided to make it green. "The first hairy tank in the world," laughed Emmanuel. It provides food for even more birds and insects—as Pocheco is also a leading LPO (League for the Protection of Birds) refuge in the Nord-Pas-de-Calais area, with dozens of birdhouses installed all around the plant. With the roof, the company is self-sufficient in water with a gray-water system (water not in contact with skin) that is used for toilets and cleaning.

At the same time, profits are reinvested to regularly modernize the machines and the production facilities. According to Emmanuel, the latter is now the most modern in the world in this sector of activity. "It means we can ensure even better targeted, more efficient service, and take on the fierce competition throughout all of Europe." These improvements were also made to increase safety and relieve the strenuous aspect of the work. The priority is to create an environment in which the employees are working in the best and safest possible conditions. This goes without saying for Emmanuel. The employees feel good at work and they are also more efficient. As he often says: "We spend one-third of our lives sleeping and another third working. So you have to have a good bed and a good job."

The entire process is now called a "circular economy." For the Pocheco staff, it's the backbone of twenty-first-century industry. Emmanuel explained: "In the past, industries extracted raw materials, transforming them to produce objects, which soon became waste and was thrown away. It's the capitalist principle: creative destruction. With the well-known downside: landfills we don't know what to do with; waste everywhere, and not only in the landfills; polluted oceans and rives; and depleted raw materials. So the industry of tomorrow, which we've been doing here for twenty years, must be radically different. Raw materials will no longer be extracted, but taken from the landfills of the twentieth century. They will be used, transformed using solar power, to produce an object that can be repaired, must be sustainable, and when its life is over, can once again be recycled to sustain this circularity."

Concerned with actual results and sometimes challenged for producing paper that is considered less necessary with the advent of digital technologies, the Pocheco team took things one step further by commissioning a CNRS study on the life cycle of paper mail over that of an email. It showed that emails can be from fifteen to twenty-three times more polluting, due to the enormous energy use of servers, digital infrastructure, and paper printouts made by users. Emmanuel and his colleagues maintain a keen awareness of the precious value of resources. They have not only planted 200,000 trees per year since 1997 through their partnership with the Finnish paper supplier, but they have also created a reforestation nonprofit in the Nord-Pas-de-Calais, a French department that has been badly scarred by deforestation. Nearly thirty thousand trees have already been planted. In addition, a partnership with two local farmers was formed, and crates of vegetables are distributed to employees and village residents. This initiative boosted the farmers' income from €500 to €1,200 per month.

It all may seem impossibly idyllic, yet this is not about philanthropy. What Emmanuel calls eco-economy has also resulted in savings for the company of €20 million, with €15 million slated for investments—or a net gain of €5 million, not to mention the social and environmental benefits: thousands of tons of CO_2 stored or saved, a revived biodiversity, and conservation of natural resources. By systematically reinvesting, Pocheco has amassed its own funds of several million euros to ride through bad years and remain independent of the dictates of growth, which currently ranges between o and 2 percent. Meanwhile, 100 percent of the jobs have been maintained over the last fifteen years.

3. Currency: From monoculture to diversity

Interview with Bernard Lietaer

Even if Emmanuel and his colleagues had proven the feasibility of stepping out of the exponential logic discussed by Pierre, we wanted to pursue our investigations further to understand why our entire economy was systematically pushed toward growth and created so much disparity. We wanted to know if there were more structural solutions that did not depend on good will and the humane qualities of exceptional entrepreneurs, but ones that could bring the majority of us along with them.

We would soon get an explanation.

"I live here for the view," says Bernard Lietaer as we walk into the living room of his apartment. In front of us, large windows overlook Brussels. Numerous African objects are scattered all around the room. On the wall, huge shelves are groaning under the weight of hundreds of books. I discovered this cheerful, mischievous economist in a TEDx conference filmed in Berlin. I had never heard about the subject he was discussing. His presentation seemed so wild to me that I wanted to find out more about him. In reality, he is neither a wild-eyed conspiracy-theorist nor an enlightened crackpot. Bernard Lietaer is an economist and author of a thesis published by MIT, where he studied with the economist and Nobel prizewinner Paul Krugman. He has been a professor and researcher at several Belgian and American universities (including Berkeley), a consultant to major companies, and a high-ranking official at the National Bank of Belgium, where he implemented the ECU, the precursor of the euro. He has been working for forty years to promote complementary currencies as a tool for economic development and resilience around the world. It's a groundbreaking and totally revolutionary approach. When we asked him why the world had so many economic problems, why we were torn apart by so much inequality, our conversation got off to a good start.

BERNARD: I believe that most of the problems we encounter are linked to our mechanism for creating money. Until we solve this problem, I maintain that we will not solve any of the others.

CYRIL: How is our system on monetary creation problematic?

BERNARD: Henry Ford, founder of the Ford dynasty, once said that if Americans understood how the banking system and money functioned, there'd be a revolution overnight. I think he was right. The real problem is that no one understands it, not the Europeans, or the Chinese, or the Brazilians. How many of you, for example, know how money is created?

CYRIL: I know, because I did my homework; as for the others, I can't say!

BERNARD: Most of the money we use is created by private banks, when they extend credit.

CYRIL: What does that mean?

BERNARD: Suppose you want to buy an apartment and you need €100,000. You go to your bank and ask for a loan and, if accepted, the bank gives you the €100,000. In other words, it enters a figure into a computer, crediting your account.

CYRIL: That's it? From nothing?

BERNARD: Yes, it's what we call "fiat money," derived from the God's words in the Bible, *Fiat lux*, "Let there be light." This ability to create something from nothing, which is a divine attribute, was also granted to the monetary sector of the banking system. The bank merely has to have a certain amount in its accounts. In theory, it should have one unit to be able to create 0.8 units. Let's say one for one, to make it simpler. But given the multiplier effect of credit, it's possible to create more than six "virtual" euros from one real euro.[1]

CYRIL: What do you mean by "multiplier effect?"

BERNARD: When the bank creates these €100,000, you then give them to the person from whom you bought the apartment, who will put them in his or her bank. With these €100,000 in its account (which didn't exist before you took out a loan), this bank could then create an additional €100,000 by giving credit to someone else. This third person will give them in turn to someone else, who puts them in a bank, and on it goes. Calculations have determined that, on average, from an initial €100,000, 600,000 will be created.

CYRIL: But where do the initial €100,000 come from?

BERNARD: Central banks, in coins and bills. Approximately 15 percent of the money in the euro zone is created like this. The remaining 85 percent is created by private banks, through credit and interest. That's the first point.

1. https://en.wikipedia.org/wiki/Money_multiplier.

CYRIL: Okay, so far.

BERNARD: When the bank creates these €100,000 for you, it expects you to reimburse them with interest. Suppose that you took out a twenty-year loan at a relatively high rate, you would have to reimburse €200,000. The problem is that this second €100,000 doesn't exist.

CYRIL: How is that?

BERNARD: When they create money, banks create the amount for the loan, but they don't create the amount for the interest.

CYRIL: Which means that nearly all the money in circulation around the world is created by loans plus interest, but that the money we need to reimburse this interest doesn't exist?

BERNARD: No. To reimburse your interest, someone somewhere else has to borrow money to create the necessary volume of money. New economic activities have to be created.

CYRIL: Hence the need for growth.

BERNARD: It's essential. People who think that we can move toward zero growth do not understand the monetary system. This would lead straight to bankruptcy! Especially because when you have reimbursed your €100,000, they are deleted from the computers. Other loans are therefore necessary to maintain a sufficient monetary mass. So we always need more growth.

CYRIL: But we can't just keep growing indefinitely.

BERNARD: Exactly, and we have known this since 1972, when the Club of Rome published its report on the limits to growth.

CYRIL: To sum up, this system places us in a position of economic struggle to go get the money we need from others to reimburse our interest payments, forcing us to pursue economic growth—two situations that are not sustainable.

BERNARD: The current monetary system is not compatible with sustainability for multiple reasons. The first is the mandatory growth we talked about. The second is the short-term view. When the money you create must earn interest, the future doesn't matter. No one is interested in getting one million euros back in a hundred years. This is one of the reasons companies are programmed to think short-term. I was discussing this the other day with a German CEO. I asked him how far down the road he thought about in terms of his children. He answered, "Twenty-five years." And when you step into your office in the morning? "Two or three quarters. And if I don't, they'll throw me out and replace me with someone who does." It's the hard reality.

The third problem is that money tends to destroy the social fabric. We pretend that it is a passive, neutral instrument that exists only to facilitate exchanges. But it's absolutely not true. Money is a programmer, with a certain number of values, which involve relationships, among others. When you purchase something and pay for it, no relationship has been established.

CYRIL: Do you mean that the monetary exchanges prevent us for creating relationships?

BERNARD: Exactly. It tends to replace the relationship, do away with it. If, for your wife's birthday, you give her a €100 bill instead of a gift, it's not okay. The social fabric is created through gifts. When I do something for you for free, to help you out, we create a unique relationship. If you pay me for the same service, we don't necessarily have to interact with each other. A community is the space in which gifts are accepted and honored. The more we conduct trade, the more relationships become impersonal, and ultimately dissolve.

CYRIL: Is this contributing to the decline of communities in Western countries?

BERNARD: It is always the "most advanced" societies that have promoted trade, because that's how we define development: an increase in the volume of trade in conventional money, currency. A study was conducted in the United States on this phenomenon: the places that still have strong communities are the ghettos, where money is scarce. The same model holds true at a family level: in southern Italy, the *famiglia* includes seventy, eighty people. It's a clan that spans several generations. But in many so-called "developed" families, we are down to just the nuclear family. More than half of the children in the United States live in single-parent households. When a grandfather has to pay rent to live with one of his children, the family no longer exists.

CYRIL: So we shouldn't use euros or dollars anymore?

BERNARD: Yes, we should. I am not against currency as such, but against the monopoly it holds. There is an entirely appropriate arena for this type of currency: trade, the worldwide place of major companies. That's where it functions the best, where it finances innovations, creates jobs, and lets people living in the "developed world" achieve a standard of living that, just a few centuries ago, only royalty could hope to achieve. We would never have been able to create and finance the economic explosion of the Industrial Revolution if we hadn't had the money from bank loans. We have now reached the limits of this industrial era; we still use the same tools, whereas we no longer have the same problems. As long as we force the world to use this type of single currency, we will continue to have them.

CYRIL: Are there problems that this type of currency cannot solve?

BERNARD: Aging populations, unemployment, monetary instability, increasing inequality, explosion of debt. But even more, climate change and the extinction of species, which will have an enormous impact in every sector. For the first time, humanity is endangering the entire biosphere. Yet I argue that all our problems have well-known, time-tested solutions, but that they cannot be funded by the conventional system. They are not applied at the necessary scale and speed because we supposedly do not have the means. If you take energy, for example, we know how to develop renewable energies, but who will pay for them? Not the private sector, which continues to hold massive stakes in nuclear energy and fossil fuels, nor governments, whose coffers are empty (primarily because of their debts). So we don't do anything, we wait.

CYRIL: It's true, we always hear that countries have huge debts, that they have to pursue austerity policies. And yet when you look at the global economy, you see an enormous amount of money in play, companies making mind-boggling profits, and people with huge fortunes. How is it that this money is not available to finance such crucial projects?

BERNARD: One of the effects of the conventional monetary system (creating money through debt with interest) is the concentration of money. If you have money, it's easy to make more. If you don't have it, it gets increasingly harder to obtain any. In short, what is interest? The transfer of money from someone who doesn't have enough of it and who must borrow, to someone who already has more than they need, because they can offer you a loan. It's an automatic machine that sucks resources to the top tier of society. It's a fairly logical way for an elite to defend its position. This system was in fact invented three thousand years ago in Sumer, when patriarchy developed, with this goal in mind. But other societies soon saw the dangers of it. What was called the "sin of usury" was only legalized in the Western world some four hundred years ago. Before, interest was viewed as unlawful, in Christianity, Islam, and even in Asia.

CYRIL: For you, is this monetary system associated with a patriarchal system?

BERNARD: Yes. Every patriarchal system in history has done what we're doing today: a monetary monopoly with interest. All matrifocal societies have tended toward monetary ecosystems, with the use of several types of currencies at once. There's one type of currency that's identical to the one used in patriarchal systems, which can be saved, and used to earn interest; and another one that penalizes accumulation, a simple medium of exchange available to everyone.

CYRIL: How do we recognize a matrifocal society? When did these types of societies exist?

BERNARD: A good way to tell is to look at images of the divine. If it's an old man with a beard who created everyone on his own, without a woman, it's a good chance you've found a patriarchal society! But more seriously, there are three particularly interesting periods. Egypt during the first millennium BCE was dominated by the figure of Isis; the High Middle Ages in France, also known as the "age of cathedrals," was dominated by the Virgin Mary; and the Tang Dynasty in China, from the eighth to the tenth centuries, when a woman had become empress. They all correspond to eras when major projects were possible to achieve and when the standard of living was higher than in preceding or subsequent periods. In Egypt, for example, even slaves had money. Everyone had the means to purchase goods and for trade.

CYRIL: But no one talks about that. I studied economics for several years and I never heard anything about it.

BERNARD: Single currencies form the cornerstone of all our economic theories. Economics courses brainwash you into thinking that we must have a single currency, because it's more efficient. I don't dispute this efficiency, but it's much more fragile. And not as resilient as it should be.

CYRIL: This idea of resilience comes up all the time with the people we've met. Does it mean that having diverse currencies creates a resilience in economic systems, just as a diversity of species creates resilience in a biological ecosystem?

BERNARD: Absolutely. The similarities between how biological and economic ecosystems function is the subject of a study in which I am very involved in the United States, with my colleague Bob Ulanowicz, one of the founders of quantitative ecology. He has spent his life measuring in grams, per square meter, and per year, what is happening in extremely different ecosystems like the Amazon, the Serengeti Plain, or a small puddle in a backyard. Wherever life exists. The question we raised was this: What do all extremely diverse ecosystems have in common? What we discovered is that they do not allow a monoculture. They need diversity. We can look at how an ecosystem functions and apply it directly to the economy, even though everything seems different. But we have created a global money monoculture. Even the Soviet system and the Chinese system are based on the same principle: the creation of a single currency on a national scale by creating debt with interest. All money functions like this. So we have a global pine forest, in which some pines are bigger than other ones, but they're all pines. What does that mean, practically speaking? Don't light a match. One wrong move and it all goes up in flames. And that's what we're doing; this is not a metaphor.

CYRIL: What exactly will happen if we drop a match on the pine forest of currency?

BERNARD: What we barely escaped in 2007–08, when we were within a hair of a systemic collapse. And many people currently believe that we are once again in a similar situation. We talk a lot about this crisis because it had such a serious impact on us, but it is not the only one. So long as we have a monopoly and a monoculture, the system is going to regularly break down. According to the IMF, between 1970 and 2010, there were 425 systemic crises and 208 monetary crises in the world. Ask the Latin Americans, the Russians, or the Asians. It's far more frequent than we think. A system needs diversity and connectivity to be sustainable; it is a law that applies to every system with complex flows—which is the case of the economy and the monetary system. The law therefore applies.

CYRIL: We now hear that global finance has more power than political parties or governments. Is this because of the mechanism through which money is created?

BERNARD: Historically, the mechanisms for creating money were established by banks to meet the needs of states looking to finance their wars. The Central Bank of England was created in 1694, in the aftermath of the war between England and France. The terms of agreements are always negotiated within this context; in other words, when governments have the least power. It started in England, which allowed the country to win the war against Napoleon, launch industrialization, then construct an empire. It's also what happened during World War II. The Americans took over England's role and set up new monetary rules, known as the Bretton Woods system. Once again, these laws were negotiated in a context in which governments were powerless. It was a question of survival, of finding the necessary resources to conduct a war and finance reconstruction.

These laws have been in place ever since. We have formalized them. The treaty that led to the monopoly of the euro in the European zone is a modern version of it. It triggered the situation that we now know: governments can no longer borrow from central banks and must borrow from private banks at higher interest rates.[1] From that point on, they had to pay interest costs they hadn't been paying before, or at least interest payments were set at a very low rate. And, of course, their debts then exploded.[2]

CYRIL: What to do if we want to create this monetary diversity and give states the power to act once again?

BERNARD: Above all, eliminate a certain number of rules that prevent people from doing something. That's it. I don't see why cities can't issue a currency, one that could be used to pay taxes and therefore solve local problems. I don't see why companies can't create currencies that would help support their activities. In fact, these systems already exist in some places. It's one way to solve the unemployment problem, because that's where we need to start. The same holds true at a national level. If we take Greece, for example, why can't the Greeks remain in the euro zone for tourism and exports, but use a national or local currency to purchase a kilo of olives? And if a Greek man wanted to buy a German car, well then, he'd

1. According to Article 123 of the Treaty of Lisbon, "Overdraft facilities or any other type of credit facility with the European Central Bank or with the central banks of the Member States (hereinafter referred to as 'national central banks') in favor of Union institutions, bodies, offices or agencies, central governments, regional, local or other public authorities, other bodies governed by public law, or public undertakings of Member States shall be prohibited, as shall the purchase directly from them by the European Central Bank or national central banks of debt instruments." Article 123 was originally Article 104 in the Maastricht Treaty, which was also identical to Article 181 in the Treaty establishing the European Community.
2. The public debt in France exceeded €2 trillion in 2015. It represents nearly 95 percent of GDP. All of the tax revenue would still not be enough even to pay off the interest on this debt. Every second, France's deficit grows by €2,665.

do it in euros. We keep both currencies, operating in parallel. When people object that it's not possible or it's too complicated, I'm sorry to have to tell them that the English have been doing this since the introduction of the euro. When you're an English company and all your customers and your suppliers are in the euro zone, you can perfectly well do your accounts and pay your taxes in euros. And every quarter, the central bank issues a conversion rate between the pound sterling and the euro. A monetary monopoly, a monoculture, is an ideology that gives control to people who want to keep it. But it is not a technical necessity.

CYRIL: So all these currencies should work together?

BERNARD: Personally, I believe we need the euro; we even need a nonspecific global currency, and we need a local currency. That's an ecosystem. No one says that we shouldn't have pine trees in an ecosystem; it's just that we need other kinds of trees, too. Otherwise, the day one of them gets sick, the entire forest is devastated. On the other hand, if you have oak, beech, hornbeam, and birch, some of the species will be stronger than others and your ecosystem will be more resilient.

CYRIL: What's the first measure to be taken or the first ban to be lifted?

BERNARD: I think we should introduce a rule that would allow experimentation for a period of five years. There obviously have to be controls, and taxation on these exchanges. But we would lift all the prohibitions. It already exists in German law, where an experimental special status exists. But you must publish your results, that's that condition. And while holding this status, the rules established to maintain the former system are suspended.

CYRIL: What's preventing this from happening?

BERNARD: The truth is, it's already happening in business. There are highly efficient complementary currency networks, but in sectors that do not address the current problems of our society. Air miles, for example, are anything but marginal: more than 15,000 trillion are in circulation. This experience demonstrates two things: first, that it's possible to do things on a very large scale, very cheaply, and which encourage people to act in a certain way. Customers remain loyal to the same airline companies so that they can earn more miles. It's great for the companies, but we now have to use the same technology to deal with our ecological, social, employment, aging population issues. It's all feasible. Concerning jobs, for example, we have to create a job currency, which helps small- and medium-sized companies (which are the largest job creators in the economy). We are now in a period where technologies will continue to significantly reduce human labor in production. China has accelerated this process, but is not the cause. To solve this problem, the solution is not to look to the past. Reindustrializing Europe is a lovely utopian idea, but I don't think it would create jobs for everyone, especially as technology is going in the opposite direction, with 3D printers at home and small shops replacing heavy industry. Not only do we need job currencies, but we also have to create a society in which our individual interests can generate activities that bring in money. There are an infinite number of things that people want to do and which are good for society, but don't think for a minute that anyone will pay you in euros for it. Growing lettuce on my terrace will never be competitive as compared to a guy with 25 acres and machines. We can create an economy that justifies this activity, but not with a monetary monopoly, because right now, the salad here on the terrace and the salad there on the farm are not the same thing.

CYRIL: Do governments then have to take the first step?

BERNARD: I don't think that governments themselves should change things, but when people are ready to change them, you should let them do it. I don't believe in revolutions. The entire history of humanity shows that revolutionaries turn into the new oppressors. I believe that we have to allow creativity to flourish. In the information era, it's a bit crazy to use criteria that were developed five thousand years ago. Money is, above all, information.

CYRIL: Which needs to circulate.

BERNARD: And fulfill its function! Imagine a Martian who lands on our planet, sees what's happening, and also that people know how to solve our problems. He'd end up asking, "Why don't you do it then?" And people would say: "Well, we don't have the money." "What's money? We don't have any on Mars. How does it work?" "The real definition of a currency is that it is an agreement within a community to use a standardized tool as a means of trade." "And you're waiting—for that?" He would leave the planet shaking his head: "There's no intelligent life here."

CYRIL: If we don't act and if an economic crisis does break out, what could happen?

BERNARD: Over the last three centuries, every time we have been in a situation like this one, we have gone to war. The solution to the Stock Market Crash of 1929 was World War II. Roosevelt admitted it himself: it wasn't the New Deal, it was the preparations for war that pulled the world out of the crisis. I hope, perhaps naïvely, that it doesn't come to that.

WIR: The sixty thousand SMEs
that created their own bank

I still remember Laurent, Antoine, and Alexandre's expressions when we left the eleventh floor, and the concern on their faces, stark in the white neon light. I watched them in the elevator's mirror, crammed between crates of equipment. We walked to the truck without saying a word, still feeling a bit stunned, but once we started talking again, there was no stopping them. As if everything we had seen up to that point suddenly took on a larger meaning. The mechanisms for creating money were the source of the financial world's power, the lack of funds to implement a genuine environmental transition, and income disparity. Bernard Lietaer's words provided a theoretical framework for all that we had seen and heard during a good part of our travels: all systems need diversity to be resilient, whether they are organic or organized by human intervention. This was demonstrated by permaculture at Bec-Hellouin; this was the story told by Detroit's reconstruction; and this was the possibility offered by energy mixes derived from multiple sources.

All this made sense, intellectually at least. We therefore asked our expert in complementary currencies for tangible initiatives proving that monetary diversity was more efficient than monoculture. For him, the most successful experiment is in Switzerland, the land of bank secrecy, located nearly opposite the Bank for International Settlements (BRI), the bank of all banks, where all international regulations are set forth, in the quiet city of Basel.

When we arrived, we found ourselves facing a large modern black building, displaying the words "WIR Bank"[1] in gold letters. Through the windows on the ground floor, we could see two focused employees behind the counter, a man in a suit and tie, a woman in

1. WIR is an abbreviation of the German word Wirtschaft, which means "economy"; "wir" also means "us" in German.

a suit. From the outside, the world's most reliable complementary currency system looked just like any other bank. Bernard Lietaer suggested we meet with Hervé Dubois, the bank's director of communications for nearly twenty years. He had retired a few months earlier and had risen at dawn to travel the several hundred miles from his home in the mountains to his former office. He was wearing a leather jacket, a small gold cross visible under his shirt, the top button undone. With his dark glasses, large mustache, and curly hair, he looked more like a New York mafia middleman from the 1970s than a Swiss banker. Yet as we listened to him speak, we had no doubt that he had been the right man for the job, promoting the WIR all those twenty years. Dubois was brilliant, cheerful, precise, and showed great humility. Like a certain number of other initiatives, the WIR was created during a crisis, specifically the 1929 market crash. Businesspeople in Switzerland, as elsewhere, took a huge hit from this economic collapse. Investment dried up, virtually no credit was available from banks, and companies were failing. At this point, German-Argentinean businessman and economist Silvio Gesell, who had been living in the canton of Neuchâtel since the 1920s, decided to put into practice his theories on a free economy, which he had first developed in the late nineteenth century. Gesell had been arguing that interest was a poison for the society, making the rich even richer, and the poor always poorer—an idea that caught the attention of a certain Werner Zimmermann, who then roped fourteen businessmen friends into joining the project. Together, they created the WIR, an interest-free currency that businesspeople could use among themselves to support their respective activities. As Dubois told us: "They were idealists, people who simply wanted a better world, in which small players had a chance to be able to live correctly, where it didn't require capital to become someone, to have a worthwhile life. In fact, this was just one idea among others that reflected their philosophy. They also introduced housing cooperatives in Switzerland." While everyone looked at these two pioneers as misguided dreamers, the idea was a huge hit among businesspeople—so much so that thousands of other small- and medium-sized enterprises joined in. After just one year, three thousand clients were using the WIR. Economic difficulties and unemployment were so serious that a large number of businesses were willing to borrow from unorthodox sources. It was so successful that it became difficult to obtain credit. Swiss authorities took a long hard look at the bank, but instead of curbing or banning the initiative, twelve months later they legalized it, by granting the WIR a banking license. "But," explains Dubois, "it wasn't because they thought it was a good idea; quite simply it was because if they had a banking license, they would be subject to the laws regulating financial establishments, and therefore to the control of federal authorities."

This control encouraged the founders to profoundly reshape their system to give it more security and sustainability. Eighty years later, sixty thousand small- and medium-sized Swiss businesses use the WIR, or more than 20 percent of the country's companies, for a monetary value of about one billion Swiss francs. The system is simple: it is a means of exchange (1 WIR Franc equals 1 Swiss Franc) that is used only within this network. As Dubois says, "the mutualizing factor is the driving force of this system." He gives us a practical example: "Imagine a carpenter who needs special saws. He is a WIR member and will try to find a producer who also works with this currency. He needs to spend his WIRs. He will order the saws he needs from a producer he doesn't know, perhaps some two hundred miles from where he lives, because he'll pay 50 percent of the cost in WIR Francs. Because it's January, the saw manufacturer decides to go skiing at his usual ski resort, and he checks to see which hotels accepts WIRs in payment for his room and meals. He will easily find some, because there are a lot of them—and they will charge him 50 to 80 percent of the bill in WIRs, some even up to 100 percent. At the end of the season, the hotel owner, who needs to renovate some of his rooms, will look for a painter who works with WIRs, and the painter will go get his paint from a specialist rather than a home improvement superstore (because these stores will never accept WIRs; they don't want them in their system). Some also use the WIR as a marketing tool. The hotel owner who needs to fill rooms in mid-season will offer promotional deals with total payment in WIRs. He'll easily find takers among the sixty thousand clients, who can use their WIRs and don't need to spend their Swiss Francs—currency they need for transactions abroad or with clients outside of the system. All the businesses make deals among each other; without the WIR, they would never have come into contact. This is the principle of mutualization. And everyone wants to quickly spend their WIRs, given that they don't bring in interest on assets. There is no incentive for investing this currency. It even loses value due to inflation. This is one of the key driving forces. It's in your best interest to keep them circulating as quickly as possible, to reuse them. It is this rapidly circulating currency that creates such a dynamic system."

The WIR therefore functions in the opposite way from a traditional economy, where money tends to be concentrated and desert the economy (because of investments, tax havens, etc.), as we learned from Bernard Lietaer. The system helps companies function during normal economic cycles to increase the activities, but it is even more relevant during downturns. Three studies, one conducted by Lietaer, and two others by James Stodder, demonstrated an increase in the ability of companies to withstand economic and financial shocks. For Dubois, "It is a fairly anti-cyclical system: the stronger the recession, the greater the dynamism. On the other hand, the better the economic climate, the lower the dynamism. During each crisis, hundreds of small- and medium-sized enterprises (SMEs) survived thanks to the WIR." With the exception of the 2008–09 period, when the membership increased slightly, the number of businesspeople using the WIR has remained stable for twenty years, because the Swiss economy has been strong. But, like Lietaer, Dubois is convinced that this system will provide powerful resilience in the event of a crisis, particularly in what are called "weak economies." "Greece, Portugal, Spain, and even Italy come to mind. It would be a way to stabilize entire regions. There's an interesting example in Sardinia, which was inspired by the WIR. Several years ago, a group of young people came here to learn about it, and in 2010 they launched the Sardex. Today, some fifteen thousand SMEs are in business thanks to this system. This is generally a poor region, one in which Rome shows little interest. So it's a little bit like a makeshift economy; without it, they wouldn't be able to survive. Since the introduction of the Sardex, many SMEs are doing better and the island's economy is stronger." And for Greece, Dubois is convinced, as is Lietaer, that an initiative like the WIR could lift the country out of its morass. "It's entirely possible to set up a complementary system that's some-what different from the WIR. Here we were focused on the SMEs, but we could shift this focus in another region, so that everyone par-ticipates: citizens, businesses, towns. Take Greece, for example. By creating a Greek WIR, they could restart the economy, given that this currency could not be used in Switzerland, America, or London, especially not on any of the stock exchanges. Because there's abso-lutely no point sending off billions of euros in forty-eight hours, once again removing them from the country, to have them land in the accounts of speculators in the major European and American banks. They need a currency that is constantly circulating within this weak economy so that the wealth produced can remain in the country. This is the first benefit. The second is that this is free money, which is not listed on international money markets. This means that the state can issue them and not continue to accrue even greater debt, so much so that it becomes impossible to repay. It would be up to the Greeks to come together to keep a monetary mass that's ideal for their economy. Initially, they could work via governmental or parliamentary decree, by announcing, for example, that 50 percent of civil servants' salaries and 50 percent of retirement payments for former civil servants would be paid in Greek WIRs. Then, another decree would make it obligatory for all companies in Greece to accept the Greek WIR as a method of payment. It wouldn't take long to get a system up and running that would benefit everyone in the country." And, as Lietaer pointed out, euros would continue to be used for international exchanges, notably in the tourism sector.

The example of the WIR is exceptional because, as opposed to all other global initiatives, the WIR bank has a license, and the WIR is an ISO-certified official currency, recognized by the World Bank. This situation could certainly not be replicated today, at least not in France, where licenses are extremely hard to obtain. Yet the status of the WIR bank means that it can play an active role in the country's economy. As with a traditional bank, the WIR bank issues currency, in electronic form only, and controls the volume of money in circulation via interest rates on loans.[1] Currently, loans have very low interest rates (less than 1 percent), while savings do not earn any interest. To optimize the system, the WIR bank has also been offering loans in Swiss Francs since the 1990s. "Especially combined loans," explains Dubois, "to finance projects that can't be paid entirely in WIRs, like a home, a local business, or a factory. The rates on the Swiss Franc are the same as elsewhere, while the rates on the WIR are minimal. In the end, it means far lower interest payments. This helps businesses undertake projects they wouldn't have had the means to do otherwise." In addition, the system provides loans to sectors of the economy that do not usually receive encouragement from the traditional banking system. "For certain sectors, like tourism and the hotel business, it's very hard to get loans. It involves too much risk for traditional banks, whereas for a cooperative SME bank like the WIR, the same argument doesn't

1. The role played by central banks in traditional economies.

The door of the Bristol Pound offices.

apply: if an activity has a chance of survival, then the businesses will certainly obtain their loans in WIRs." This is the interest of monetary diversity, the multiple forms of accounting vaunted by Lietaer. Advocates of the WIR are fully aware of this. "The WIR is not an alternative system to the Swiss Franc; it's complementary. In fact, it would no longer present these same advantages if it became an alternative to the other system one day: it would soon be afflicted by the same ailments. It has to remain complementary so that monetary speculation is not a possibility."

Bristol, where you can even pay your taxes in the local currency

For specialists in monetary transition, creating a complementary currency requires a community of people with a community of interests. For the WIR, the community includes all the country's SMEs, with the aim of maintaining a more resilient economy in Switzerland and in its different regions. There is another, more well-known form of complementary currency, wherein the community of interests is geographical: local currencies. Lietaer suggested we visit a certain number of towns that have already introduced them, and we opted for Bristol, one hour west of London. We have to admit, Bristol seemed more hip to us than Basel. A city of artists, with Portishead and PJ Harvey, it is often compared to Seattle, the home of grunge and groups like Nirvana and Pearl Jam. Like Seattle, where organic stores have popped up alongside co-ops and other types of shared housing, Bristol has a certain culture of social innovation and protest. It's no surprise that one of Europe's most successful local currency systems was created here.

As in Todmorden, everything started with two friends attending a conference. This time, it was an economic forum, where Nath and Ciaran launched into a heated discussion about the shortcomings of the modern economy: tax havens, outrageous speculation by banks, financial bubbles, and at the bottom of the chain, unemployment and poverty. They started to think about a way to support small local businesses, which are the greatest job creators in regions. A small group was formed, which included a few people with links to the Transition Network, where the idea of local currencies is widespread. One of the first created in the UK was in Totnes (see pp. 188–191), home to Mark, who would become one of the biggest supporters of the Bristol Pound.

The project was launched in 2010. For Ciaran Mundy, director of the organization, it was out of the question to launch a small alternative initiative that would not have any real impact on the local economy. From the beginning, the experiment would encompass the entire greater city area, with one million residents. Discussions were undertaken with the Bank of England and financial authorities. Apparently no laws prevented the initiative, which expanded at a surprising rate. By 2012, several hundred businesspeople had already joined the process. According to Ciaran, anyone can create their own currency, but "for it to function, you have to aim for a sufficiently large scale, which includes all the goods and services we need in our everyday lives: food, electricity, and transportation. You need a community of people who trust each other and trust the system." For Ciaran, as for Lietaer and Dubois, money is above all about trust. To maximize it, the Bristol Pound staff chose to involve the local authorities early on, particularly by the then mayor George Ferguson. A former local businessman, he was strongly committed to the success of his city's SMEs. He therefore viewed this initiative as a useful economic and communications tool—so much so that he soon opted to receive his salary as mayor (£51,000) entirely in the local currency—a world first. All the local stakeholders outside the mayor's office soon joined the project. According to Ciaran, the explanation is simple: "It very hard to disagree with the idea of a local currency. It supports local businesses, it also keeps large companies from hiding their money in tax havens, it stops delo-calizations, it reduces the supply chains, and it creates shorter sup-ply chains among producers, distributors, and consumers—which also cuts backs on CO_2 emissions and makes our economy more resilient. Does anybody disagree with that?" For two years, Ciaran, Mark, Katie, Nath, and their entire team went all over town to talk with local businesses. Instead of launching a system without them and then trying to get them to join, the team asked them: "If the Bristol Pound existed, how would you like it to work? What pur-pose should it serve first? What would the bills look like?" They gathered all this feedback and tried to devise a system that was best adapted to the needs of the businesspeople.

As with the WIR, they decided to keep it simple and establish parity with the pound sterling. Several dozen exchange spots were set up around town, in stores, and the Credit Union.[1] Once the pound sterling are taken out of circulation, they are stored at the Credit Union, where they can be used as security against loans at very low interest rates granted to people in the greatest financial need. Bristol Pounds can then be used in the network of eight hun-dred participating shops and businesses, either electronically or in the form of bills—a critical innovation that was missing from other experiments of this kind, according to Katie Finnegan-Clarke, who is in charge of communications with local businesses. "When we launched the Bristol Pound, we had studied existing experiences in England—Totnes, Lewes, Brixton—to understand what worked and what didn't. The fact of having to convert bills was a major obsta-cle for many users." Now, they can pay via a simple text messages in shops that have the "txt2pay" system. Hence the importance of

[1]. Not-for-profit cooperative bank, which belongs to its customers. Credit Unions provide low-cost banking services for people with low incomes. Their money is not invested in financial markets and certainly not in tax havens, as opposed to most of the major private banks. The money is entirely protected in the event of a financial crisis.

letting shop owners use these Bristol Pounds to pay their suppliers or to purchase essential goods. For the bookshop to be able to pay its staff in Bristol Pounds, employees need to be able to use them to pay some of their electricity bill, buy food, clothes, appliances, and computers, or go to a café or a restaurant. That explains the main success of Bristol. Today, most of the sectors of the local economy are represented. Since June 2015, even energy bills can be paid in Bristol pounds to a 100 percent renewable energy supplier, Good Energy. For Juliet Davenport, the company's founder, it's a world premiere.[1] It's been so successful that universities are starting to study the model and experts have come from London to assess the economic impact of the Bristol Pound. According to several shop-keepers we met, the system started off slowly, but Bristol Pounds now represents 20 to 25 percent of their transactions.

The current goal is to expand the volume of these financial exchanges, which currently represent £700,000 (for one million issued). To do so, the team is primarily targeting hospitals and the municipality. "Every year, the city spends £500 million, including 200 million supporting SMEs. If it agreed to convert them, even partially, into Bristol Pounds, we would absolutely reach another level," says Ciaran. Today, the organization earns its income by taking 2 percent on the amount of physical and electronic conversions. In the future, they plan to offer loans at very low interest rates, modeled after the WIR. "Ultimately," says Ciaran, "the goal is to give power and control over the economy back to local citizens. If you want to construct a more democratic economy, where people can see what's actually happening, they have to feel as if they have more of a stake in what's going on. Large multinational companies have no interest in the places where they do business, and it is impossible to know what's happening. You don't see the

---

1. Steven Morris, "Bristol Pound gets Boost of Energy as Power Company Signs Up," *The Guardian,* June 16, 2015, www.theguardian.com/uk-news/2015/jun/16/bristol-pound-powered-renewables-good-energy-signs-up.

impact of these companies to which you give your money. There is a discrepancy between their power and their self-interest in maintaining a well-functioning and healthy society."

We were walking through the shops in the covered market, most of which accept Bristol Pounds, and I asked Ciaran what inspired him to get involved in local currencies. His answer was persuasive: "My initial training was in ecology and agronomy, particularly soil biology and the impact that conventional agriculture can have on it. And I was always facing the same problems: the reason that soils are declining, fish are disappearing, trees are cut down—it's the economy. So I wondered: Do we have any control over this economy? And can it stop? The answer to these questions was always the same: Money does what money does. Most people do not see the impact that the economy can have on all living organisms, including humans. Chopping nature up into small pieces, killing thousands of species so that people can buy stuff they don't need, selling them by making people believe that if they didn't own them, they wouldn't have any standing in society—none of this is sustainable for very long. So I told myself I would give up my research on environmental protection and concentrate on a subject that would truly have some impact: business and economy." For Katie, to whom I asked the same question, it was about starting a real revolution, a positive one: "I sometimes participated in huge demonstrations in London. We were caught up in the crowd, we truly thought we were going to change the world. And when we went by the same spot the following day, the world was still moving along as if nothing had happened. With the Bristol Pound, we are building something solid, which can't disappear from one day to the next. It's a revolutionary approach, but it's peaceful. It's radical and exciting, although it doesn't look like it. Yet it's about overturning the financial system, turning it head over heels, but in a nonviolent way." Ciaran agrees: "The essential problem we're trying to solve is that of infinite economic growth and the capitalist system as it exists today. If your hold on to your money and put it in the bank so that it works for you, if you invest in the idea of having a rapid return on your capital, you need to have a constantly growing economy, no matter what. But money doesn't need to be created in this way. It's possible to exchange wealth without forcing the economy to expand endlessly. We don't want an economy that is growing nonstop, but an economy that meets the needs of people."

As Rob Hopkins, founder of the Transition Network in Totnes (where the first local currency in the UK was launched), explained: "To have a more resilient economy, we have to have money that cycles as much as possible. Every time you spend a pound in the local economy, it circulates more times and generates £2.50 of activity in the local economy, whereas if you shop in a supermarket, it maybe leads to £1.40 worth of local activity. That money just leaves. Local currency is a really useful tool for building resilience and keeping some of this money, preventing it from being sucked up by large international companies, capitalized and leaving behind entire sectors of the economy that need it. The Totnes pound isn't worth anything in the town up the road; it has to be used here. It's not to get rid of sterling, it's a complementary currency, it runs alongside it." In Totnes, the founders of the Transition Movement printed a 21 Totnes pound note. A touch of pure English humor that we much appreciated: "Because we can, so why not?" They weren't just thumbing their noses at the monetary rigorism and supposed seriousness of international finance, but for the supporters of local currency, these new bills were a way to celebrate their regions, cultures, and diversity. The pound note for the London neighborhood of Brixton features famous people who were born there, like David Bowie ("so much cooler than the queen for me," says Rob), or stayed there, like Vincent van Gogh. In Totnes, Ben Howard, a local singer who's becoming very well known internationally, graces the £10 note.

When the first Totnes pound was printed, no other local currency was yet in use in England. The group initiating the project decided to form an advisory panel of "eminent alternative economists" to determine the legality of the venture. A memory that still makes Rob laugh: "When we asked them: 'Are we allowed to just print a Totnes pound and pretend they're worth a pound?' They looked at each other and said, 'no idea; do it and see what happens.'"

It was only when Bristol set up a system in a city with one million residents that the Bank of England decided to have a little talk with the budding counterfeiters. Since then, the organization has printed an official notice concerning local currencies and their legality. They are now considered to be like vouchers or loyalty points, like an airline's frequent flyer miles—a first step leading to a new kind of creativity.

For advocates of complementary currencies, resilience at a local level is extremely important for keeping the entire worldwide economy afloat. To be able to trade fairly without endangering their respective integrities, economies must first of all ensure their own good financial health. Like cells in a body. But also a kind of equivalency. For Hopkins, "When two economies interact, and they're both completely dependent on buying everything from all over the world, and they don't make anything themselves, the quality of how they interact is very different from places that are very resilient, that have a very strong local food culture, generate a lot of their own energy, manage their own water really well. For me, if we grow up without knowing how to produce some of our own food, how to repair things, or maintain our economy, it leaves us much more vulnerable and we lose something about ourselves as well."

This statement could well raise questions for countries like Algeria, which imports nearly 75 percent of its food, or France, which, as discussed earlier, is 91 percent dependent on energy imports.

Rob displays a few currencies from around the world.

Food riots in 2008 were directly correlated to these two phenomena. With the surge in oil prices (due to excessive speculation), many rich countries turned to producing large quantities of biofuel, abandoning food crops. In 2008, 30 percent of corn production was used to power vehicles at the expense of human or animal food.[1] Grain reserves diminished and prices increased by 84 percent in four months. Countries like Egypt, Côte d'Ivoire, Senegal, and Burkina Faso were hit hard. As their agriculture is widely based on exports rather than meeting local needs, food in these countries represents more than 70 percent (and sometimes up to 90 percent) of household budgets. Food prices became prohibitive. Similarly, when a city or a region is heavily dependent on a multinational industry to provide its population with jobs, it has little power over the decisions made by the company's board of directors. France has experienced this situation, as when ArcelorMittal in Florange (a steel manufacturing company) and Goodyear in Amiens decided that producing in other, less-expensive countries would be more profitable to the group. Despite all the efforts by the French government, despite all the demonstrations by trade unionists, nothing could be done to stop them.

To combat this situation and return economic power to citizens, localist movements are developing all around the world. We saw this in France, England, Switzerland, India, and the United States, where 35,000 businesspeople, members of eighty networks spanning the entire country, have been meeting together for a dozen years. BALLE (Business Alliance for Local Living Economies) has set itself a goal: "Within a generation [BALLE envisions] a global system of human-scale, interconnected local economies that function in harmony with local ecosystems to meet the basic needs of all people, support just and democratic societies, and foster joyful community life." In Oakland, we met several hundred of them who

1. Catherine Coquery-Vidrovitch, "Les émeutes de la faim en Afrique, prélude à la débâcle," *Liberation*, October 10, 2008, http://www.liberation.fr/futurs/2008/10/10/les-emeutes-de-la-faim-en-afrique-prelude-a-la-debacle_114081.

had come together for their annual conference. Judy Wicks, whom everyone calls "BALLE's Mama," is co-founder of the organization. Her story demonstrates, once again, that most movements are created on the initiative of an ordinary person who one day decides that he or she can no longer keep working within an incoherent system running on values counter to his or her own.

In the early 1970s, just after Judy had moved to the historic area of Philadelphia, she learned that part of her neighborhood was slated for destruction to make way for a shopping center. She was attached to the area and decided to join local residents who had already mobilized to stop the work. After several months of opposition, they won. Inspired by this energy, Judy became increasingly involved in the area, and in 1983 opened a small storefront establishment in her building: the White Dog Café. Thanks to her dynamism, it became extremely popular, and in just a few years expanded to nearby buildings. After six years, it became a restaurant serving two hundred people. Already attuned to environmental issues, Judy initiated some renovation work, and the White Dog soon became the first business in Pennsylvania to source 100 percent of its electricity from wind power. She set up a recycling and composting system and installed a solar water heater for cleaning all the dishes. But the spark for BALLE came from another source. Like any restaurant owner, she faced the issue of sourcing her food, and was particularly concerned with the treatment of animals. In 1998, she decided she wouldn't serve any meat from animals that had not been able to walk or see the light of day, shackled animals or those packed in cages, given GMO feed, and stuffed with antibiotics. She therefore sought out local, organic producers, whose chickens, pigs, and cows were free range and fed a healthy diet. She was able to find people to provide all the meat and dairy products the restaurant needed. This approach led her to do the same

_____

Traces of the resistance in Bristol against the creation of a Tesco supermarket.

for her fruits, vegetables, and grains, and within a few years, 95 percent of her fresh produce was sourced from local farms located with a radius of less than 50 miles. She wanted to go further and have an impact on producers throughout the region, so she created White Dog Community Enterprises, a nonprofit dedicated to connecting producers with restaurant owners. To ensure its operation, she funneled 20 percent of her company's profits into it. In just a few months, a regional network of farms, restaurants, and grocery stores was set up. Judy wondered how to expand it to include other activities. She set out to meet businesspeople in the region and, in 2001, the Sustainable Business Network of Greater Philadelphia was formed. Today, SBN Philly has more than four hundred members representing sustainable agriculture, renewable energy, ecoconstruction, waste management, ecological cleaning, clothes manufacturing, independent media, and retail shops. She then met Laury Hammel, a sort of alter ego, who in 1988 had founded the New England Businesses for Social Responsibility. Together, they dreamed of creating a national project for their networks that could inspire thousands of other businesspeople. Throughout the summer of 2001, they invited several dozen of them to reflect about this idea, along with two economists who were particularly concerned with the issue of relocalization: David Korten and Michael Schuman. By the end of the conference, they had decided to create BALLE. Other networks have since developed throughout the country, based on the Philadelphia model. One of the most dynamic is in Bellingham, Washington, where we met with Derek Long, co-founder with his former wife, Michelle, who is now BALLE's executive director.

4. Local first!

Bellingham is located in the far northwest corner of the United States, a few dozen miles from the Canadian border. It rains so much there that locals quip that they have webbed feet. Arriving straight from California, we were happy to see the water, the greenery, and just how refreshing this small town looked against the backdrop of mountains, but, as compared with Detroit, where we had three days of rain, the sun was shining brightly. We weren't about to complain. Bellingham proper has some 85,000 residents,[1] and an open-mindedness that seems to pervade coastal regions. Located between Seattle, the city of grunge and organic shops, and Vancouver, one of the world's most environmentally friendly cities, along with Copenhagen, the mindset here is highly conducive to the development of a local economy—to such as degree that it has become something of a small paradise.

After spending several days wandering around and talking with shopkeepers, a good part of the crew still couldn't believe that such a place existed in this land of free trade and ultra-liberal economics. It seemed somehow fake. But the proof was right in front of us: Bellingham had succeeded where many other European cities had not even begun to try. Crammed into Derek's car and a rental pick-up, we started our visit with Wood Stone, which manufactures pizza ovens that are now sold all over the world. As in Bristol, the idea of the American localists is not to eliminate international trade, but to anchor companies within a community and a territory, to produce locally everything that possibly can. When Keith Carpenter and Harry Hegarty met in 1989, one of them was selling restaurant equipment, the other incinerators. In 1990, they decided to pool their skills to make pizza ovens. "It's the village oven that we have simply modernized," says Merrill Bevan, one of Wood Stone's vice-presidents.

1. And about 200,000 in the county.

Success followed and in twenty-six years, the factory has grown from 16,000 square feet to 117,000 square feet, and from two to one hundred thirty employees. "We had opportunities to relocate production to China a thousand times," continued Merrill, but this is where we want to create jobs, where we want to put down roots, and pursue our values. Ninety percent of everything that goes into making our ovens comes from Washington State: high-temperature ceramics, stainless steel, charcoal grill."[1] The ovens are sold in eighty countries, but most of all locally, including La Fiamma downtown, where we went to eat the enormous pizzas that you'll only see in America.

In 2006, Sustainable Connections, the nonprofit run by Derek (similar to the Sustainable Business Network of Greater Philadelphia, created by Judy), organized the "Green Power Community Challenge," which encourages the development and use of renewable energy in the region. Derek and his staff focus on two factors to convince local residents, elected officials, and businesses: economic incentive and competition. For the former, they propose assessments on energy savings and the profitability of renewable installations. Solar panels, for example, last twenty years and pay for themselves after six or seven years—which leaves thirteen years of "free" energy. And then competition, because Americans love being "number one," and the idea of becoming the country's leading city in terms of renewable energy production has motivated the entire town of Bellingham. Wood Stone decided to compete as well and joined the challenge. They installed solar panels on the roof to produce their own electricity. They hired Itek Energy for the work, another local business whose employees[2] make solar modules used in the city and throughout the entire state. Most of the people in the manufacturing facility are

1. Since our trip, Wood Stone has partnered with Henny Penny, an Ohio-based company specializing in food-service equipment. To guarantee the continuation of their values, the two firms decided to become an employee-owned company.
2. There were fifteen employees in 2012, and there are now more than eighty, to meet the region's growing demand for renewable energy.

twenty-five to forty-five years old, and are happy to get together for the group photo that we will use at the end of the film. After just three years in business, Itek has manufactured more than 90,000 solar modules that produce 24,000 megawatts per hour. Some of them were installed by Mike McCauley, a superintendent with Chuckanut Builders, a local construction company that does energy renovations. We meet up in front of a typical 1960s house they have just completed work on. From the energy sieve that it was, the house has become a positive building that produces more energy than it uses. The walls were insulated, windows replaced, spaces redesigned to create one large room instead of several small ones, the roof weatherproofed, and solar panels installed. Most of the materials came from local companies and or resources. Or both.

The reason companies like Itek and Chuckanut Builders were created so recently and have so many orders is because the challenge launched by Sustainable Connections was more successful than anyone expected. In just six months in 2006, the city's purchases of green energy grew from 0.5 to 12 percent of the total power used. From 2007 to 2009, Bellingham was the number one EPA certified Green Power Community in America.[1] The city council voted unanimously to purchase 100 percent green power for all public buildings and facilities, and more than one hundred businesses, like Wood Stone, have installed solar panels on their rooftops or asked their utility suppliers to adopt renewable energy options. Thanks to the amount of green energy the city purchases, a bulk discount of 40 percent benefiting all residents was negotiated. The farmer's market (one of the largest in Washington State) is a case in point; it installed a row of Itek panels to provide power to the stands. Derek is very proud to show us this bastion of fresh,

1. It has since been relegated to 12th place in terms of the power usage, and 21st place in terms of percentage of green power, with 15 percent of its overall mix, far behind Hillsboro (near Portland), which is 2nd in usage, and 1st in percentage, for the same number of inhabitants and a 50 percent mix of renewables. See "Green Power Communities," EPA, https://www.epa.gov/greenpower/green-power-communities.

local, organic food. At first sight it doesn't look like much to us, as we're used to local outdoor markets in France—except that on closer inspection, nearly every single stand is run by local farmers. No greengrocers who purchase products from around the world at wholesale food markets. The meat, eggs, bread, fruit, vegetables, flowers, and honey all come from within 60 miles, often less. These farms sell here, to locals, but also supply shops and restaurants in town, like Mallard, which has been making artisanal ice cream from local organic ingredients since 2011. In a few years, Mallard has become one of the largest customers of Growing Washington, an organic farm, and Cloud Mountain Farm (one of the farms we saw at the market), from which they buy hundreds of pounds of berries and small fruit, apples, grapes, and pumpkins. In all, six nearby farms supply Ben Scholtz and his team as they produce a seasonal menu of more than twenty-five flavors, in addition to vanilla, chocolate, coffee, and pistachio—which come from farther afield.

Our tour could have gone on forever because a local version of almost everything is available in Bellingham, like the clothes designed and made by Teresa Rampal from organic cotton and fair-trade hemp in the basement of her downtown shop. As we visit here and there, Derek tells us great stories about Bellingham, which run counter to everything that we have heard elsewhere. "Here," he says, showing us a street corner, "was a Kentucky Fried Chicken. The neighborhood reeked of deep-fried oil, so a young couple in the neighborhood bought the building and transformed it into a fantastic bistro, with a beautiful terrace covered with vines, surrounded by flowers. They serve local food—and now it smells good!" A little farther along, we walk by WECO, the Whatcom Educational Credit Union. "It's basically the town's largest bank. It belongs to its members and helps to keep the money local, so that our economy can grow. Deposits are recycled into loans used for personal or business-related projects, here in Bellingham." We turn the corner to Woods Coffee: "There are twelve or thirteen in

Bellingham County. It's a local chain! The father opened the first one. When his kids grew up, he wanted them to stay close by, so he expanded his business." Mélanie asks: "And how many Starbucks do you have?" Derek half smiles: "Just one downtown, and maybe one or two others around the county."

This type of unreal story, in which local businesses replace or displace the international chains that have clobbered everything in their way everywhere else in the world,[1] is a familiar one to Derek and his staff. For more than ten years, Sustainable Connections has been doing everything in its power to support local businesses by creating networks, running ad campaigns among the general public—like "Think Local First"—and by providing technical and administrative assistance. They run successful programs in multiple fields: farming and food, energy, construction, and waste management. Today 70 percent of Bellingham's residents know about the Think Local First program and 60 percent of them have changed the way they shop. The city ranks second in the United States for the proportion and vitality of its local, independent businesses. Nearly seven hundred local businesspeople are affiliated with the organization and some two thousand profit directly or indirectly from the work of Sustainable Connections. It's enough to keep a downtown record store in business, where we have a good time sharing our music tastes in CDs and vinyls. Whatever anyone may say, Bellingham is a great place to live, as confirmed by a 2014 Gallup-Healthways Well-Being Index, which ranked the city number one in the "small town" category, for health and well-being.[2] Local residents display "fewer

1. Starbucks opened an impressive 700 new shops around the world in 2011–12. The number of establishments in Paris doubled between 2011 and 2015, growing from 44 to 90. See Mathilde Visseyrias, "Starbucks s'attend à une nouvelle année record," *Le Figaro.fr*, September 23, 2011, http://www.lefigaro.fr/societes/2011/09/22/04015-20110922ARTFIG00744-starbucks-s-attend-a-une-nouvelle-annee-record.php.
2. Ben Miller, "Seattle, Bellingham are 'Healthy' Cities," *Puget Sound Business Journal*, March 26, 2014, http://www.bizjournals.com/seattle/morning_call/2014/03/seattle-bellingham-are-healthy-cities.html.

chronic illness, lower rates of obesity, exercise more, smoke less, and generally have a more positive outlook about their community."

Michelle Long is Derek's former wife. With Derek, she founded Sustainable Connections before becoming executive director of BALLE. During the Oakland conference, we had a long conversation with Michelle, Michael Shuman, one of the movement's economists and theorists,[1] co-founder Judy Wicks, and Nikki Silvestri, once of the forty fellows best representing the vision of the organization. We wanted to understand what this idea of "local" meant to them. Even if the concept of "relocalization" is growing in France and around the world for the many of the legitimate reasons already discussed, relating to both the environment and society, it sometimes conveys the idea of withdrawing and disconnecting that is one of the bywords of the extreme right. So it is about returning to some earlier time? Putting an end to the globalized economy? Have local economies proven themselves to be truly effective? These are the questions we were looking to answer.

Interview with Michelle Long, Michael Shuman, Nikki Silvestri, and Judy Wicks

CYRIL: In your opinion, what is not working with the current economy? Why put so much energy into transforming it?

NIKKI: The American economy can't continue down this path. It was built on the genocide of the Native Americans and the slavery of my people, which has never recovered from it. African Americans went from slaves to sharecroppers, then to prisoners. One in

---

1. Michael Shuman is an economist, lawyer, and entrepreneur. With a BA and law degree from Stanford University, he has written eight books and hundreds of articles for *The New York Times*, the *Washington Post*, and other publications. He also ran the Institute for Policy Studies, one of the most influential independent think tanks in Washington, from 1988 to 1998.

three African Americans will be jailed at some point in their life. And a large share of our economy still uses the free labor of these prisoners to rake in profits. Our entire food system depends on the work of illegal immigrants. They represent 50 percent of the labor force, are exploited, threatened with deportation if they complain, and are treated as sub-humans. Our clothes and some of our products are manufactured on the other side of the planet by human beings working in totally unacceptable conditions, for starvation wages. We need to restructure our economy. Until it can function without an underlying slave class, until it closes the unbelievable gap in which 90 percent of humanity owns less than 10 percent of the wealth, things cannot get better.

CYRIL: Would you also say that consumers are, to a lesser extent, slaves of this system? That they must work their entire lives to keep it functioning, by producing and consuming? The very word "consumer" is already a way of redefining a human being as an economic variable.

NIKKI: Yes. And unfortunately, many of us don't know that there's any other way.

MICHELLE: For me, the essential problem is that everything is separated, as if everything wasn't interrelated. When I did my MBA, I argued so much with my macroeconomics professor that some students said, "I've never seen a teacher spend so much time with a single student." I couldn't understand how an economic system that excludes variables like people and nature[1] could function. I asked him: "Can this thing be applied somewhere, or is it just a theory?" Success in the business world is represented by a simple bottom line. But the question of whether we are doing well or if our lives

---

1. Variables that classical economics calls "externalities."

are improving is not factored in. It's totally crazy to measure economic success by the number of microwaves per household, rather than the happiness of the population. This type of economy does not really benefit people; it creates more inequality, it destroys nature. ... What affects me the most is the rate of suicides; people feel like they no longer belong to anything at all.

CYRIL: How does a local approach answer these challenges? It's entirely possible to have a local business that destroys nature and treats its employees poorly.

MICHAEL: Obviously, just because it's local doesn't mean it's perfect. People behave badly everywhere, but we now have irrefutable proof that local economies perform better in many sectors. A study by the American Environmental Protection Agency examined the probability of factories allowing a certain amount of toxic pollution produced by their operations. It showed that a factory belonging to a distant company would tolerate ten times the amount of toxic emissions than a locally owned factory. When a company acts badly and you meet up with the manager or the owner at church, at the store, or at school, you can tell him what's going wrong. And pressure from the community can influence his company's actions.

MICHELLE: We don't feel the impact of a tree cut down in the Amazon; however, we can clearly see it when it happens on your street or behind your garden. We are often more fully motivated to act and make a difference on a local scale. The larger and more remote a company becomes from where it operates, the less the people in control have a sense of what they're doing. On the other hand, local entrepreneurs will try to add value to the places where they live, for the people they live among, for the rivers, the schools.

MICHAEL: In terms of jobs, which is everyone's number one priority during every election, we have amassed a very large number of studies showing that local economies are the key to job creation. One of them was published in the *Harvard Business Review* in July 2010. It was a retrospective study on hundreds of metropolitan areas throughout the country; it demonstrated that cities with the largest proportion of jobs with local and independent companies were those that created the most jobs per capita.[1] The Federal Reserve conducted another study in August 2013. It showed that an increase in per capita income is directly linked to the existence of small, independent companies. Dozens of other studies corroborate these results. On the other hand, the worst way to support job growth is what is being done in the name of economic development all across the United States, which is to pay massive amounts of money to attract or retain global business. That is a proven loser for economic development. We know, for example, in a bunch of studies that have been done at the community level, that for every dollar that a person spends at a locally owned business, it means two to four times more jobs produced by locally owned business, as compared to a non-locally owned business.[2] It also means two to four times the impact on income and wealth, the tax collection coming into the local government, the charitable contributions that people give. A study in the city of Cleveland[3] (population: 390,000) showed that redirecting 25 percent of food purchases to local producers would create more than 27,000 new jobs in the region (which corresponds to putting one in eight people back to work),

1. In this case, "per capita" refers to jobs "per company" rather than per person.
2. A study conducted by the New Economic Foundation in the UK confirms these figures. It refers to "LM3," or the local multiplier effect. See Justin Sacks, *The Money Trail* (New Economics Foundation, 2002), http://b.3cdn.net/nefoundation/7c0985cd522f66fb75_oom6boezu.pdf.
3. [o]Brad Masi, Leslie Schaller, and Michael H. Shuman, *The 25% Shift* (Cleveland Foundation, December 2010), http://www.neofoodweb.org/sites/default/files/resources/the25shift-foodlocalizationintheNEOregion.pdf.

increase the regional annual production by $4.3 billion, and generate $126 million in additional tax revenue for the city. And this study only looked at the food sector.

MICHELLE: To sum up, the major transnational companies are very good at raking in dollars, but they end up in just a few hands. A path leading to a maximum of wealth benefitting a maximum number of people involves a greater density and diversity of local and independent companies in a given place.

CYRIL: For you, is the future 100 percent local?

JUDY: This is our vision: rather than a global economy, controlled by multinationals that shop products around the world, we could create interconnected local networks that are as autonomous as possible, where every community would develop strong food, energy, and water security. They would no longer depend on large companies to meet their basic needs and could trade their surpluses, their own strengths. People are mistaken when they think that our movement is only local. Our idea is "Local First": whatever we can produce and which corresponds to our basic needs, we should do. But by trading fairly with other communities, we can also support local economies on the other side of the world, without exploiting the natural world or people. All lives are interconnected, whether they be human, animal, or plants. We need to make our commercial, economic, business, and consumer decisions based on this reality; we have to act for the good of the community, not for individual greed.

MICHAEL: I believe that the economy of the future will share three characteristics. First, a very large majority of jobs (somewhere around 90 percent) will be in local and independent companies. Second, I agree with Judy: every community should be autonomous in terms of its basic needs. I often hear people say: "If you create a world where every community is autonomous, you're going to destroy the global market." But it's not true: this kind of community has more wealth to spend. I live in Washington, and when I transferred my savings account from Bank of America to a local Credit Union, I saved several thousand dollars a year, and with that, I bought French wine! And the key to lowering CO_2 emissions is to simultaneously promote local businesses and to charge a carbon tax so that less fossil fuel is used for the exchange of goods and services. Third, we need companies that are committed to the triple bottom line: environmental, social, and financial concerns. This is what all the BALLE companies do.

CYRIL: To achieve this, is it just consumers who have to change the way they purchase items, or do we need legislative changes?

MICHAEL: We need both. For example, I am in favor of real economic liberalism, so that when a major company is about to go under, it's not the taxpayers who pick up the bill because it's supposedly "too big to fail." In 2008, we saw that major financial institutions were neither efficient nor sustainable. But the fact that the government intervened to keep them from going under means that it did not act on behalf of the collective interest, nor of the market, but on behalf of these institutions. We have to treat them like small businesses, let them go bankrupt if they are inefficient. The rhetoric of all American political leaders, regardless of their party, is that small companies are the life blood of the economy. So their politics should be in sync with their speeches. For example, we should prevent big companies from becoming monopolies. Walmart[1] treats its suppliers like a monopoly, in violation of our anti-trust laws, which no one forces it to comply with. Amazon is allowed to sell

1. In 2014, the world's largest retail company in terms of revenue.

its books online with charging taxes, even though all independent bookstores pay them. There are very simple measures that can be taken, if we believe in liberalism. In a market that is truly free and fair, local businesses would do very well.

CYRIL: But we are hearing, all over the world, that multinationals have a decisive influence on political leaders and on laws.

NIKKI: That's true. If big companies continue to act as they do, we're going to see more and more money in politics. The people who have the most money are going to get control of the lawmakers. If what we have is people power, then we have to use it.

JUDY: That goes without saying. That's why BALLE is a pro-democracy movement. We can't have a true democracy if our governments are controlled by big business. The first step is to weaken the power of these firms by no longer giving them our money and by buying from businesses in our communities. That's how we will reclaim power over the economy.

MICHAEL: We can also do our own lobbying. We recently won a legislative victory by proposing a policy that brought together both strong conservatives and strong progressives to enact some particularly interesting change.[1] In the last one hundred years, the United States has enacted what it called securities laws, which cover financial transactions. Rather than promoting security, they created two classes of investors: on the one hand, the rich, which we now call "the 1 percent," and then the other 99 percent. In short, if you are rich, you can invest anytime, in any sector, no questions asked. If you do not have a personal fortune and you want to invest in a small

1. Michael Shuman was one of the architects of the crowdfunding reforms that became the "JOBS Act," signed into law by President Obama in April 2012.

local company, it will cost thousands of dollars in legal fees intended to "secure" the transaction. The result: very few people invest. We have just changed all that in the American law; we have lowered these costs substantially for small companies, to free up investment for the 99 percent. We managed to create an alliance among local participants, like me, and the Republican's Tea Party, which still believes in the deregulation governed by stupid old laws like the securities laws. This coalition was able to get Congress, in 2012, to vote nearly unanimously in favor of this reform of the securities law. This was an unprecedented consensus, which shows that if we can be smart and find a common interest, we can hope to win.

CYRIL: What can these news laws do, in the long term?

MICHAEL: The goal is to shift money from Wall Street to Main Street. To invest our resources in companies with which we maintain a relationship. There's something crazy about the current system: we hand over a lifetime of savings to investors we have never met, who invest our money thousands of miles away in Malaysia, all because they have promised us a great retirement and a happy life. It's a fairy tale.

People involved in the Slow Money movement[1] say this: "Invest your money in companies you care about, which contribute to building the world you want to live in, which bring something to your community. If you invest locally, you will be the first to benefit from the positive results of a company that creates jobs, that protects the environment, that creates wealth." This approach gives us the ability to set up our own hedge funds. Financially, we become the masters of our own future. It's the first step, and the most important one, in recovering from the unhealthy addiction created by the global economy.

---

1. A reference to the Slow Food movement, which promotes alternatives to fast food through the meaning, quality, and health of our food.

CYRIL: Can private investment be a powerful tool?

MICHAEL: In the United States, it is estimated that long-term investments represent $30 trillion. If half of this money went to half of the economy, in other words, to local businesses, we would see a transfer of $15 trillion from Wall Street to Main Street. Which would give $50,000 to each American. The key is to get the movement started. When the first $1 trillion starts to move, the demand for shares of Wall Street companies will go down and their prices will drop. On the other hand, the demand and value of shares of Main Street companies will go up. Investment advisors and wealth managers will tell their clients: "Something's happening with these local investments; you should put some of your money into it." And trillions will be added to trillions until it reaches an equilibrium with two $15 trillion investments. It could be the largest and most revolutionary flow of capital in modern history. Wall Street wouldn't even know what had hit them.

CYRIL: For you, is it essential to create new companies rather than try to change existing companies from the inside? It's an ongoing debate among those who think that we should get rid of McDonald's, for example, and those who believe that it could become an upstanding company.

MICHELLE: BALLE was created from a movement of businesspeople who tried, some twenty-five or thirty years ago, to reinvent the current model. Pioneers like Anita Roddick, who founded The Body Shop, and Ben Cohen and Jerry Greenfield of Ben & Jerry's. The best of their generation. For every businessperson, the capitalist norm involves reimbursing the capital invested, then growing it by getting bought out by a bigger company or going public on the stock market. They thought they could do it better, by creating a better version of a business that placed a higher priority on people and nature.

CYRIL: And The Body Shop was bought by L'Oréal; Ben & Jerry's by Unilever. They didn't change the big companies, the big ones incorporated the smaller ones to bolster their model.

MICHELLE: Yes. These were great people with visionary outlooks, but the system swallowed them up.

CYRIL: Why? Why couldn't they transform it?

MICHELLE: There are lots of reasons: the way the companies are financed, inertia, habit. We have learned from sociologists and theorists that when a large system becomes corrupt, whether it's a human organization or an ecosystem, it has a very hard time looking at itself in a new way. It does what it does; it effects small, marginal changes (as do companies with their sustainable development or social responsibility departments), but it cannot entirely remake itself. To create something new, you need to create a secure space, outside of the dominant system. This is what we're doing with this network of small, local companies that are spread out geographically. We are pioneers trying to imagine what our economy could look like in the future.

CYRIL: Why are you so involved in all these operations? What do you tell yourself when you get up in the morning?

MICHELLE: I like businesspeople and their energy, innovation, and ideas. I like business when it's a tool for creativity and service. Not when it exploits people's talents to make money. My friends who work in large companies are miserable, they're like zombies. They rack up numbers, but aren't connected to anything. Entrepreneurs have ideas, gifts, and they bring them to their communities. What matters to me is reconnecting. Here in Berkeley, scientific studies have shown that a person is happy (whether they're French, American, young, old, Republican, or Democrat) when he or she feels connected, has a meaningful purpose, feels linked to other people, to nature, generosity. And I want to be happy.

NIKKI: My family taught me that we are part of a whole. If our family is going to do well, our community has to be doing well; for our community to do well, the society has to be doing well; for society to do well, the planet has to be doing well. I feel the responsibility of all that. This is my planet, my people, all of them.

CYRIL: Do you have faith that we can achieve this?

JUDY: We will win. And if we don't, it will be the end of civilization as we know it. Nature will continue to be destroyed, inequality will continue to grow, and we will be engulfed in chaos. It's a suicidal path. This is what we want to avoid by returning power to everyone among us. Power to the people.

Stop this suicidal path. ... I haven't had a drop of alcohol in two weeks. That hasn't happened for nearly fifteen years. Without drinking to the point of being completely drunk, I had gradually started to drink wine like some people are addicted to coffee: one to four glasses a day, or even a lot more at parties and dinners. For me, drinking is a powerful, cultural, familial addiction, linked to the fantasies of many of my heroes. Freeing myself from it seems like a good way to take control of myself. And I hope it will lead to other transformations. The direction the world is going is tearing me up; despite all my efforts, I can clearly see that there is nothing I can modify in the long term. Drinking alleviates the need to confront this suffering on an everyday level; it deadens me, cuts me off from myself. Not drinking has brought me back to this reality and to other benefits. The desire to meditate is slowly coming back. The need for a mental cleansing that washes away the frenetic activity of my thoughts, allowing me to access a sense of plenitude. Simply being in the present, pure attention; meditation, long walks among trees, strolling around the city, sexual bliss, hugs, contemplation are the most significant, fulfilling experiences I have ever had. And the impetus for all this is never linked to any material possession. Love for another person, the emotion of looking at a work of art, the inner gratitude when in contact with nature: none of this depends on any financial transaction. Once the basics (housing, food, access to energy, clothing, mobility) and the small extras (access to culture, travel) are taken care of, nothing should keep us from being profoundly happy. That's what I understand from the struggle that Judy and the others are pursuing. It is, above all, a struggle against ourselves. Or rather for ourselves.

5. Repair it, reuse it, build it: The maker movement

This movement to reappropriate the economy is also at the heart of the approach adopted by makers, whom we were able to meet in Oakland during the BALLE conference, but also in Detroit when we visited the urban vegetable gardens. In a context of an ultra-consumerist society, where everything is disposable, concepts like planned obsolescence[1] limit the life cycle of products to just a few years, and repairing is often more expensive than buying a new product, makers have opened places where people make,

1. The policy of designing a product with an artificially limited useful life so as to shorten the replacement cycles, thereby generating greater sales.

repair, and learn how to produce things on their own; they're called "fab labs." With inventions like the 3D printer, these urban workshops have become, in just a few years, mini-factories that can produce small series of objects of varying sizes. From the impossible-to-find part needed to repair your refrigerator or your printer, to musical instruments, cups, wheelchair ramps, bottle holders, toys, and telephone cases, nearly everything can now be produced, without requiring mass-production plants or large companies. In recent years, a car,[1] houses,[2] and a building[3] have even been designed and constructed from 3D printers. According to Alastair Parvin, the designer of WikiHouses—homes made from open-source plans, which everyone can download and build their house—"we're into this future where the factory is everywhere ... If design's great project in the twentieth century was the democratization of consumption—that was Henry Ford, Levittown, Coca Cola, IKEA—in the twenty-first century, I think design's great project is the democratization of production."[4]

This approach is especially interesting in Detroit, where the twentieth-century industry has partially collapsed. In addition to being a world leader in urban farming, Detroit has become a major hub in the Do It Yourself economy. The city and its region are home

1. The Strati, presented at the Detroit Auto Show on January, 2015. See "Une Voiture Fabriquée en 44 heures avec une imprimante 3D présentée aux Etats-Unis," France Soir, January 16, 2015, http://www.francesoir.fr/culture-medias/une-voiture-fabriquee-en-44-heures-avec-une-imprimante-3d-presentee-aux-etats-unis.
2. Like the bioclimatic solar wooden house built in two weeks in Barcelona in 2012 (www.maison-bioclimatique.info/maison-solaire/) and the Chinese houses constructed by a 20-foot-wide 3D printer: "Vidéo : une imprimante 3D qui construit des maisons," January 23, 2015, http://www.directmatin.fr/economie/2015-01-23/video-une-imprimante-3d-qui-construit-des-maisons-698327.
3. A five-floor building in China, built by a 3D printer, 33 feet high by 20 feet wide, see "Chine : un immeuble et une villa bâtis avec une imprimante 3D," January 21, 2015, http://www.leparisien.fr/high-tech/chine-un-immeuble-et-une-villa-batis-avec-une-imprimante-en-3d-21-01-2015-4465801.php.
4. "Alastair Parvin: Architecture for the People by the People," TED Talk, YouTube video, May 23, 2013, 13:11, http://www.youtube.com/watch?v=Mlt6kaNjoeI.

to multiple places occupied by makers: i3 Detroit, The Robot Garage (Lego and robotics), Omnicorp Detroit, and TechShop. We visited one of them, the Mount Elliott Makerspace, run by Jeff Sturges, a delightful forty-something who looks a bit like Tom Cruise and has seemingly endless energy. As he likes to say, Jeff was an industrial designer: he made toothbrushes. "One night I went home and said to myself: We don't need more new toothbrushes! Nor a lot of other stuff, for that matter. We do, however, need food, water, shelter, clothes, transportation, exchange systems, waste management. We must have access to these things and the means to create them as easily as possible. Once we have solved these basic issues, we can then look into other things that are necessary in the hierarchy of needs:[1] music, a creative life, meaning, and so on." He then invested totally in the dynamic of fab labs and opened Mount Elliott Makerspace, "a community workshop where people come to learn how to make and repair just about anything, together."

It's an unusual spot, housed in the basement of a church that looks pretty much like a haunted house. It's light years away from the images of the trendy fab labs on the Internet. But step inside, and it's clearly a dynamic scene. The bike workshop is next to a large common room with rows of computers and tables. There's a spot for sewing and, behind some glass, another room with work benches and walls covered the wood- and metalworking tools. When we visit, two men are fixing their bikes, a woman is making potholders, an entire tableful of people are learning how to build mini-speakers with Post-Its, and young girls are playing Minecraft. Jeff is sorry we hadn't come the previous day, when it was three times busier. For Jeff, this is an educational spot, but also a way for people to free themselves. "In Detroit, there are very rich people and very poor people, with very few middle-class folks in between. The very poor become dependent on the rich who own or produce

1. Abraham Maslow created the theory of a pyramidal hierarchy of human needs.

things. Which leads the poor to take jobs they don't like, so they can buy these things. Here, we are trying to create a world where we make the stuff we want and need ourselves, within a community. We want to decrease our dependency on large companies that don't always have our best interests at heart."

Next to him is a boy about sixteen years old, who explains to us that he's been coming here for two years. He has built his own bike, fixed his cell phone, and made new friends. It's not the worst place to hang out after school. The same goes for a young girl who, two tables over, is finishing up her homework. Her family has been attending this church forever. At first she stayed at Mount Elliot because she had to, then she started making her own dolls. She's now trying to get the most out of this place. She is eleven years old, African American, clearly from a family of modest means, and talks to me about melting ice, the acidification of the oceans that is eating up some of our oxygen, and about humanity in general that could disappear. She tells me that she dreams of a world where diversity would be accepted everywhere, where segregation, violence, and crime (like the situations in her own neighborhood) no longer exist. She dreams of going to Princeton to become a lawyer, to defend the poor. As she explains: "In a newspaper, the paper is white, but the letters are black; we all need each other. A single race can't control the world." Behind her, the woman making potholders runs them through a sewing machine, one after another. She has been a volunteer, teaching sewing classes for four years. With her, children learn how to sew on buttons, repair pants, shirts, socks, and also make their own clothes. "I teach them independence," she smiles. Young and old help each other. Jeff tells us how a twelve-year-old girl have, over the last three years, trained dozens of adults how to solder—it's a different way of learning than what we experienced in school. "One of my friends, Joi Ito, runs the MIT Media Lab. He often says to me: 'Don't talk about education, talk about learning.' People reject education because it's forced on them, it comes from the outside. Learning, you do it for yourself, because you want to or need to. These kids don't have to be here. They come because they want to. In the future, I hope that maker spaces and schools will be interchangeable. We will call them learning centers. People will be happy, they'll have fun as well as learn and exchange with others."

This need to relearn "how to do it by ourselves"—which Jeff shares with Rob Hopkins and the Transition Movement discussed earlier—is deep-seated. When we ask him why it's useful to work so hard to make a small object, when the world is full of products manufactured for peanuts, he takes off again: "For me, it's about the crux of our human capabilities. We are made to create things, digitally and physically. It's really important to use everything that we have available—our minds, but also our hands, eyes, noses, mouths. We have to reconnect ourselves to all our facilities and reconnect to other people. Consumerism is now the norm. But extracting all these resources is becoming problematic. We have to ask ourselves if we can produce them ourselves by recycling, repairing, repurposing." He shows us objects that have been created by members of the fab lab, using his small 3D printer: missing Lego parts, a small seeder used on urban farms, and his favorite, an artificial hand a father is making for his son. For Jeff, the maker movement can transform society by giving every single person the tools to free up their creativity. "Thousands of people in their homes, creating electronic parts, works of art, food. If we develop the proper tools while allowing people to express their talents, we can change everything. Maybe most people don't see it yet, but it's already happening."

In 2015, the Maker Faire in Detroit brought together several hundred makers and more than 2,500 visitors over two days. It featured all kinds of projects, notably those concerning sustainable energies. Over the last ten years the city has lost 25 percent of its overall population, but downtown Detroit has 59 percent more university

---

Alexandre and Fabien (who replaced Raphaël during a shoot).

graduates under the age of thirty-five, according to a 2011 *New York Times* article.[1] A sign that the energy in the leading post-industrial large city, which attracts journalists and tourists from around the world is incredibly contagious.

6. Toward a decentralized sharing economy– Interview with Jeremy Rifkin

Several factors were becoming clear to us from our travels and all our encounters. Everyone stressed the need to decentralize economic power: whether it involved monetary creation, entrepreneurship, investment, innovation, or industry, they all highlighted the importance of organizing our models into multiple networks in which every person would have a stake and responsibility in the operation of the global system. We can't continue supporting behemoths that concentrate more and more power and wealth. In this respect, Bernard Lietaer's analogy about natural ecosystems really hit home and echoed the philosophy of permaculture. Perhaps the first thing to do is to draw inspiration from how nature operates to create efficient and resilient economic systems. Thinking back, most of the initiatives we saw were built around this model: renewable energies are trying, however imperfectly, to reproduce photosynthesis; "Zero Waste," circular economies, and the makers are inspired by the ecology of forests in which waste material is constantly reused to produce new resources; and complementary currencies and the BALLE network are drawing on the principles of diversity and interconnectivity that Bernard Lietaer discussed as essential factors in the resilience of any ecosystem. They all spoke

1. Jennifer Conlin, "Detroit Pushes Back With Young Muscles," July 1, 2011, *The New York Times*, http://www.nytimes.com/2011/07/03/fashion/the-young-and-entrepreneurial-move-to-downtown-detroit-pushing-its-economic-recovery.html

of autonomy as crucial to obtaining greater freedom, achieving equilibrium in our relationships, and guaranteeing genuine democratic values.

All around me, in the NGOs, universities, and media, I was also seeing the emergence of a vast movement based on an economy of sharing, on the idea that we no longer have to own all our goods, but that we could share these things. For most of these people, the movement toward decentralization, toward a more lateral society (a break with the pyramidal and vertical model we now know) resulted from the major cultural and technological transformation ushered in by the Internet. For the first time, a majority of human beings could connect to each other directly, have access to information and services, and create them on their own, without having to go through centralized organizations (even though the concentration organized by Facebook, Google, Amazon, and Apple is starting to look like the vertical capitalistic model of the twentieth century). The Internet makes it easy to share information, objects, services, energy, and for Jeremy Rifkin, whom we met at the start of our journey, it is a key aspect of a widespread revolution. He believes that it fosters the emergence of a collaborative economy, the first radically new economic model to appear since capitalism and socialism in the early nineteenth century—and one that is about to take on a decisive role. For those who don't know him, Jeremy Rifkin is a sort of worldwide guru of the future. An economist, consultant, CEO, president, and co-founder of the Foundation on Economic Trends, he has, in the past dozen years, become one of the most influential experts on the future in the Western world. To his credit, long before many other people, he came to certain realizations that inspired him to fight for many essential issues. In 1973, he organized one of the largest anti-oil demonstrations, foreseeing the need to shift to renewable energies. In 1988, he brought climate scientists and environmental activists from thirty-five countries to Washington DC for the first worldwide conference on greenhouse gases. That same year, he gave a series of conferences in Hollywood to raise awareness among actors, producers, screenwriters, and directors on the challenges posed by climate change.

In 1992, he launched "Beyond Beef," a campaign supported by a coalition of six environmental organizations, including Greenpeace, Rainforest Action Network, and Public Citizen, with the goal of reducing the consumption of beef by 50 percent. All these subjects are now, in 2015, known to all, but they were well under the radar at the time. It's always wise to pay close attention when he forecasts developments for the upcoming decades. As special advisor to Chancellor Angela Merkel, the European Parliament, and the European Commission, he managed to get them to officially adopt his strategy: a third industrial revolution, based on the conjunction of renewable energies and the Internet. Even if the success he projects requires a certain number of preconditions, we wanted to compare this vision with everything we had discovered about the economy. Jeremy Rifkin met with us during a trip to Paris, where he was making a stop as part of an international book tour. And it was a somewhat different experience from what we had seen up to this point.

Walking down the corridor of the five-star hotel, we spotted Jeremy Rifkin walking a few feet ahead of us. I hurried up to catch him and introduce myself; he responded with cold indifference. He was stressed, putting in thirteen-hour days, repeating the same story over and over again to journalists in any number of languages, and felt that he didn't have any time to waste. He explained to me, without having the slightest idea who we were and why we wanted to interview him, that he could only give us twenty minutes, not sixty. I reminded him that we were making a feature film, that we wanted to go more in-depth than just a quick media interview. After talking to his press attaché, he agreed to thirty minutes, but without any questions so that he could present his position from start to finish. In the end, he stayed the full hour with us, without the slightest interruption. Here is a large part of what he told us that day.

"The great shift was in the first and second industrial revolutions in the nineteenth and twentieth centuries; we created a vertically integrated world: centralized, top-down power, centralized industry, and agriculture with even larger means of production, distribution tools, and centralized communication (fewer media and owners, purchasing center and superstores), centralized systems for banking, insurance, transportation, and logistics. This was the most efficient way to create economies of scale, achieve the immense projects of this period, and better our lives. But we have now reached the limits of this model for all these reasons we know. We have to embark on a new revolution. With the Internet, we can overturn the way we communicate, the way to exchange and distribute energy, the way we get around. The architecture of the Internet is distributive, collaborative, open, transparent, and rewards lateral economies of scale. It allows millions of people to come together, to produce, and to share with each other. The value created by all these small players overwhelms what the large twentieth-century companies could do. Let me give you three examples: one for transport, one for energy, and one for industry.

"With the Internet, it is now easer to share a car rather than own one. Millions of young people who have no interest whatsoever in ownership, but want access to mobility have been car sharing in the last five years. With your smartphone and GPS, you can find a car or a driver in just a few minutes, you go to your destination, and then you pay online. Think how this benefits the environment. Larry Burns, who was executive vice-president of General Motors, did a study on the impact of car sharing at the University of Michigan in Ann Arbor. Right now, even with the incipient nature of the infrastructure we now have, we could have the same mobility with 80 percent fewer vehicles on the road. We now have one billion vehicles in the world. We could reduce it to 200 million and make sure they are not only car shared, but also electrical and fuel-cell operated, and manufactured using 3D printers.

"Which brings me to industry. We now have a makers' movement, a generation with 3D printers who are sharing software and plans for free on the Web, producing all kinds of objects. And you know what they're using for their material? Garbage: recycled plastic, paper, metal that they melt down and reuse. No patent costs, no raw materials costs; once the printer is paid for, it costs them nearly nothing. In a few years, they will power their 3D printers and little factories with their own solar panels and wind turbines—and again, once the panels are paid for, the energy will be basically free, at near zero marginal cost.[1] Solar energy is abundant; the sun doesn't send you a bill. As products are produced on demand, we can avoid the immense waste generated by the current consumer and industrial society, whereby we have to produce as many units as possible to keep costs down, even if it means throwing stuff away. Not everyone will be creating sophisticated products, but if, as President Obama wants, every school has a 3D printer, it won't be long before young people will be able to make smartphones, houses, and more.

"It's the same thing for energy. In Germany, 27 percent of the electricity is now solar and wind, at near zero marginal cost, and the country is aiming to reach 35 percent green energy by 2020. On one Sunday in May of 2014, 75 percent of all electricity powering the third biggest economy in the world was solar and wind, at negative prices all day, which sounds like an oxymoron. A solar watt used to cost 66 dollars to produce in 1970; it's 66 cents today, and is going down toward zero. We now have millions and millions of small players in Germany: individuals, small businesses, medium-size companies, citizens' cooperatives, nonprofit organizations that are all producing their electricity at near zero marginal cost. This is a revolution of unprecedented magnitude. How can fossil

---

1. Marginal cost is the cost of producing an additional unit of a good or service once the fixed costs have been covered.

fuels and nuclear stay in the game? Within ten years, we'll have tens of millions of people around the world, and twenty-five years from now, we'll have hundreds of millions, producing their own electricity, locally and regionally, through biomass, geothermal, wind, solar, hydraulic, and sending it back to a digitized energy Internet. It will happen, it's inevitable. We can already see the trend lines. And the giant vertically integrated, centralized national companies won't be able to keep up. In Germany, over the last seven years, the four big power companies produced less than 7 percent of the new electricity. They're used to dealing with centralized power so their economies of scale are vertical. But the new power is horizontal, distributed, the energy is everywhere, available and free. All these millions of small players have to do is take little bits of it, store it and share it. When you put it all together, in lateral economies of scale, it overwhelms any that a nuclear power plant can produce.

"Every businessperson has always been looking to find new technologies to increase productivity, reduce marginal costs, to put out cheaper goods and services, win over consumers and market shares, and bring some nice profits back to the investors. But none of us in our wildest expectations ever imagined a technology revolution so extreme in its productivity that it could actually reduce marginal cost to near zero, making them essentially free and abundant. The very thing that created the great success of the capitalist system is now turning against it.

"A new term appeared a few years back: social entrepreneur. The older generation would say that this is an oxymoron, that you can't be social and entrepreneurial, because Adam Smith said that each individual only pursues their self-interest and doesn't care about the common interest; but by pursuing their self-interest, they improve society. But apparently, the younger generation never read Adam Smith, because they firmly believe that by contributing their own talents, their own creativity, and their own skills, and by freely giving it to the sharing economy, that this improves not only everyone else's life, but their own as well. When a young person judges a government, a political party, a school system, or any institution, they ask the following question: 'Is this institutional behavior centralized, proprietary, patriarchal, top-down, enclosed? Or is it distributive, collaborative, open, transparent, and does it reward lateral economies of scale?' Not only are they very entrepreneurial, but they have a different idea of power. This is power to the people.

"Of course, all these companies, which are still immensely powerful, will try to monopolize the tools of progress: telephone and cable companies, access and energy providers, the huge Internet companies. Google records six billion searches per day (two-thirds of the research engine market in the United States and 91 percent of all searches in Europe); 20 percent of the people on the planet are on Facebook; Twitter has 300 million users; Amazon is the world's supermarket. We already have major problems about data security and personal privacy. The real battle will therefore be democratic; we have to make sure to maintain net neutrality. It's going to be rough, but it's the price to pay to create a society that is truly in harmony with the planet, a place where our children and grandchildren will be able to live. We don't have much time, barely three decades to make it happen."

Laurent and his boom mike.

4

REINVENTING DEMOCRACY

1. Background–Interview
with David Van Reybrouck

David Van Reybrouck is an author; this activity, for which he is best known, is the most recent in a long string of careers. *Congo: The Epic History of a People*, the English version of his book, *Congo Een geschiedenis* (2010) was published in 2014 to widespread acclaim. The French edition (2012) won the Prix Médicis Essai and the Prix du Meilleur Livre Étranger. Before that he worked as an archaeologist and ethnologist. After studying archaeology and philosophy at the Université Catholique de Louvain, he earned a Master's degree in world archaeology at Cambridge, and completed his doctoral thesis in 2000 at Leiden University, titled "From Primitives to Primates. A History of Ethnographic and Primatological Analogies in the Study of Prehistory." From 2010 to 2012, he focused on issues of democracy and co-founded the G1000 in Belgium and the Netherlands, a platform created in response to the G8 and G20; it included one thousand people who were invited to work together to develop broad guidelines for their countries. At the same time, he was conducting in-depth research on this issue, which led to his book *Against Elections: The Case for Democracy*,[1] a passionate examination on what our democracies have been, are, and could be in the future.

We spent two hours with David in his Brussels apartment, just after meeting with Olivier De Schutter and Bernard Lietaer. And kept learning one thing after another.

DAVID: Initially, I didn't have any desire to write about politics or democracy.[2] I thought it was a problem that was pretty much solved, that everything about it had been examined and that the solutions

1. David Van Reybrouck, *The Epic History of a People*, trans. Sam Garret (New York: Ecco/HarperCollins Publishers, 2014).
2. According to Websters, "democracy" (from the Greek *demos*, "the people," and *kratia*, power) is "a government in which the supreme power is vested in the people."

we had found were the best, or at least, the best of bad options. I was happier writing poems and plays.

But it is very hard to write when the roof is leaking. And the roofs of our European democracies have started to leak so severely in recent years that I began to feel responsible, as an author, a researcher, a citizen, to look at the question and participate in a debate that I view as essential, even crucial, for the future of our societies.

CYRIL: In your opinion, what is the main problem our democracies face? We've just come from traveling to many different countries, and one of the major obstacles we've seen everywhere is that citizens have lost their power, mostly to economic and financial Goliaths. The people we met told us that there needs to be a political framework that facilitates the emergence of new economic, energy, and agricultural models; at the same time, they say that many elected officials are under the influence of transnational groups with deep pockets. We're going in circles!

DAVID: There is growing mistrust in every Western country toward political parties, parliaments, and power in general. And it seems to me rightly so. People feel excluded. There is a sense of theft, of loss. Citizens have in some way lost their say, their involvement in their governments. A recent study published by Princeton essentially concluded that America is now no longer a democracy, it's an oligarchy.[1] That's downright incredible. We are not talking about some tiny band of extreme left wingers, but Princeton University!

CYRIL: What sources did the study use to reach such a conclusion?

[1]. Study drawing on data concerning 1,800 public policy issues from 1981 to 2002. See "Study: US is an Oligarchy, not a Democracy," April 17, 2014, www.bbc.com/news/blogs-echochambers-27074746 and Martin Gilens and Benjamin I. Page, "Testing Theories of American Politics: Elites, Interest Groups, and Average Citizens," *Perspectives on Politics* 12, issue 3, September 2014), https://doi.org/10.1017/S1537592714001595.

DAVID: It compared what people actually want (expressed primarily in opinion polls) with government actions and the preferences of the economic elite. And it reached the conclusion that public decisions are nearly systematically in sync with the desires and appetites of the economic sphere. And not with the wishes of the majority of the population. But a situation like this cannot last. Today, everyone sees how this is working, and elected officials have lost the trust of citizens. If I were president of a political party, I'd be a bit worried. Every two years, Transparency International publishes a report on the perception of corruption. Its most recent publication states that in every Western country, the organizations that are the most mistrusted by the public are political parties. Even in Norway, 41 percent of the population believes that the political parties are corrupt or extremely corrupt—41 percent! And it's not just in Norway. In Belgium, it's 67 percent; in France, 70 percent; Spain, 80 percent; and in Greece, it's over 90 percent. We have a serious problem when the primary actors in our democracy are considered to be the most corrupted elements in our society.[1]

CYRIL: How did this happen?

DAVID: We, as citizens, vote for members of parliament; the parliament appoints a government, and it is this government that is supposed to run the country. But if we compare the level of power held by our governments and our parliaments as opposed to what this was in the past, we see that things have changed drastically. The national level has lost a great deal of power, first of all to a higher level. Much of the political jurisdiction and authority shifted to the

1. According to an IPSOS France poll in 2014: "For 65 percent of French people, most male and female politicians are corrupt. Eighty-four percent believe that politicians work primarily for their own self-interests." For 78 percent "the democratic system is flawed, [their] ideas are not well represented." Seventy-two percent of French people do not trust the National Assembly, 73 percent mistrust the Senate. For 88 percent of the people polled, politicians "don't pay attention to what people think."

European level (which is still somewhat democratic) and to a trans-national level of finance, American ratings agencies, the IMF (which is not at all democratic anymore). At the same time, we have seen a major shift of power downward, with citizens much freer than they were in the past and who no longer trust their elected officials. So the level of power that held the reins of society for some two hundred years now no longer has power, nor does it enjoy trust. We are in the midst of a crisis of legitimacy and efficiency.

CYRIL: But we should legitimately be able to force our political leaders to regain control and do what we really want or want is necessary. Why can't we achieve this?

DAVID: Because our current model of democracy is not designed to give power to the people, to the majority.

CYRIL: What do you mean?

DAVID: Our electoral democracy is based on the principle of delegation. In the late eighteenth century, after the French and American revolutions, it became necessary to find a way to govern these countries that no longer had a sovereign. The distances were enormous, the people fairly uneducated, and the technological tools for spreading information widely and rapidly did not yet exist. An aristocratic process, elections, were deliberately set up to create a kind of delegation. Which means that today, I, as a simple Belgian, French, or American citizen, I make my choice on election day, by which I have handed over my power for four or five years.[1] We have completely

1. Abbé Sieyès (one of the chief political theorists of French Revolution) declared in a speech on September 7, 1789: "Citizens who designate representatives abandon and must abandon making the laws themselves; they have no particular will to impose. If they dictated their will, France would no longer be that representative State; it would be a democratic State. The people, I repeat, in a country that is not

reduced democracy to elections only. I studied the history of the Congo in depth for my eponymous book, and when people used to say: "We have to introduce democracy in the Congo," what they really meant was: "They have to hold elections like we do." The same goes for Iraq and Afghanistan. I know that this may sound a bit heretical to say, but it's the truth. If you studied the history of elections as have Bernard Manin and other major French thinkers, you'd see that it has always been an aristocratic procedure. Aristotle said it, as did Rousseau and Montesquieu. And in fact, in French and in many other languages, the words "elections" and "elite" have the same etymology. An election is a procedure that puts in place a member of the elite; we have often forgotten this.

In the mid-eighteenth century, while Rousseau and Montesquieu were supporting the idea of drawing lots as being more democratic than elections, the French and American revolutionaries deliberately chose elections, one generation later, to evict the monarchy and replace it with a new form of power. The hereditary aristocracy was replaced by an elected aristocracy. We can compare it to the Egyptian revolution, which we know better as it is more recent. The people got rid of the authorities in power, and in the months following the revolution, the second-string politicians, who were already organized, took the place of the leaders. This is exactly what happened after the French Revolution. The elections served the purpose of conferring a certain degree of legitimacy to these secondary officials.

But the masses who stormed the Bastille, who created the Revolution, the lumpenproletariat as Marx called them, have always been disempowered. In the nineteenth and twentieth century, attempts to make elections more democratic involved giving the vote to expanding circles of the population. First the workers,

a democracy, (and France cannot be one), the people can only speak, can only act via their representatives."

the miners, the farmers, then women, and young people. And even later, migrants. Yet even in an era where nearly everyone has the right to vote in the West, the thirst for democracy has still not been quenched.

CYRIL: But how do elections maintain an aristocracy in power. Today, you could say that anyone can run for election and will potentially have the ability to get elected.

DAVID: In theory, everyone can run for election. Therefore, philosophically, the system is neutral and open to all. But when you look at it in practice, it's very different. Ninety percent of elected officials are university graduates, with a large number of lawyers. This is already a fairly specific form a representation. And when you look at the overall population, in France for example, you see that less than 2 percent are members of a political party.[1] Less than half of these members are active. And within this small percentage, an infinitesimally small number will run for office. And ultimately, in this tiny group, a few will be elected. And we call this a representative democracy? It's a bit over the top, don't you think?

CYRIL: So, what should we do? Stop voting? More and more people are raising the question. People may feel that there's no real point to it anymore.

DAVID: I wrote a book called *Against Elections: The Case for Democracy* and I still vote. When I was working on the history of the

---

1. In 2015, French political parties recorded 451,000 members, or 1 percent of the French electorate (44.6 million in 2014, according to INSEE). And this may figure may even be overestimated. In 2014, Stéphane Robert, a journalist with France Culture, suggested, according to the membership fees received, that the Socialist Party membership was probably closer to around 30,000 (while it claims 60,000); UMP, with 130,000 (with claims of 213,000).

Congo, I saw people die to have the right to vote. So I do not underestimate this act, even if it has become somewhat symbolic. But I fully understand that there are more and more people who no longer vote. I think that we have the right to a political strike, just as we have the right to an economic strike. Yet absenteeism will not solve all the problems. One day, I suggested the idea that if 40 percent of people are no longer going to vote, we could leave forty of the seats in parliament empty, if only to send the message to those who are elected that the legitimacy of their mandate is approximate at best. Because in our current system, even if 1 percent of people vote, the parliament is always full. Finally, deputies do not attend sessions all the time, yet their seats are always reserved! [laughs!] But the innovation in democracy can't be limited to keeping seats empty; this would be a form of civic nihilism. I think that we have to try to find new ways to get people to speak. For the time being, we have elections, referendums, and opinion polls. I think these mechanisms are fairly outmoded, fairly primitive. During an election, we can merely select a candidate. With a referendum or a poll, we can respond by a yes or a no. It's a pretty limited system.

CYRIL: Especially when you don't choose the questions.

DAVID: Exactly. And you can wonder about the validity of a democracy that asks its citizens to say yes or no in a referendum, and any reply is good, as long as it's a "yes!"

CYRIL: That's what happened in France in 2005.[1]

1. During the referendum on the European Constitution in 2005, 55 percent of French people voted against its ratification. Three years later, the parliament ratified the text in an altered form (a treaty), with the same wording, but without a new consultation. For this to happen, the French Constitution was revised by a vote of parliament on February 4, 2008, at the Château de Versailles.

DAVID: That's right. And as for polls, it's hardly any better. We are asked to give an opinion on a theme that we are often unfamiliar with. It's 6:oo p.m., a mother is at the stove cooking spaghetti sauce when IPSOS calls: "What do you think about the new policy on immigration?" "Um, um, I'm against it!" They will call a thousand people like that, and this result will influence the political decision-making in France and elsewhere. It's absolutely unbelievable! The influential American political scientist James Fishkin said, in essence: An opinion poll asks people what they think, when they are not thinking. It would be more interesting to listen to what they think when they have had the change to do so. He is one of the inventors of the system of deliberative democracy: you contact one thousand people, as with a poll, but instead invite them to come talk to each other, meet experts in the field, get informed about the subject. Then, after debates and dialogue, they are once again asked for their opinion. And the answers are inevitably more informed. This new form of democracy shows enormous promise.

CYRIL: Has it already been used elsewhere?

DAVID: In lots of places, yes. An incredible thing happened in Texas, the American oil state par excellence, which at one point organized a series of democratic discussions on renewable energy, particularly wind turbines. They asked people beforehand if they would be willing to pay a bit more to have a sustainable economy. Of course, very few people had the slightest desire to pay more. They began with citizens drawn by lots. They provided them with information on climate change, green energies, profitability, pollution, and so on. During and after the sessions, the number of citizens willing to pay a bit more skyrocketed. Today, Texas has more wind turbines than any other state in the United States. It's incredible! But if we had broached this issue with elected politicians only, who are closely tied to the oil industry, Texas would still be entirely tethered to oil.

CYRIL: And, more broadly, what could the democracy of the future look like? What new story can we tell ourselves?

DAVID: I think that the future of democracy lies in new ways of representing the population. Up until now, we've had only one form of representation: elections. But I think that our democracies deserve better than this extremely selective and repetitive procedure. The actual act of voting is becoming totally obsolete. Elections have worked relatively well during periods when information moved slowly or they took place in fairly limited circles. But in the last dozen years of so, information has been moving at considerable speed and is accessible to everyone. That creates a whole different ball game. For the first time, we have the possibility of letting people express themselves in a radically new context. What's more, the West has been experimenting with democracy for some three thousand years now, and we have been using elections for just two centuries. There are rich democratic traditions that preceded the monopoly of elections.

CYRIL: For example?

DAVID: There's another way of representing the people: by drawing lots, which I discussed earlier. Society has always used this system in one, extremely limited context: jury selection. They do that in Belgium, in Norway, in France, in the United States. And even if the system is far from perfect, we almost always see that these juries take their job very seriously. This example demonstrates that ordinary citizens are capable of becoming alpha citizens, who take charge and work for the well-being of the society. If we were to combine drawing lots with a deliberative democracy, we could then reach far better decisions than what the political parties are able to do today.

I'll give you a concrete example. In Ireland in 2014, a process called the Irish Convention on the Constitution came to an end. This Convention was formed of thirty-three members of the Irish parliament, sixty-six randomly selected citizens, and a president. They worked together for fourteen months on eight issues relating to the Irish Constitution, notably a reform concerning same-sex marriage. The debates were streamed live, and regular reports were published by the press; the population was encouraged to participate by sending contributions to the one hundred members. The result: in Ireland, a Catholic country, the Convention's official recommendation was to modify this article of the constitution, legalizing same-sex marriage.[1] While France during this same period underwent a year of political instability around this issue, with one million people in the streets and considerable social tension. The difference is that in Ireland, this debate took place in a calm atmosphere, and people could contribute their opinions—not only the sixty-six people drawn from the general population, but all those who wanted to participate. Thousands of reports and recommendations were submitted from citizens, churches, gay organizations. For me, it is a really interesting decision-making process that show that when you put randomly selected people together with elected officials, they find solutions that exceed what is currently possible in the political "particracy" that we now have (a democracy reduced to political parties). It's a tremendous way to increase the efficiency and legitimacy of our decisions.

---

1. Since we met, the government took on the issue and organized a referendum. While the Catholic Church took an official position against it, the "yes" carried the day on May 22, 2015, with 62 percent of the vote making the extremely Catholic Ireland the first country to adopt this measure via referendum.

CYRIL: Are you worried that some will say that the people selected by drawing lots do not have sufficient expertise? That we should leave politics to the professionals?

DAVID: When we talk about new forms of democracy, deliberative democracy, drawing lots, these are not just ideas. Hundreds and hundreds of experiments have been conducted by universities and researchers. And they invariably report that the people randomly selected by lots are able to look beyond their own self-interests. They may have less expertise than the elected politicians, but they have more freedom than a member of parliament has. They are not bound hand and foot to an entire series of business interests or their political party. Plus, we see that people are able to make decisions on complex issues, upholding the common good of the society.

CYRIL: How could we institutionalize this principle of selection by drawing lots?

DAVID: Personally, my dream is for a House made up of elected citizens and a Senate of citizens drawn by lots. The terms of office for elected officials could remain as they are today, but perhaps with a limit on the number of terms. And the randomly selected citizens would change every six months or every year. I think that the two institutions would be able to run the country better than it's being done currently, and that it would be a good thing for political parties to be in regular touch with a constantly new batch of reasonable citizens. It would help to calm the hysteria of the current system, which is maintained by the media.

CYRIL: Do you think that the media play a harmful role in our democracy?

DAVID: When the electoral system was invented, after the French Revolution, there weren't yet political parties, no right to vote, no mass media, and obviously no audiovisual or social media. All that came later. Yet we keep on with the same system as if the political ecosystem has not changed. But it has changed enormously! Every society needs a channel running from the base of the population to the top, where decisions are made. The civil society used to play this role: unions, employer organizations, and so on. They were useful in transmitting information. Now, their power is far less, while the power of the commercial media and social media has grown considerably. As a result, the dialogue between those who have the power and those who hope that society will change is seriously contaminated by this media filter, influenced by financial and economic interests. The media's role in the current dysfunction of democracy is phenomenal. Elections are won in televised debates. And they are designed to attract viewers. Yet a democracy is fairly simple: citizens get together and make decisions concerning the future of their society. It's nothing more than that. And we have created an entire array of devices that make this dialogue impossible. It is urgent to once again find the means, the tools, to foster this dialogue among citizens.

CYRIL: How to begin? Because, listening to you, I still feel that these initiatives (the use of a lottery system, deliberative democracy) should be introduced by political leaders themselves, but there is really no self-interest for them to change the system. Or, even if they want to, they are paralyzed by the apparatus itself and the financial stakes that we discussed. The example of President Obama is particularly relevant: he raised enormous expectations that have been largely unfulfilled.

DAVID: Even Obama, with all his ideals, which I believe were sincere, couldn't manage to change the system, because an elected politician ultimately doesn't have much power. Even an American president. I recently saw a diagram that compared the feudal pyramid with the neo-liberal pyramid. Obama was at the fourth or fifth level, and there was a whole slew of more powerful people above him.

CYRIL: Who was at the top?

DAVID: The global financial network, followed by the IMF, the ratings agencies, the multinationals, and so on. Today, it's the world of finance that runs the world.

CYRIL: Yes, we have already seen that. So how to begin this change?

DAVID: We can keep putting pressure on them, as nineteenth-century workers did. If Thomas Piketty is right, if the gap between the richest people and the rest of the people is becoming like the Victorian era,[1] we will have to return to the mass unrest of that era. I think that we will see an increase in the number of people saying no. It has already started, on a small level, with people who no longer vote. And it is continuing with those who are organizing themselves—like the Constitutional Assemblies that are working to raise awareness among the population and establish new rules for living together, as Étienne Chouard is organizing in France. I think citizens will change the situation by putting on more pressure. This would help elected officials feel more supported by the population. There is a Flemish proverb that says: while citizens and politicians fight over a bone, the financial world simply picks it up and walks off with it. This is why it's crucial to create new partnerships between the political sphere and civil society. I don't think it's enough to just be angry with our politicians. They have lost a huge amount of power too; we need a new coalition of dedicated people.

1. A reference to inequality during the reign of Queen Victoria in England.

They exist among the general population, in the world of politics, and even in the economic world. There are CEOs who are not at all happy with what is happening now.

CYRIL: During our travels, the assistant mayor of Copenhagen told us that cities could become the true world leaders, replacing nations. Do you think that cities are better placed to change democracy? That we should return to a smaller scale?

DAVID: In terms of democratic innovations, it may be important to start on a small scale, yes. It's no coincidence that it is the small European countries that are now in the avant-garde: Iceland with its 320,000 people, Ireland with its 4.5 million, Denmark, Finland, Belgium. But I don't think that the entre future of democracy lies at the local level. It has always developed from the local to the global. It started in Athens, which was no larger than a small French town, and now India has become the largest democracy that has ever existed on the planet, with one billion people. If someone had said to Pericles, in the fifth century BCE, that one day one billion people would be living in a democracy, he would have said, "Wait, hold on." And yet it's happened. And it's tremendous, because India is now becoming the most interesting laboratory in the world in terms of democratic innovation.

Cyril: You were talking earlier about Constitutional Assemblies; is changing the constitution the way to transform the system and return power to ordinary citizens?

DAVID: In many European countries, particularly Spain and France, there is a push to rewrite the constitution. It's a long-standing republican dream. I have a great deal of sympathy for these initiatives, as our constitutions have always been created by elites who then take advantage of them. Although the words "political party" do not exist in constitutions, it is always the ones holding the power who have written the document that gives them this power. It's problematic. I therefore support these movements, because it is an important document. But I also have a lot of questions. The downside of a constitution is that once it has been revised, we're stuck with it for another fifty years. And I think that's a shame. I am more in favor of evolving constitutions, that are less stuck in the constitutionalist dream, which is very nineteenth century. We now live in a flexible, fluid time, and the idea that by rewriting a constitution we would achieve a new society does not seem very realistic to me. I would argue in favor of flexible, open constitutions. Like open-source software, individuals are constantly improving it, in a collaborative way. It's a little like what happened in Iceland, where a spectacular process gave the population the opportunity to rewrite the constitution. It was very impressive. In a "particratic" system, it has never been possible to achieve such a rapid, convincing result.

2. Revolution in Iceland: Citizens vs. finance and the first crowdsourced constitution in history

During our trip to Iceland, we were able to meet the leading figures of this extraordinary experience. They gave us a step-by-step overview of the Pots and Pans Revolution.

When the Lehman Brothers bank went bankrupt on September 15, 2008, it plunged Iceland, a tiny country of 320,000 people, into an immense financial hole, said to be one of the largest bankruptcies in history. Until that time, Icelanders were not merely living on credit, they had taken this mode to unprecedented levels.

As described in Hördur Torfason, actor, musician and initiator of the revolution: "Since the 1990s and 2000s, the lifestyle of Icelanders had become totally mad. People were only consumers; all they did was borrow from banks, buy houses, a new car, clothes, travel." Katrín Oddsdóttir is a lawyer. She was among a group of citizens elected to draft a new constitution. Sitting in a small café near her office, she smiled and said: "We thought Iceland was perfect, and we were protected from corruption by this great democratic system. We were totally unaware of what was really happening in our country and what is still happening all over the world with a global capitalism that is slowly, surely destroying us. We were happily watching our plasma television screens, going abroad, spending money, busy being rich and happy. And then one day, we realized that everything we believed was reality, was fake."

The fall was brutal. In just a few months, the Icelandic króna lost half of its value; unemployment, heretofore unknown, climbed to 9 percent, while the GDP recorded a steep drop, losing ten percent in two years. The country's three bank collapsed. Thousands of Icelanders lost their homes to foreclosure. For French researcher Philippe Urfalino, an expert in the Icelandic crisis and a Reykjavik resident (who met us in a small café near the parliament, where we also met, by accident, the singer Damien Rice, one of Mélanie's close friends): "The Icelandic crisis was one of the largest and fastest-growing financial bubbles that has ever existed. In just a few years, the country's corporate and bank debt had grown to four to five times the national wealth. And during the three years immediately preceding 2008, this debt doubled. Banks were loaning money to companies too easily, and with insufficient controls in place. All of this within a euphoric system, exponential growth, and speculation. Collapse was inevitable." The situation was so serious that pandemonium broke out in the Icelandic society. As Joseph Stiglitz wrote in late October 2011: "The utter despair in Iceland made any orthodox approach impossible, giving the country the freedom to break the rules."[1] The government and parliament adopted an emergency plan that consisted of closing the country down to protect it, with a control of capital flow, a refusal to socialize losses, and expansion of the Minister of Finance's power. The political authorities decided to allow the banking sector to collapse, while saving their domestic activities (deposits owned by Icelanders), which was soon taken over by new banks created to manage national operations. For once (and in total opposition to what happened in the United States), the Icelandic citizens came before the banks.

At the same time, another "revolution," a popular one, was in the works. "After the collapse, there was this silence," remembers Katrín Oddsdóttir. "We could hear people around us talking about solutions. It was an extraordinary opportunity, because everyone thought that this should never happen again. And that we had to get together. For a nation, it was a unique moment. Most of the time, people are battling over small, unimportant problems and don't see that what unites them is stronger than what separates them."

Starting in October 2008, Hördur decided to act. "When the crash happened, on Monday, October 6, 2008, I decided to go to the parliament building at noon, that following Saturday. I wrote to the people who followed me on Facebook to ask them to join me. I had two questions: 'Do you know what happened to this country?' and 'Do you have any ideas on what we can do about it?' There weren't a lot of people that first day, and people said I was an idiot to stay standing there. But I came back to the parliament building every day at noon, and stayed for twenty to thirty minutes. With my questions. On Monday, the members of parliament came out for lunch, so I asked them questions. But they didn't know how to answer. So I got to work organizing an open-air meeting, like in ancient Greece. I rented a car, sound equipment, called my friends. People were shocked, angry, completely lost. You could see that

1. Pascal Riché, *Comment l'Islande a vaincu la crise* (Paris: Versilio and Rue 89, 2013).

certain types of food were starting to go missing off the shelves in the grocery stores. The newspapers were publishing photographs of America from the 1930s with huge lines. That Saturday, thousands of people joined us, and we started to think about what we could do, all of us together."

They planned another rally for the following Saturday, at the same time. And the next. Instigated by Hördur and poet Birgitta Jónsdóttir (who would become an MP representing the Pirate Party after these events), the demonstration in front of the parliament began a regular event, held every Saturday at 3:00 p.m., for a half an hour. The protesters had three demands: the resignation of the government, the resignation of the board of the Central Bank and the resignation of the board of the Financial Supervisory Authority. Hördur chanted to the crowd through a megaphone: "Is this what you want?" "Yes!!!" yelled back the protesters, after each one. The crowd grew larger with every passing Saturday. And, from just a few people after the collapse of the banks, they numbered five thousand by late 2008. After the parliamentary break, Hördur organized a major demonstration to remobilize the troops after the Christmas holidays. "I asked everyone to come back with pots and pans, symbolizing our need for food. It's an idea I got from Argentina. On Monday, January 21, there was a huge crowd. We stayed from noon to midnight; it was completely peaceful. Then the police came after us to get us out. There were a few confrontations, but everyone ended up going home to sleep. Twelve hours later, we were all back."

The crowd continued to grow, fueled by Facebook. The liberal government was paralyzed, faced with the largest popular movement since 1949. The prime minister, jeered by people on the streets and by other political parties, initially refused to resign, until his primary ally, the Social Democratic Alliance abandoned him, thereby splitting the coalition. On January 23, he called for pre-term elections. Yet this was not enough to appease the protesters:

the concert of pots and pans continued. "It was fun," continued Hordür, "we then had drums along with the pots and pans, as well as whistles, huge cans people were drumming, all lined up in front of the parliament. We could see frightened MPs watching us from their windows. Unfortunately, there were a few anti-police incidents that day; people who were a bit tipsy stirred up trouble. I appealed to everyone, via TV, to stop the violence, and we set up a security service, dressed in orange, to form a cordon around the police to protect them." On the next day, Sunday January 25, the largest demonstration to date took place. "Everyone was very quiet. It was incredibly tense. We had met with the ministers and given them letters on which we had written; 'You are fired.'" On Monday, January 26, the prime minister and the government resigned, as did, in subsequent days and weeks, the boards of the Central Bank and the Financial Supervisory Authority. The demonstrators' demands had been met.

For the first time in the country's history, a woman, Jóhanna Sigurðardóttir, was elected prime minister, ushering in a massive influx of women into the political apparatus. Two women took over the leadership of two of the national banks and, during the elections in April 2009, forty-three of the elected parliament members were women. More than in any other European country, except Sweden.

But during this time, discontent was growing in the international community. Deeply angered that the Icelanders had refused to reimburse the investors and speculators in their country (for a sum representing 60 percent of Iceland's GDP), the British and Dutch (the major creditors) decided to use strong-arm tactics with their small neighbor, with the support of the European Union. Not a single bank would loan a penny to Iceland. Driven into a corner, the new government agreed to negotiate a reimbursement of the debt over fifteen years, starting in 2016, a plan approved by the parliament. For this, every Icelander, children included, had to bear the cost to the tune to €13,000, although the country was already hobbled by unemployment and a twofold increase in prices. The Icelanders baulked and launched an online petition, which was signed by 26 percent of the population. The president decided to hold a referendum on the issue. On March 6, 2010, 93 percent of voters said no to the repayment plan. Ordinary citizens had stood up to the international financial sector that was demanding its payment. The agreement was put back on the table. The rate was reduced from 5.5 to 3 percent, with a reimbursement over thirty years. The president once again opted for a referendum and this time, it was rejected by 60 percent of the voters. In December of 2011, the European Free Trade Authority Surveillance Authority lodged a complaint against Iceland with the EFTA court. Against all odds, on January 28, 2013, the court ruled in favor of Iceland, due to the exceptional circumstances of the bankruptcy. "Yes, yes, yes. We have all won, together. A victory of direct democracy in Iceland," tweeted the new MP Birgitta Jónsdóttir. The taxpayers would not be responsible for reimbursing the debt; the liquidation of the Iceland bank Landsbanki would cover two-thirds of the debt. Another major development was that, on the advice of the IMF, the Icelandic government decided to write off the excessively high debt of households and companies. Seizing their property or pushing them into bankruptcy would have been extremely counterproductive for the economy.

Like every self-respecting revolution, the Pots and Pans Revolution set the stage for rewriting the constitution, and introducing protective measures that would prevent any recurrence of this type of situation. "The idea was to write a constitution by the Icelandic people, for the Icelandic people," Katrín said. A group of twenty-five "ordinary" citizens had to be elected, with support for the constitutional Assembly consisting of a few specialists, in charge of ensuring the legal basis of the proposals. The initiative for the constitution seems to have come from multiple sources: it may have been in the mysterious corridors of power. The convocation of a Constitutional Assembly was the condition demanded by the Progressive Party (allied with the right-wing party in power in 2007), in exchange for its neutral stance in the formation of a left-wing coalition led by Jóhanna Sigurðardóttir, who had, herself, widely supported the process and worked to place it in the hand of citizens. Yet it is the revolutionaries who claim it as their own. "Some of the parties deny that the initiative came from the people, but I can tell you that this is what happened. I participated in every demonstration, from the very first one after the crash, when there were only a dozen of us. There were more foreign journalists than protesters. I followed the entire process and I understand the spirit of the reform: it is about creating a true separation of powers, to prevent elected officials from acting in their own self-interests, and to protect our natural resources," insists Birgitta Jónsdóttir.

It all started with a major "national forum." On November 6, 2010, one thousand people drawn by lots met for a major "constitutional brainstorming event," to define their country's top priorities and values. Among the directions proposed was "one person, one vote" (at present, one urban MP represents twice as many voters as a rural MP), and the fact that the natural resources "belong to the people."

On November 27, 2010, a group of twenty-five citizens was elected from among 523 candidates (mostly people from higher social and professional categories) from the general public; MPs and ministers were not allowed to run). But in an unexpected turn of events, the Supreme Court declared the elections null and void on the basis that they had not complied with the electoral laws. According to Michel Sallé, who holds a PhD in political science and specializes in Icelandic affairs, this was a hostile reaction from the judges, who had nearly all been appointed by the Independence Party (a conservative party opposed to the process). The parliament then transformed this group into a Constitutional Council, but without a binding mandate.

Yet the group got to work and, for the first time in history, citizens were participating in the writing of their constitution, by proposing reforms, submitting comments, requesting clarifications via Facebook and Twitter, attending meetings, or following them on YouTube. Every week, a working version of the project was published and submitted for feedback. Four thousand responses were received in three months, which is extrapolated to a country as large a France, would be the equivalent of 750,000 people. "A lot of really good proposals came to us from all over the country and the world, and we used them in our first draft of the constitution," said Katrín. "And we were able to work in a totally new way. Usually, the majority keeps the minority down. It's a warrior mentality. In discussions, we generally think that one of us must be right, you or me. Me, certainly," she laughs. "We decided to work differently, according to a consensus model. And it produced amazing results. This gave us the opportunity to find a brilliant solution, even better than the one proposed by one side or the other. Politicians should explore this path. They have to stop thinking that because they have the majority, they can do whatever they want. We have to listen to other choices. We had three major issues to deal with in our constitution: the equal distribution of power, transparency, and responsibility. We were trying to see how to redistribute power so that there would not be so much corruption. We have to stop thinking that power lies with the administration or the law; now, it lies essentially with money and the media. Most people are not intentionally bad, but when you give them too much money or power, they become corrupt. It's just a sad fact. And power tries to maintain itself. So we were trying the break it up. We also wanted to develop a direct democracy. Get rid of this stupid system by which, every four years, you vote for a party without having any guarantee of what will happen in those upcoming four years, nor

Nighttime demonstration in front of the parliament.

the direction the country will take. It's like playing the lottery. We had included a number of provisions, for example: 10 percent of the population could request a referendum and ordinary people could propose laws to parliament. It was radical, but it's the future and it has to happen."

After working for just four months, thanks to the enthusiasm of its members and the multiple contributions from the population, the group adopted a text unanimously. It was submitted to parliament on July 29, 2011: 114 articles and nine chapters, which proposed transforming Iceland from a parliamentary regime to a semi-presidential regime, and introduced several methods of direct democracy, such as referendums based on popular initiative. In May 2012 (after being blocked for several months by the right in Iceland), an advisory referendum was held concerning the six main points of the new constitution. The "yes" vote was overwhelming (67 percent in favor of adopting this text as the new constitution, 83 percent in favor of making natural resources public property, 74 percent in favor of the referendum on popular initiatives), but fragile (with only 49 percent of the population voting in the elections). The next step was for the parliament to ratify the texts. And this is where the main problem kicked in. In the spring of 2013, new legislative elections were organized, which were won by the Independence Party (the party in power during the banking crisis).

Once the financial situation had returned to normal, a form a liberal conservatism once again gained the upper hand in public opinion, jeopardizing months of work and mobilization. The recently elected party was opposed to the project for a new constitution, and blocked it for two years. We were taken aback. As were Hördur and Katrín when they told us about these events. How did the Icelanders manage to put back in power the party that had dragged them into such a situation and which was openly prepared to block the result of all these years of work and mobilization? As Philippe Urfalino explained: "In the story of the Icelandic crisis, the intellectual elite, committed people, had promoted constitutional change, but the fact is, that's not what the majority of the population was interested in. The recent success of the Progressive Party and the Independence Party in the last legislative elections can be explained by a measure the prime minister proposed: offering debt relief to the middle-class, which had not been a priority in the preceding government's protective measures. You were telling me about the failure of the major climate summits, about a huge grassroots movement on these issues. But for now, I don't see any large grassroots movement; I only see the involvement of the intellectual elite, who are growing more aware of the problems. Activists are doing their work, but it is still small. Change will be easier to implement when people feel a greater sense of urgency, and when the leaders see that it is in their own interests to do more, if they want to win elections."

The fate of their country is now in the hands of the Icelanders. Under pressure from the street, they could finalize what would be one of the most innovative constitutional processes, and bolster their popular sovereignty by forcing the parliament to adopt the new constitution. A first step has already been made. While the Constitutional referendum in 2012 was non-binding, it has become so, through to the work of MPs like Birgitta Jónsdóttir and Katrín Jakobsdóttir, former Minister of Education, Culture, and Science. It's a first step prior to the adoption of the entire text. "We have done the work, and we will be ready when the next crisis occurs. Just like the Patriot Act was ready in the United States after 9/11. The most important was the creation of a community, the discussions that occurred among the Icelandic people. All this was not in vain; everything in its own time," says Birgitta Jónsdóttir. "Every ten years, we should bring the parliament together with the people to reform our constitution. So that it grows gradually, in sync with the country. And that our energy is not dissipated in conflict, but is transformed into change, if we want change," added Katrín Oddsdóttir. "Power belongs to the people, not the MPs, not the large companies. We can't forget this."

Fittingly, the final word goes to Katrín Jakobsdóttir when she tells us: "I don't think that we can say that political leaders are unnecessary ... but with greater participation on the part of the population, you will clearly have a better political system."

So the ball is back in our court. Once again. Blaming political leaders and big companies is not enough. We also have to demonstrate that we are willing to get involved on a daily level, so that our democracies, and our economic, energy, and agricultural models operate well, to make them fair, sustainable and fulfilling. Perhaps we had to learn about what Elango, whom we'd meet on next trip, calls "citizen self-governance."

3. Kuthambakkam: Self-governance

Roland, our production manager and friend for this final film sequence in India, told us we couldn't drive in India. As soon as we get out of the airport, this precautionary measure makes perfect sense. Chennai, the city closest to the village we were heading to, has a population of eight million living in a chaos and turmoil that is barely comprehensible for the Westerner that I am. The streets seem to have been organized in an entirely anarchic way, whether in terms of urban planning, traffic, or business. Buildings are packed tightly together, apparently built according to necessity, without any prior planning. Some of them don't seem to be finished; others seem based on wacky architectural plans; while most of them look like what happens when you build in a rush, when necessity trumps reason. The sidewalks, which do exist on certain streets, suddenly disappear on others; the most diverse range of vehicles throngs the streets in a dance of wheels and a cacophony of horns. Settled into a wobbly old minibus, we watch as our driver slaloms between the tuk-tuks (yellow, three-wheeled taxi-scooters), cars, trucks, pedestrians—who regularly spill out into the streets—and animals that cross without warning. With one hand he wields the steering wheel; with the other, the horn, nearly nonstop. Every driver uses this method to warn others of his or her arrival. Drowning in this sea of noise, they seem to be guided by a sense of intuition. This is what we end up telling ourselves, tired of clutching our seats at each new intersection, terrified to the point of uncontrolled fits of laughter. And indeed, we are fine.

As David told us, since 1950, India had become the world's largest democracy. But for Shrini, our guide, interpreter, and local production assistant (and, incidentally, the man with the most infectious laugh I have ever met), it is still crippled by corruption, inequality, and the caste system. A look out the window confirmed his view. Immense slums stretch out under the bridges on the banks of the Cooum River. On the sidewalks, swarms of people step over the maimed, the disabled, and the needy. Huge billboards featuring equally huge faces are everywhere along our route. When we asked Shrini what they're about, he replied simply: "That woman is prime minister of the State of Tamil Nadu. She's a former Bollywood star. She's now in prison for corruption, pending her trial." We were obviously surprised that her portrait still held pride of place on the streets. This time, Shrini just laughed. Once we reached the village of Kuthambakkam, where other portraits awaited, we started to get an idea of the atmosphere that reigned in the country's politics. Indians like their leaders, just as they like gurus. Displaying their faces, portraying them on the streets gives them a quasi-mythological status. And there are so many voters that these leaders need to make themselves known, to be present, even in the most remote areas. When elections come around, the farmers, who don't know policies any more than most French people do when they go to vote, are tempted to choose one of these faces, the one that seems to keep the most promises. Which made the experience we were about to have even more extraordinary.

Elango Rangaswamy is an untouchable, a Dalit,[1] as the Indians say. If, like us when we arrived, you are unfamiliar with the Indian concept of castes, here's a brief overview. Throughout India's recorded history, the society has been divided into four castes: Brahmins (the priests, the highest caste), Kshatriyas or warriors (next in line), Vaishyas (today, mostly merchants), and Shudras (servants). For reasons that no one really knows (although several theories exist), this hierarchy structures Indian society, granting superiority to some on a hereditary basis. A fifth caste can be added to the list: the untouchables. Historically, they did the jobs that were considered to be degrading or impure, usually related to the slaughter and butchering of animals, death, garbage removal (butcher, fisherman, hunter, beggar, cemetery guard, midwife, etc.). For this reason, they were pushed outside the social system and were not supposed to even be touched by members of the other four castes. Untouchables also could not touch the water or the wells, nor the food of the other castes, and had fewer rights concerning freedom of movement and sanitary conditions. Since independence in 1947, it has been illegal to treat anyone as an untouchable. In reality, this ancient tradition is still strong in Indian society. This is why it is hard to imagine that an untouchable child could one day became a rich chemist; mayor of his village; train hundreds of other mayors, including members of the higher castes; and influence hundreds of thousands of Indians, and dozens of mayors around the world. Indeed, his reputation had spread so far and wide that news had reached us, and we were about to film him.[2]

Elango was born in the early 1950s, an untouchable, and his family were still living in hellish conditions, in the neighborhood

1. Dalit means "downtrodden."
2. I discovered Elango's amazing story in Bénédicte Manier's excellent book, *Un million de révolutions tranquilles.*

Cotton Street in Chennai.

of this excluded population. Schooling was only available through fourth grade; starting in fifth grade, he had to go to the main elementary school, where untouchables and children from the upper castes had to cohabit as best they could. Elango, as per tradition, could not have any physical contact, even indirectly, with anyone except for children of his own caste. Not once did a teacher even deign to give him a glass of water.

One day, an event occurred that would determine the entire course of his life. "A boy, an untouchable, had suffered an accident. His head was bleeding and he was dying in front of all the other students, teachers, and the families of the upper caste. The Dalit children were crying and shouting, begging the adults to do something. But no one wanted to touch him. He died in front of my eyes. I couldn't understand why not a single person even offered a cloth to stop the blood. When our parents learned what had happened, they rushed to the school and started throwing stones at the houses of the upper castes, breaking their windows and their walls. And I started to cry again, I yelled at them to stop, not to add to the violence that had just occurred. That day I realized the extent of the caste problem. I told myself that something had to be done. Though I was only a small boy at the time, I promised myself to do something."

Elango was a brilliant student and was able to continue his education in Chennai, in the middle of the huge city. He became a chemical engineer, found a job, and stayed there about ten years. His parents hoped that he would pursue a successful career and earn lots of money. But he couldn't get the images from his childhood out of his head.

"I saw the misery in my community; it was worse than ever. Something in me just couldn't accept this, it went around and around in my head, day and night. Someone had to put a stop to this injustice, this inequality. I was desperately waiting for the government, the parliament, the ministers to handle it. But nothing happened."

In 1992, the 73rd amendment of the Constitution of India definitively decentralized the world's largest democracy, thereby strengthening local power. It established the system of Panchayats, local councils, and Gram Sabhas, popular assemblies. This was a catalyst for Elango. "With local governments, local democracy could be stronger. We could set up a system in which we voted and participated, as in Gram Sabhas, the citizen's assemblies. We elect the city council, the mayor, and everyone participates in the assemblies, gives their opinion and influences the politics."

Elango saw this as a golden opportunity for transforming his village as he had always dreamed. He decided to leave his job and return to Kuthambakkam with his wife. As soon as he got back, he took time to go meet all the castes, the untouchables, the young people, and share his decision to run for mayor. Armed with his diplomas and ten years' experience as an engineer, he managed to rally members of the upper castes and Dalits to his cause. Against all expectations, he was elected in 1996. Those who did not vote for him were worried: an untouchable as mayor could create problems for them, perhaps he would even take revenge for the years of frustrations and humiliations. But to their great surprise, Elango did exactly the opposite. It positioned himself as a leader who would unite people, and decided to use the new institutional tools to propel the entire population toward true change. "In the traditional system of democracy, people vote and that's the end of it. But that's not democracy! They have to fully participate in local politics. Having representatives is not enough. Our representatives spend their time doing things other than what we expect of them, in India at least, while Gram Sabhas are true people's parliaments. We vote, we govern. If a leader makes a bad decision, we can propose others, we can even veto them. The assembly has the power to change the agenda. The true concerns of the local citizens are taken into account."

He started by preparing a five-year plan (corresponding to his term in office) and presented it to the assembly. "When I read the plan, every line, every project was discussed in depth with the community. Some were doubtful, others enthusiastic, while still others wanted to wait and see. Three months later, I returned to Gram Sabha, the assembly, with the initial results we had achieved on the subjects discussed during the previous session. This was how I was able to build trust and get local residents to support me. Little by little, everyone started to contribute to the program and then to the initiatives. It became the villagers' plan, and no longer my own."

His program was conceived to deal with the primary problems facing Kuthambakkam: unemployment, poverty, garbage, lack of infrastructure, illiteracy. And once the process began, everyone got involved to help set it up. The residents started by cleaning up the village, while the mayor's office provided garbage bins for the streets, public lighting, and a system for harvesting rain water. In five years, the schools were upgraded and families encouraged to send their kids to school. Before that, the dropout rate was almost 40 percent by the time children reached sixth grade; now, nearly all of them go every day and continue through secondary school.

Elango raises money and creates hundreds of jobs, which primarily benefit women who have often been unemployed, victims of domestic abuse, and sometimes reduced to selling illegal alcohol. They are now part of a federation that proposes various microcredit options. Each of the 1,500 women members can now borrow up to 50,000 rupees to start a business. In the workshop adjoining Elango's home, several dozen women were assembling burners for gas stoves and making compresses for the hospital.

The assembly then decided to lay pipes for water. According to Elango: "To construct the pipes, the city council estimated that we needed 500,000 rupees,[1] but we only had 170,000 rupees. We

1. €7,000.

needed 330,000 more. We found some financing, but we were still short by 40 percent of the amount. The assembly decided that the villagers would provide it. The richest people gave some money and the poorest offered their labor. All they needed was to be fed. So the wealthiest farmers said, OK, we will provide your food. In this way, the work was able to start and, with just 60 percent of the budget, we were able to achieve 100 percent success."

But Elango's proudest achievement is his work among the castes. He decided to take on the slums where the untouchables were forced to live. He submitted an ecological and architectural renovation project to the assembly. With him, everyone would work to refurbish the neighborhood, including the upper castes. Where people had been living in tumbledown shacks with dirt walls and zinc roofs (sometimes patched together with bits of tarps or posters picked up off the street), more than one hundred and fifty homes were constructed from local, ecological materials. Elango found low-tech yet highly efficient tools, like a mud and cement brick press and a tile mold that could produce thousands of units in just a few weeks. They were then assembled and painted in multiple colors by the residents themselves, who all contributed to this transformation of the living areas. Real roads were built to replace the dirt tracks. To thank the residents for their help, the untouchables dug the drainage ditches for the neighborhood themselves, saving the town €31,000, and they will maintain the roads and the town's wells.

Elango drew on this initial experience to launch a new program in 1998 to create a place where the upper and lower castes would live together. Many untouchables as well as some members of the upper caste were homeless (castes have nothing to do with a person's wealth; there are rich untouchables and utterly penniless Brahmins), and new homes had to be built. "In general, if you're creating a township, there must be a separate township for the upper castes, the lower castes, and the untouchables. And I thought: Why can't we try to have all the poor live together, whatever their caste? I raised the issue at one Gram Sabha, and after lengthy debate, most of the poor people agreed. When I discussed this with the Chief Minister of Tamil Nadu, he was thrilled. It was historical for India, no one had ever done such a thing."

A decision was taken to construct fifty twin houses (one hundred homes in all), with a family of untouchables living on one side and a family from one of the other four castes in the other. So they had to live together. The Chief Minister was so enthusiastic that he came to inaugurate the neighborhood himself; he called it Samathuvapuram, which in Tamil means "Equal Living." He supported reproducing this model, and more than three hundred such Samathuvapurams were constructed in the state. "From these places a new generation is emerging, where there are barely any differences among the castes. We are planting seeds so that, within two or three generations, we will be living in a completely casteless society."

After one term in office, his achievements were already immense. But, as Elango was reelected, he decided to go even further. "With the help of the Panchayat, we were able to provide roads, we were able to upgrade the schools, install solar street lighting, better housing, fresh water for everyone, but I found that our community would only truly be happy when every family was generating sustainable income to live well and feel secure." He then sought ways to create more jobs in the village. The answer appeared on its own: to relocalize the economy. Many goods and objects could be produced in Kuthambakkam rather than be imported from elsewhere in the state or the country. Once again, the Gram Sabhas participated. Everyone obviously wanted to work, and the community set out to identify just how this process could begin. The first phase involved food: rice was already grown around the village. But at the time, it was sold outside, as there were no facilities for dehusking the rice on site. And then rice was imported back for food. They had to find

Elango and a local resident in front of the school.

a way for the village to dehusk it. And once again, Elango and the assembly came up with low-tech tools that not only dehusked the rice, but also ground it into flour. The same process was used for coconut oil. Major efforts went into construction. The idea was to both increase jobs and prevent speculation, which makes products too expensive for the villagers to buy. Elango conceived of a program whereby ten to fifteen villages can join together to produce most of what they need. Depending on their resources and typology, some would concentrate on certain activities that were complementary to others in the network and exchange surplus goods.

It is a highly ambitious project. While some of it has already been achieved, Elango estimates that it will take another dozen years to achieve the self-sufficiency that Gandhi himself promoted. For him, "meeting our own needs by ourselves is the real meaning of independence, one of the surest ways to freedom. The way society is developing now is centripetal; it attracts energy, money, and power to the center. Sustainability comes from greater self-sufficiency within each community."

In 2001, after two terms in office, Elango decided to step down from the mayor's office and work instead on transmitting his experience. He wanted more villages to promote citizen participation, more Indians getting involved in democracy. He created the Panchayat Academy, a place that trains mayors from other villages to implement the experiences conducted at Kuthambakkam. In ten years, he has taught nine hundred elected officials about the principles of citizen self-governance. His idea is to create Gandhi's "republic of villages," where democracy is strong at the very smallest level. "I continue traveling, meeting with institutions, developing new methods. And applying them to Kuthambakkam.[1] Mayors come here,

1. Even though he is no longer mayor, Elango is still highly respected and works closely with his successor.

look at how and what we have done, and replicate what seems relevant to their own villages."[1]

When we met, Elango was trying to set up a program to solve the health and social problems caused by a lack of toilet facilities. His goal was to have 240 million installed throughout the entire country in the following few years, with support from the national government. After presenting a prototype to the residents of his village during a Gram Sabha, he invited other mayors to show them the project. More than six hundred mayors and city councils are already participating in his network, and some of them, like his home town, have already implemented many of his principles. For Elango: "It is empowering citizens who can lead a beautiful democracy. If people are not empowered, it will be chaos. With the grassroots institutions, we have a tremendous opportunity to educate citizens, to fully empower them. Once there are enough of them, they will be the ones to lead, to build their own democracy." Like Shane in Detroit, Morten in Copenhagen, Pam and Mary in Todmorden, and Emmanuel in France, Elango believes that no one is going to come save us and that it is up to us, whether we are elected officials, businesspeople, or citizens, to initiate the transformation of our societies.

This is also the philosophy of Vandana Shiva, a philosopher, physicist, and Indian activist who is famous for her fight against the biopiracy and takeover of seeds by multinational companies. For her, the struggle for a real democracy in her country, India, as in many countries throughout the world, is a real battle. Meeting Vandana Shiva for the first time is an unforgettable experience. Vandana is under 5 feet tall, wears brightly colors saris over which she drapes a shawl in cold weather, and at first sight, is not necessarily

---

1. What Indians call villages can include many thousands of inhabitants. One of the mayors we met governed a town of 20,000 people.

Cyril with one of our small auxiliary cameras.

impressive. Yet the minute she sits down and gazes across at you with her dark eyes, with her enormous third eye in the middle of her forehead, a sense of extraordinary, nearly magnetic, power emanates from her face, her hands, her voice. Vandana is both an exceptional fighter and speaker. Never, among all the people we have interviewed, did anyone answer our questions so specifically, decisively, without any hesitation, saying just what was necessary and with impeccable timing. For those who see her on film, you can certainly perceive her power, but also the implacable toughness of this woman, who is harassed and denigrated by the multinationals she is fighting, most of all Monsanto. We could not end our Indian trip without asking her what a true democracy could be.

4. Meeting Vandana Shiva: Obeying higher laws

VANDANA SHIVA: For me, elected governments no longer represent the will of their people. Democracy is supposed to be "of the people, by the people, for the people." Because of twenty years of globalization and corporate rule, multinationals now literally control government decision-making. They write the laws, they write the policies, they pay the politicians to do what they want them to do. And so we now have a representative democracy that has mutated into "of the corporations, by the corporations, for the corporations." One of the most striking examples concerns food. In over half a century, we have seen how losing control of the food system is creating communities, societies, individuals who are not free. My own journey of awareness and commitment began with the GATT, the General Agreement on Tariffs and Trade, which led to the creation of the World Trade Organization. A Monsanto representative is on record in 1990, saying: "In writing this treaty, we achieved something unprecedented; we wrote it, we took it to our government, the United States, and had it imposed on the rest of the world."[1] This, then, is what led them to say: "We were the patient, the diagnostician, and the physician, all in one." They defined the problem and the way to solve it. One of the major problems was that farmers could save their own seeds. Their solution was to criminalize this through intellectual property, by patenting seeds. Few people are aware that seeds are what allow us to live on this planet. Without seeds, we have no food, no clothing, no wood. Taking control of seeds is about taking control over all of society. The agreement on agriculture, which introduced free trade in agriculture (which in effect means the destruction of local food systems and local farmers), was written by the lead negotiator for the United States, who was also Cargill's Vice-President (the world's second largest seed multinational, after Monsanto). It's a new form of dictatorship. The Transatlantic Trade and Investment[2] currently negotiated with little transparency, is setting up "the new generation of free trade." It has a single goal: to dismantle the protections built into European laws as a result of democratic movements of people. For now, multinationals can't sue France or Italy, because of the laws of their constitutions. They are therefore trying to create a transnational legal sphere, where they could sue for a violation of free trade. So that a government that refuses the use of GMOs or Roundup could be accused of unfair practices toward a company that sells them, while favoring others. This type of case has already occurred in Australia, where the tobacco companies sued the government for their anti-smoking campaigns. We are at a tipping

1. James Enyart, "A GATT Intellectual Property Code", *Les Nouvelles* 25, no 2 (June 1990): pp. 54–56, cited by Vandana Shiva, *Éthique et agro-industrie* (Paris: L'Harmattan, 1996), pp. 12–13.
2. A treaty that would create the world's largest free-trade zone between the United States and the European Union.

point of humanity losing its power to act democratically to defend the future. States very often willingly give up that power because the individuals (at least some of them) have a lot to gain. We have built a society where individualism takes precedence over the society. The more that governments give up, the weaker they get. This is the tragedy of our times.

CYRIL: So what can we do? We have met experts who have shown us that other democratic models are possible; we have seen that it's possible in Ireland, in Iceland, and in India. But what I hear from you is that we must also fight back, prevent this massive takeover of power.

VANDANA: I think we have to devote 90 percent of our time developing alternatives in every field—agriculture, energy, economy, and especially politics. In India, we have created Navdanya, an organization so that farmers can produce and exchange organic and traditional seeds for free. In two decades, we have created 120 community seed banks. But if we don't spend the remaining 10 percent keeping an eye on the political system, we implicitly accept that the power of governments and elected officials is subject to gigantic multinationals. And this quasi-militaristic machinery will criminalize and restrict our freedoms, again and again.

CYRIL: So do you think we need to disobey? That this is one of the keys for the future?

VANDANA: What we have to do is obey higher laws, and there are two sets of higher laws. One law comes from the earth: the laws of Gaia, the laws of diversity, the laws that we must protect the earth and all her resources and all her gifts, this system to which we owe our lives. The second set of laws comes from human rights, from democracy, from our constitutions. And any law that interferes with the natural equilibrium or that interferes with us fully free and independent human beings, must not be cooperated with. We must fight them. We must replace dead democracies with living democracies, where people participate at a daily level. And the only way you can have that participation is by reclaiming democracy locally. You can't have democracy at a national level if all local democracy is dead.

CYRIL: How to fight these laws? I know that you do it in India, but here, it's very hard to mobilize people.

VANDANA: It's not always easy in India either. But you have to find a way to show people that it concerns them directly, in their everyday lives. And you have to be patient, stubborn, never give up. In 1987, I was fortunate enough to attend a supposedly secret meeting of industrialists who laid out the plans of seed multinationals concerning legal and intellectual appropriation. So as soon as our government was pressured to pass these measures into law, we were ready. We had created communication tools, and went to see every member of parliament to inform them about everything. The government then appointed me head of a drafting committee of the law on plant varieties. We established the Plant Variety and Farmer's Rights Act, which includes a clause stipulating that it is a farmer's right to save, exchange, produce, reproduce, sell, and breed their seeds. And that this fundamental right can never be alienated.

In 2004, there was an attempt to undercut this law and create a new seed law, criminalizing local seeds. I traveled throughout the country, informed farmers, organized large meetings. We collected 100,000 signatures, which I took to our prime minister and told him: "We are in the land of Gandhi. When the British tried to impose laws for salt monopolies, he walked with thousands of people to the sea, picked up the salt and said: 'Nature gives it for free, we need it, and we will continue to make our own salt.' We must continue his struggle for our seeds. We have received these seeds from nature and our ancestors. We owe it to future generations to pass them on. We will not obey these laws, so you might as well not pass them." The parliament got involved and the laws were never passed. We are inspired by two of Gandhi's major ideas: "auto-organization," which can also be called "internal democracy," the art of self-governance, and the "fight for truth," which means refusing to apply harmful laws. Like those that criminalize the use of seeds or plants for medicinal purposes.

CYRIL: I have often heard you say that the primary requirement of a democracy is to ensure that people can feed themselves, self-sufficiently.

VANDANA: For me, it is a crucial issue of democracy, because we are what we eat. If farmers don't have the right to keep their seeds and reproduce them, if people don't know where their food comes from and how it was grown (as in the United States, which does not have a labeling law), if corporations control what we eat, then we lose the most personal aspect of our freedom—that of sustaining our bodies, maintaining our heath. In comparison, all the other aspects of democracies are just pretty decorations on the wall.

The next step to establishing a true food democracy is therefore to recognize this link between health and food. A link that should be obvious, but which is increasingly neglected by our civilizations, even denied and removed by law.

CYRIL: Given this financial political and economic steamroller that holds nearly all the power, do you think it is really possible to change our society in a nonviolent way?

VANDANA: I come from a country of nonviolence. It is a principle that works, that contributes true change. I am committed to it for both ethical and philosophical reasons. Even though it is only a tactic, it is the one I would choose. Nonviolence sends a message to those who are not involved in these actions. We can no longer remain merely a club, a very good underground army, but one with very few members. If you want to expand the circle of people involved, nonviolence is the right path. Most people do not want violence and chaos.

CYRIL: Do you think we will have to experience catastrophes for change to occur?

VANDANA: When a catastrophe happens, people don't change, they panic. These are situations when dictatorships or political coups can take power. The idea that the most exploited people at the bottom rungs of society will miraculously rise up is not realistic.

Solidarity, however, does work. Opposition to all forms of exploitation forms a link among all these people and can bring about genuine transformation. At least that's what we've seen wherever change has taken place.

CYRIL: You think that getting people to change is a process and that a catastrophe wouldn't be a wakeup call to transform overnight?

VANDANA: No, it's impossible. Especially not now. Things used to be simpler: we needed to eat, have a place to live, clothes to wear. Now, we don't even know where our food comes from, nor what type of seeds were grown to produce the wheat in our bread. Everything has become extremely complicated. It is unrealistic to think that a single catastrophe could raise awareness in one day. It is a process that requires educating people, which is why the work we all do is so important. I believe in human potential. We can be a destructive force on this planet, but we can also be a creative, caring force. It's the principle of quantum physics: nothing is fixed, nothing is separated, everything can be transformed, nothing is certain. This is why we must expand this human potential by educating generations today and of the future about all these challenges.

5

A NEW STORY OF EDUCATION

1. Background

All through our journey, many of the people we met brought education (either for children or adults) as a kind of "root action" that would have an impact on all the others. If the origin of our problems comes from within us, our heads, our neuroses, our wounds, then this is where we need to start so that we can eventually help our civilization transform in a sustainable way.

As Pierre Rabhi told us: "For me, change is determined by our awareness of a situation. Expanding this consciousness in everyone is already an act of education. I believe that there can be no true change in society without a profound change in humanity. Our political and activist choices are not enough: we can eat organic, demonstrate against nuclear power, recycle our waste, return to nature, and yet still exploit our nearest and dearest—unfortunately these are not incompatible. We must manifest the original utopia within ourselves. Tangible projects and tools will only be factors for change if they are derived from a consciousness freed from the limited and primitive arenas of power, fear, and violence. The profound crisis we are now experiencing was not caused by tangible deficiencies. It can be tracked down to ourselves, to the intimate core that determines our vision of the world, our relationship to others and to nature, the choices we make, and the values we uphold. For me, personifying utopia means above all realizing that a different being must be constructed. An aware and compassionate being, a being who, with intelligence, imagination, and physical effort, pays tribute to life—of which he or she is the most sophisticated, the subtlest, the most responsible expression. And educating children is crucial to the construction this being."

Malik, one of the urban farmers we met in Detroit, was a school principal for many years before getting involved in organic market gardening. For him, "The American model of education is fashioned after that of factories, of the Industrial Revolution. It consists of repetitive tasks, a hierarchical organization, and obedience to orders, and has very little tolerance of critical thinking. I believe that there is a real difference between educating and schooling a child. Education sometimes happens in school—but only sometimes. Educating comes from the Latin words *educere*, which means "to lead forth." Education should consist in bringing forth the qualities that we have had within us since birth. Not filling us up with knowledge as if we were empty vessels. Each one of us has our own qualities, gifts, and attributes that are important to recognize and cultivate, so as to offer them to humanity. One of the responsibilities of school should be to identify them."

Muhammad Yunnus shares this vision. Seated on a red couch in the hotel where he greets us, his entire body seems to come alive when we bring up the subject: "Our educational system is all wrong. We manage to teach mathematics, physics, chemistry, history, but we do not help young people discover who they are or the role that they could play in the world. Today, the implicit goal of school can be summed up like this: Work hard, get good grades, and fight to get the best possible job. It's fairly narrow in terms of a goal for a human being. It's even pretty depressing. Human beings are not born merely to work for someone else, to earn a salary; we are unique creations in a world full of creations. And this unique aspect is completely excluded, crushed, standardized. Education should mean telling children: You are a being full of potential, you have the power to become and do whatever you want. Here are the tens of thousands of options that you have. What kind of world do you want to live in? What kind of society do you want to help build? Today, it's as if we gave a script to every school kid and asked them to dutifully act out their role in society. Most of our institutions work to transform them into machines, into robots. We have to change this."

When I ran Colibris, we did an IFOP survey[1] before the 2012 presidential elections. We wanted to ask questions that no one was raising in traditional surveys. To the question "What purpose do you think schools should serve?," 41 percent of the respondents answered that it should "Help everyone find a job when they get out of school and become a member of society," 39 percent that it "Transmitted essential knowledge (reading, writing, arithmetic) to everyone," and just 20 percent that it could "Help everyone thrive according to their own talents and abilities, regardless of their grades." For Jeremy Rifkin, "What we really teach [in schools], at any given time, is the consciousness of an era."[2] In other words, school is a reflection of our society. We train children to become stakeholders in the world in which they live, with its beliefs, its dogmas, and its social organization. The people we talked to had received a twentieth-century education, with all this it implies.

For centuries in Europe, education was primarily reserved for an elite, thereby perpetuating the class system. When schools became more widely accessible to the working class, they were primarily run by the Church, which viewed them as a way of maintaining a Christian view of the world. Jules Ferry's institutionalization of secular, free, and compulsory education in 1881–82 represented a major move toward a democratic approach in France, opening the doors to education for the largest number and promoting "freedom of conscience." Initially, this was genuine progress. The late-nineteenth-century society was enamored of precisely this type of "progress." As Rifkin points out: "The public school movement in Europe and America was largely designed to create a productive work force to advance the Industrial Revolution."[3] This has led many

1. "Etude IFOP pour Colibris : ce que veulent les français," Colibris, https://www.colibris-lemouvement.org/projets/campagnes-precedentes/campagne-tous-candidats/etude-ifop-pour-colibris-ce-que-veulent.
2. Jeremy Rifkin, *The Third Industrial Revolution* (New York: St. Martin's Press, 2011).
3. Ibid.

critics of school, including Ivan Illich in his book *Deschooling Society*, to say that it is more a way of training good little soldiers for the system than free-thinking, non-conformist minds—a viewpoint also shared by Malik and Muhammad. Yet the world has changed drastically over the last 150 years, and what we used to call "progress" has been largely dismantled. Twenty-first-century kids, born in the age of Internet and the depletion of natural resources, do not view the planet or civic responsibility as their elders do. Yet most of the education they receive is still based on the world of the past, both in terms of pedagogical methods and content.

What could the twenty-first-century school look like? In order to prepare each individual to participate in the industrial era, twentieth-century schools set up an institutional response that strongly resembled the industrial model: train a maximum number of students in a minimum amount of time, without really being able to adapt to diversity and with a strong tendency toward standardization of knowledge, and hence minds.

In the twentieth-century school, the teacher was a sort of acknowledged master of strict theoretical knowledge, whose mission was to transmit it to students. According to Kenneth Bruffee, researcher and professor at City University of New York: "A student's responsibility to these foundational classroom conventions was to 'absorb' what the professor in one way or another imparted. The professor's responsibility was to impart knowledge to students and evaluate their retention of it."[1] Learning was a solitary, mechanical, standardized act, governed by the figurehead of the teacher and the pervasive dogma of the "program." This knowledge, once it had been properly assimilated, would serve as a passport into society. Refusing to conform to these conventions meant foregoing a multitude of possibilities for further study and professional activities,

1. K. A. Bruffee, *Collaborative Learning: Interdependence and the Authority of Knowledge* (Baltimore, MD: John Hopkins University Press, 2nd ed. 1999), p. 66.

regardless of the actual knowledge that one possesses—a situation expressed by the ubiquitous maxim: "If you don't work hard in school, you won't find a job." In other words, one of the first injunctions of the twentieth-century school was a form of submission to the model, of educating for obedience. It's a trend supported by society's overall view of education, particularly in terms of the parent/child relationship.

But the students today are different. In certain respects, teachers have changed too, especially among the younger generation. We are therefore in an awkward place: teachers are becoming increasingly aware of the need to rethink the system, and are attentive to young students moving farther away from the authoritarian practices of their elders, and losing respect for the institution, but who are still caught up in a machine that seems prehistoric in a changing world. This machine has achieved such a level of complexity that it has become paralyzed, unable to envisage any real change. It is therefore vital to determine what purpose schools should really serve, and what model of society we would like them to prepare our children for.

For Ivan Illich, school is an institutional response to a societal need: "Equal educational opportunity is, indeed, both a desirable and a feasible goal, but to equate this with obligatory schooling is to confuse salvation with the Church."[1] We could say that schools are one way among others to acquire a certain amount of knowledge, expertise, and social skills. We have to rethink them in terms of a contemporary context; we should perhaps stop trying to hand over to them the entire responsibility of educating our children and find, for each one of them, the best possible path for their own fulfillment.

What do we need our children to be prepared for today?

Primarily an ability to manage the problems that we have created: to repair and care for our shared biosphere, and to establish peaceful and viable social and economic systems that are equitable to all.

1. Ivan Illich, *Deschooling Society* (London: Marion Boyars Publishers, 1970), p. 21.

They will need resources that cover both theoretical knowledge, but also a new awareness: the perception of our planet and of humanity as a single, interdependent unit. This implies developing among this younger generation such qualities as empathy, cooperation (rather than competition), and a connection to nature. Yet the major obstacle to expressing these qualities is often a malaise and lack of well-being. So that our children can find the resources to construct this ecological, cooperative and fair society, we need them to develop a capacity for happiness, fulfillment, and living skills; and to discover their own talents, passions, and practices they can put to use for the society at large, and their own communities in particular.

Certain establishments have already started to work in this direction; one such example is the Kirkkojärvi School in Finland, which we set out to discover.

2. Every student is important: Education in Finland

For more than ten years, the Finnish education system has stood out as a model in Europe, and more broadly, in all Western countries. To understand why and how this small country scores so high in the PISA[1] international rankings conducted by the OECD (second worldwide in science, third in reading, sixth in mathematics in 2009, far ahead of every other European and Western country, twelfth, fifth and sixth, respectively, in 2012 behind a slew of Asian countries and ahead of all the Western countries—with the exception of math; the Netherlands, Switzerland, and Estonia come in ahead), we went to see this seemingly exceptional establishment.

1. Programme for International Student Assessment.

Kirkkojärvi is a brand-new school, built in 2010 in the middle of a disadvantaged neighborhood of Espoo, a suburb of Helsinki. Dull public-housing building built in the 1960s, as ugly as you could find anywhere, rise all around the red-brick building with huge triple-glazed windows (for thermal and acoustic insulation) and solar panels atop the roof.

The principal, Kari Louhivuori, a former English teacher who spent part of his childhood in England, greets us at the entrance. Kari is sixty-two years old, has no desire to retire (even though he will be forced to, much to his regret), is thin, elegant and relaxed, funny, and charming and seems more Latin than Slavic or Scandinavian (the jury is still out as to whether the Finns are one or the other) in terms of conversational style. We'll learn that the Finns tend to be a quiet lot. "There's a joke about Swedes and Finns (the Swedes are our "favorite enemies," much like the English are to the French): a Swede and a Finn spend a weekend in a country house, and the first night they drink beer. The Swede raises his glass and says: 'Skal!' the Finn replies: 'Okay, are we drinking or spending the rest of the night chit-chatting away?' That's the way we are here in Finland, we don't need to talk much," laughs Kari, who is well aware that he doesn't fit the mold. As we walk into the building we are struck by the space, cleanliness, the harmony of the lines and curves, and just how quiet this establishment is. High-quality materials were clearly used, and the layout of the space seems to have been carefully considered. "To build this school, we organized an architectural competition. Sixty-nine projects were submitted. I was on the jury and was lucky enough to be able to choose the best. The winning project was designed by two brothers; one made the primary school, the other the middle school. The goal was to have the architecture support the educational program. Each activity and each age group has its own space." And when I ask him if all the schools are this beautiful, he tells us this: "Always when you build a school, you try to do the best you can. This is a fairly poor area, so it's a good way that our society has shown that it sees education as very important. Finland doesn't have any mines, no gold, no oil; all we have is wood. So our primary wealth is a good education."

There is much to say about the Finnish model, its practices, structure, and assessment methods, but the most important factor, what seems to be the secret of its amazing results, may be this: To the question, "Should students or knowledge be at the heart of the system?," the Finns opted for their children. Each student is important, and it is the system that must adapt to the individual rather than the student to a rigid system.

In Finland, the idea that happy, fulfilled students who are free to develop and work at their own rhythm will more readily acquire essential knowledge is not the utopia of a visionary educator; it is simply the tenet that underlies everyone's approach: the government, municipalities, principals, and teachers. To achieve it, the key word is trust. As Kari says: "The Ministry trusts the local authorities, who trust the principal, who trusts the teachers, who trust the students. I am free to choose my team among the teachers who apply for a job when a position becomes available. We have a very small bureaucracy. For example, we do not have inspectors who, as in other countries, come by to check that our teachers are complying with standards. Our teachers are extremely well trained; they are professionals; they are the best qualified to know how they should work in their classrooms. Of course, we get together and talk about how to improve our practices, and we assess our own methods every three years via a circular system. We start with ten things that we really want to improve, then select three, and that establishes an agenda for the upcoming three years. But mostly, we use our time for teaching, not testing." Nor is there a centralized system that manages transfers. Each establishment is autonomous and teachers stay as long as it works for them and for the staff. Kari has been principal of this school for thirty years. There is also no national testing of schools that would rank them from best to worst. "Each one must be good," insists Kari.

One of the main goals is to make sure that every student feels "at home." To do so, the schools try to stay reasonably small (300 to 400 students per middle school, and 400 to 500 per high school), with fairly large work areas, pleasant colors, and comfortable places to relax. Professors are encouraged to interact with students to create a genuine relationship of trust and partnership. When Kari walks down the halls, children spontaneously jump into his arms and he tosses them up in the air, as if all this were completely normal. And in fact, at Kirkkojärvi, it is. At lunchtime, teachers eat side by side with their students. Even in middle school, everyone is on a first-name basis. "It's part of the job," explains Kari, "it's an educational moment, when teachers and students can get closer and create a relationship that will then help in the classroom. And then they also teach them good manners," he laughs. I tell him that in France, teachers don't have the right to touch students, and this kind of familiarity could be seen as diminishing their authority. Which, once again, makes him smile. "Our authority comes from different things: professional ability, first of all, but most of all—respect. There's no need to hide behind a title. We have discipline problems, just like every school in any country, but creating this type of close relationship makes it easier. They don't want to be bad because they like you, because we are friends, and they see that we want to help them. Of course, there are always kids who test limits and push back, it's not always easy. But in my experience, punishment doesn't help. It is often more effective to talk sense to them, involving the parents, making them feel secure, listening to them, letting them make decisions also. These are ways to get them to cooperate."

When we show up in Miaja's classroom, with her fifteen nine-year-olds, we get a better understanding of what Kari meant. The kids are in the middle of a natural science class. They are study-ing pollination with large puffy dandelions. Some kids are sitting at their desks, but a bunch of them are standing up or slouching on the sofa at the back of the class, while six or seven are actually lying on the floor—one of them is observing his flower through a small magnifying glass; another is squatting; the third is kneeling; while the fourth is jumping around his friends. The hair and seeds are floating in the air, gradually taking over every corner of the room and even getting as far as the corridor. The kids are talking to each other, but it's not exactly what we'd call total mayhem in France. For Maija, "It's important to have a good feeling in a classroom. If the environment is very strict, they get worried and they can't concentrate on what they're learning. It's sometimes hard to create a harmonious atmosphere because there are so many different personalities; they have to get along, form a group in which everyone feels they belong. No one should get upset or intimidate others. It happens, but I try to keep an eye on it and tell them to let me know if something's not right. I'll do a little investigating; they talk to me." Maija loves her job, and it shows on her face and in her relationship with her students. In fact, this is what she likes the best, "Building relation-ships with them, being close so that they trust me and I can help them grow." She likes that the children come from different cultures (50 percent of the students at Kirkkojärvi come from other countries): "We learn a lot of things," she tells us enthusiastically. She also likes the trust Kari displays and the cooperation among the other teach-ers. "It's important to move in the same direction, and even when we don't agree, we always find ways to work together. We're open."

In the Finnish system, it's normal to let kids learn at their own rhythm. For example, they have up to the age of eight or nine to learn how to read, and can happily spend their earlier years honing other skills, following where their curiosity takes them. In principle, repeating a year is forbidden by law; it can be proposed if needed, but the student and the family have to agree.

The school day is organized in synch with the biological rhythms of the child and to avoid unnecessary fatigue: up to the age of sixteen—when compulsory education ends—classes are never more than forty-five minutes long, with fifteen-minute breaks between them during which students can wander through the hallways, talk in the relaxation rooms, play, perform music, or go online. Finnish schools have fewer students per classroom (from fourteen to twenty-five in Kirkkojärvi when we visited) and have more staff: teachers, advisors in high schools, and teaching assistants in primary school. There are from one to three per class, according to need. Most of the classrooms at Kirkkojärvi have assistant professors for children with special needs, those who don't speak Finnish well, or simply to give a little extra attention. The school has a psychologist, a nurse, and a class for children with special needs for physical or emotional reasons, so that they remain within the school system. All these measures are intended to tailor the teaching methods as closely as possible to the children's needs.

"Each student is different, they learn in different ways," explains Maija. "We take that into account in our teaching. It's so much easier now; we have so many resources available to us. With our teaching assistants, we can divide up the class, we have computers, books, DVDs, we can go outside in nature. For example, when they are learning to read, some of them start with the letters and they combine them; some of them start with the words and then they divide them. There are many ways to learn how to read. When I was in school there was only one way, but that way is not used anymore. But I learned; it worked too! What's important to understand is that whatever method you use, the children always learn. Some of them faster, and some of the take some time. I don't think there is only one good way; I think there are many ways. You just have to find the right way in for each student." Starting ten years ago, lecture classes virtually disappeared. Teachers are there as one resource among others, and they are expected to encourage and

---

Maija's class at work.

guide the education of their students rather than impose authority and knowledge. Students learn in small groups using the available resources that Maija discussed. For her, providing a freer space and more mobility in the class serves the same purpose. "Thirty years ago, there were forty students in a classroom, they were sitting tight, they were very quiet. The teacher was in front all the time, teaching from a platform. But now, we walk around, students are allowed to talk with others when they're working, not in a loud voice, of course, but quietly. They can walk around, sit on the couch to read. And they learn that the teacher is not an authority, not like a god. It's very important that students understand that teachers and parents are not always right. That we can say to them: "I made a mistake or I was angry and yelled at you, I'm sorry." You talk about it and move on. But they understand that we are all the same, we are equal. It's more free and more open. I think it gives students a lot more self-confidence and other kinds of skills, like how to be with other students. They learn from each other. They acquire social relationships, social skills. And that's important in life. Not just the subjects... Of course, we have to be strict from time to time, impose silence when needed. It's sometimes hard to find the right balance—not too strict, not too lenient. We're not here to be their friend." Throughout the entire period of comprehensive schooling (from seven to thirteen years old), the courses are the same for everyone. Then from thirteen to sixteen years old, students gradually take more responsibility for their curriculum by selecting from two to six optional subjects. In high school they are entirely free to create their own curriculum by selecting classes from a list available on their school's computer network and online. Traditional classes do not exist. Up to the age of nine, students don't receive grades. From nine to thirteen, they are assessed but not graded. Learning the essentials therefore occurs without stress or stigma. Everyone learns at their own rhythm without feeling like a "loser." Actual grades are introduced only at age thirteen, based on a scale of four to ten. Zero, a potentially humiliating grade, doesn't exist. The goal of assessment is to validate what has been learned, rather than what hasn't. It is therefore no longer competitive and stress inducing.

When we go to eat in the cafeteria with Kari, all the tables are full. With the kids' bright clothes and the colorful chairs, there's a rainbow of pink, green, and yellow moving in every direction. Yet the noise level is certainly lower than in other cafeterias. Kari explains that soundproofing materials were used on the walls and under the chairs, and the kids are in socks. Lunch is not bad and—surprise— it's free for all students. As are books, health care, and school supplies. Yet Finland's overall education budget is nearly the same as that of France (between 6 and 7 percent of the GDP). "Small bureaucracy," repeats Kari with a smile. He believes that the secret to Finland's success is primarily due to teaching training. It's the key to building a good system. Most of them choose this profession because they're interested in teaching itself and helping children develop, more than in a particular subject. They are truly appreciated and even enjoy a certain level of prestige in a society that is extremely attached to its education system. The Joensuu teacher training university receives 1,200 applicants every year for eighty available spots. Every teacher must earn a Master's degree in educational science (for the comprehensive school) or a Master's degree in a specific discipline (for secondary school), study one to two years of pedagogical methods, and then spend three years as a student teacher in a classroom. Then, and only then can they apply for a job in a school. As Kari explains: "They pursue in-depth studies in child psychology, and learn about all kinds of different teaching methods: Montessori, Steiner, Freinet. ... The goal is to give them lots of models, lots of ideas, a profound knowledge of children, their learning abilities, the type of learning problems they may encounter and what assistance they can provide to a child. ... They can then choose what they want to use. They also read a great deal on the history of education."

Once they have a classroom, teachers have very good working conditions and virtually total pedagogical freedom, which seems to contribute to their motivation and helps them create learning situations that are adapted to their students. And they do not just work in the classroom: teachers are also responsible for supervising students and visiting families outside of school hours. All of which fosters close relationships. And to top it all off, they are very well paid. When the gym teacher told me he earned nearly €4,000 a month, I nearly choked. It's true that the cost of living is slightly higher here, but not enough to justify such a difference with pay scales in France, where middle school and high school teachers earn an average of €2,500 per month.[1]

Thanks to these methods, young Finnish students achieve excellent results in traditional subjects (the OECD still considers Finland to have the best educational system in Europe), even though they spend ninety minutes less time in class every week than young French students—for a total of two thousand fewer hours from the ages of seven to fifteen.[2] But the goal is above all to teach them how to learn, to make them more autonomous. Today, knowledge is available just about everywhere, so Kari and his staff help each student learn how to sort through this mass of information and find the right way to acquire what they'll need in their future lives. In Kirkkojärvi, the young Finns not only learn math, Finnish, and history; they also learn how to knit, sew, make clothes, work with wood, metal, and leather, build objects, wash their clothes, clean up, cook, draw, paint, and play musical instruments. Kari takes us to see their incredible music room, where middle school kids can practice on bass guitars, drums sets, keyboards, tambourines,

1. Laurent Fargues, "L'Education nationale dévoile enfin le salaire des profs," *Challenges*, May 5, 2014, www.challenges.fr/economie/20140512.cha3642/l-education-nationale-devoile-enfinles- salaires-des-profs.html.
2. "Finlande : le bon élève des systèmes éducatifs occidentaux peut-il être un modèle ?," *Sénat*, April 7, 2010, www.senat.fr/rap/r09-399/r09-399_mono.html.

saxophones, and more, and rehearse with their bands during breaks; the shops where they make guitars and speakers, and learn how to construct bridges from popsicle sticks that can support 130 pounds; the kitchens where young boys discover the basics of a filled cake or a mushroom omelet; odd rooms where they learn how to wash their clothes in industrial-size machines. He shows us the jackets, pants, and shirts made by students in the sewing class. "We give them the basic skills in all these disciplines so that they can experiment and figure out if they are more manual or intellectual. And, regardless of what they do, when they leave school and home, they will know how to take care of themselves." Generally speaking, on leaving Kirkkojärvi, 50 percent of students opt for university and 50 percent choose a vocational path. For Kari, both paths are equally worthy: "We need all these different professions!"

The model has been constructed step by step over the last forty years. When we ask Kari how the country accomplished this (with a thought for the French educational system that seems so impervious to change), his answer is clear was a bell: "In Finland, education is not a political fight. There are commissions in parliament where all the parties are heard and agree on the major direction to take. So even when a new government comes in after elections, they don't change the education system. We change the curriculum about every six years, and it's always done together. Education is too important to become an electoral issue."

Kari thinks school should be about "preparing for life, moving on to the next stage," not just to find work, but to "learn tolerance, understanding, differences. Discovering and appreciating all cultures, all colors. Understanding that everyone is important, but that some need a little more help than others. Loving each other. That's one good thing that I hope they will have learned when they leave school."

What's interesting about the Finnish example is its scale: it is a national system that educates one million students every year.

That is why we chose it for the film. But thousands of other tremendous, albeit more modest options, exist all around the world, with some hundred or so in France. Among them, La Ferme des Enfants created by Sophie Bouquet-Rabhi, Pierre Rabhi's daughter, in the Hameau des Buis, the small ecovillage founded with her companion in southern Ardèche; the École du Colibri founded and run by Isabelle Peloux in the heart of the Amanins ecocenter; the Living School in the 19th arrondissement of Paris; or the fantastic small school, École Montesourire, in the Beauséjour eco-neighborhood in Saint-Denis-de-la-Réunion, which we filmed, but were not able to include in the film. They all stress the need to foster autonomy, cooperation, nonviolence in children (with encouragement from adults), and fulfillment as the base from which each child can discover their purpose and take care of the world around them. Creating a generation able to take on the challenges of the twenty-first century means giving them access to happiness. At least, a certain kind of happiness.

Mélanie showing the monitor images to some village children.

6

GETTING STARTED

Interview with Rob Hopkins

"Yes, but where to start?" That's what we were all probably wondering once we returned from this ten-country journey. And maybe that's what you're wondering, too, if these experiences have convinced you that's it's crucial to start something, somewhere. The answer (one answer, anyway) can be found in Totnes, a small town in southwest England, where we stopped on our way from Bristol to Todmorden. In the middle of July, glowing in the late afternoon night, Totnes looks like the ideal small town. At least by my book. The small main street runs outside the Seven Stars (a pub with multiple locally brewed beers, which is already a great sign); it's lined with perfectly English, part-medieval, part-charming old buildings. Most of the businesses are independently run; many of them sell organic, local, fair-trade, artisanal products. A lot of people get around on bikes, and a rural countryside is just a couple miles outside the town. This is where the Transition Network was founded, in 2008.

Since then, nearly one thousand two hundred cities in thirty countries have followed the lead of this small community of eight thousand people. Halfway between the Seven Stars and the square where Ben Brangwyn (one of the co-founders, and known by most of the locals as Dr. Bike), repairs bikes in exchange for thanks, a piece of cake, or Totnes pounds, we found time for a last conversation with Rob Hopkins, who initiated and inspired the movement. Rob is tremendous, luminous, with a childlike grin always about to spread across his face. But he is also calm, charming, and incredibly funny, with that unique British sense of humor. Every time I saw him, he was wearing jeans and a tucked-in shirt, and sleeves rolled up above his elbows, as if he were just about to get some new project underway. Before coming to Totnes, Rob used to teach permaculture in Ireland. The idea of transition came as he suggested that his students apply these principles to cities, as a way of addressing the challenges of climate change and peak oil, and of making them resilient. Rob radiates so much genuine humanity and was so overwhelming that he even managed to make us to cry during the interview.

ROB: It's fascinating how as a species, and as a culture, we are brilliant at imagining our own extinction and our own demise. We make films about whether we're all wiped out by zombies or nuclear bombs or diseases or robots or aliens or little funny gremlins. We love those. But where are the films about us actually turning something around, and solving a problem? We don't really have those films. We're terrible at it. Those stories are so important because when those climate scientists say: If you want to keep the biosphere on this planet within the boundaries in which human civilization emerged and flourished and everything that we associate with our history, then you need to start cutting emissions now by eight, nine, ten percent every year, but the problem is, we don't have the stories that go with that. We see that as a story of less and of moving away from something. And if you say to people, what would it look like in twenty years' time if we started cutting our emissions by that much ever year, what would that be like? For many people, it's sitting in a cold cave eating rotten potatoes.

MÉLANIE: They think it's the end of the world.

ROB: Exactly! But actually it could be fantastic! Human beings are so ingenious and so creative. We can do extraordinary things, but we need to tell stories. I remember someone once saying: Having a vision, telling a story, is like throwing a whirlpool in front of you that then starts drawing you toward it. That's what we've tried to do with Transition, tell the story of ordinary people around the world trying to build a healthier, more human culture, one that is more appropriate to the future; building places that are creative, fun, passionate, exciting. Too often the environmental movement has been about negatives and about what we don't want. And now we can express a vision of how this could be, which is thrilling and delicious and far more exciting. The mayor of Barcelona just announced this big push to be generating all the city's energy within the city and all its food by 2040. It's really ambitious, but again, it's a story that people like to tell and say, "Wow, that's fantastic, we could do that." The same with Detroit, it's an incredible story, everyone talks about it. And that's what we need, the "we can do that" stories.

MÉLANIE: I hear what you're saying, and yes, I want to do all this. But this is Totnes, the "perfect, beautiful city," with its free hugs, its local currency, its organic stores. When I think of my daily life in Paris, with my neighbors in our big buildings, it's hard to think that I could convince them to go along with it.

ROB: You might be surprised. Have you asked your neighbors?

MÉLANIE: I once suggested planting vegetables in containers in front of the building. But some of my neighbors immediately told me it wasn't allowed, it was impossible; I got discouraged.

ROB: It's worth trying again. It often doesn't work the first time you try. There was a woman who got in touch with us recently from some small town in Australia. She said: I love Transition, it's so exciting, I'd love to do Transition here, but nobody else around here is interested in that kind of thing. She put an advert in a local paper: Hello, my name is so-and-so and I'm interested in Transition, anybody else? And she got 120 letters. In Portugal, there are fantastic examples of people living in apartment blocks thinking that they're the only people interested, and they put out an invitation and they started all kinds of fantastic food gardens. And also, it doesn't need everybody; you need enough people to get something started. And you never know where the tipping point is. A few people get started, and even people who tend to be quite cynical sometimes love to see people with a good heart, with good motivation, doing something. It gets people involved.

CYRIL: I imagine there are certain aspects of Transition that are much harder to implement in cities, and which are simpler on a smaller scale, like here.

ROB: There are some aspects of Transition that work much better on a city-wide scale. In Liège, in Belgium, for example, some people started "Vin de Liège." They raised 1.85 million euros to start a community supported vineyard. They are connecting the city with the land around the city. And it's just a group of people, it's not everybody in Liège. Look at some of the Transition initiatives in London, which work at a neighborhood level; they often break London down into places like Totnes. They do local currencies, they grow food on the underground stations. It always starts with a group of people. So if the idea of creating a vegetable garden doesn't work, maybe you could look at putting renewable energy on the roof.

MÉLANIE: Yes, and I thought that maybe I could ask people who want to do it, then do it with them. When others see that it works, they will join too. It's just that sometimes I feel sad and tired. I see that every time I talk about this documentary to my friends, who are smart and aware, they just don't care. They roll their eyes. I don't know how to explain it and motivate them. You don't feel tired sometimes?

ROB: Of course, sometimes. But I see so many examples of people and where it works. I talked to a woman in a place near London recently, and they wanted to do Transition streets (like those we started in Totnes). She had a little four-minute video explaining the idea and she put a notice through the doors of everybody on her street saying: "I'm going to have a party next Friday, come around, I'll make some cake, I'll get some drinks and I'm going to show you a little video and just see what you think of it." She didn't expect anybody to come, but then she couldn't fit them all in her house, there were so many people. They watched the video and then all said, "When do we start?"

MÉLANIE: That's amazing.

ROB: Sometimes we try things and they don't work, so we try something else. There was a Transition group near here having a hard time getting people together. And they said: What is it that unites people in this town? Is it peak oil? Is it climate change? Is it beer? I think it could be beer. So they started a community-supported brewery and raised money; people bought shares in it. All these people then feel like it's their brewery, and then that's how they introduce people to these ideas and get them involved. It's simply a way in. What is important is not to focus on a single-issue campaign, because either you agree with it or you don't. With Transition, you have lots of different way to interact. You may be interested in food or in plants. Or you might be very good at business or finance. Or garbage! People get involved not just because it's about climate change, but because it's fun. They meet people. The other day I was talking to a woman in Totnes, who told me: "I've lived here for twenty-two years, but the two years I've been involved with Transition, I know the place so much better than I ever did before." One guy said to me: "Even if this Transition group stopped tomorrow, I know two hundred people that I didn't know before." When we started doing Transition, we imagined it as an environmental process, an ecological process, a sustainability thing. Now we really see it as a cultural process. How do you start to change the culture of a place? You now often see letters in the local newspapers saying: "Seeing as how we're a Transition town, surely we should ... etc., etc." Whether people are involved or not, the culture starts to change around them.

CYRIL: Do you ever get discouraged at how much work this all takes? Everything you do is amazing, but given the collapse of an entire civilization, it may seem like a tiny step.

ROB: What we're seeing around the world now, whether it's Transition or whether it isn't, is a quiet revolution. Many people might not be aware of it, but it's happening underneath their feet. People are not waiting for permission; they're rolling their sleeves up and doing things. They're creating new local economies, new renewable energies, infrastructure, and businesses; they're reimagining their food systems. They're taking the power that they invest in the economy they want to see every day they go shopping, deciding what they want to support. There's a big shift happening. We know the solutions, we know how to do it: the difficult thing is to mobilize communities and people to make them happen, while paying attention to the resilience of the group, of the people who are doing this. The conventional activist model that I grew up with was that you keep going until absolute burnout, then you get up again and go a bit further, then you collapse again. That's not going to get us where we need to go. Transition draws from lots of different sources and says: we need to come together, we need to get diverse people together in the same room, give them permission to take risks, to experiment, to celebrate, to be creative and imaginative.

CYRIL: What motivates you to do all this, why are you so committed to it?

ROB: I have children, four sons. For me, it's really important that when they have children, I can tell them that during this time I did everything that I could do, where there was still a window of opportunity. That I spent my every waking hour trying to actually turn it around, trying to find a different way to engage people, trying to get away from the old way, when we made signs and stood outside demonstrating. What motivates me is a mixture of rage against the people who manage to do the degree of damage that is being done to the world, and its systems and its people, and promote the kind of injustice that we see. And an incredible degree of optimism and power that comes from seeing what people can do on the ground. People are doing incredible stuff; no one's given them permission, no one's written them a big check. They've just said: This isn't okay, what can we do about it. I love the fact that I can walk about my town and see how different it is from six or seven years ago. That's so nourishing on a really deep level. And I'm also very stubborn. I don't let go of things very easily. I can see, in Transition and in other movements, the seeds for a sustainable future that we so desperately need to create. I can see the potential that's there. I want it to flourish and grow and expand and be everywhere.

CYRIL: Do you still believe in political leaders?

ROB: For me, there are two approaches to take in terms of politicians, government leaders who get together at these international summits. The first, when we tell politicians that we need change, that we're putting so much of our energy in this, so why aren't they doing this, and they should do that. It's often very frustrating. But there's another way, where we just say: "Listen, you do what you do, while actually, outside your offices, your conference centers, all over the world people are just getting on, living as they need to in

---

Rob and his now-famous 21-pound Totnes bill.

order to stay below two degrees. And in doing so, they are making friends, having more fun, creating new enterprises, they're eating better food, they're having better parties, they're drinking better beer, they have lower energy bills, they feel part of something historic. And to the politicians, we could say, you do what you want to do, but you could get behind this, put your energy in to help make this happen, but it's happening anyway, with or without you. It's a quiet revolution. And so, come on in, be part of it." For me that feels so much more productive than saying: "You are this, why don't you do that." Look, we've got a 21-pound note, we're having a great time, we don't care!

CONCLUSION

Maybe it all comes down to that. Ensuring that human beings work together, mobilize, stand side by side to build another world. According to one of my friends, Jean-François Noubel: "The greatest challenges facing humanity are not hunger, poverty, sustainable development, peace, health, education, economy, natural resources, ... but our ability to organize collectively to be able to solve them." There is certainly no perfect school, nor a perfect economic or democratic model, but what we seemed to see emerging from this trip was a new vision of the world—one in which power and authority are not concentrated in the hands of a select few at the top of the pyramid, but where everything is connected, interdependent, networked, as in nature; a more complex world, where diversity is a genuine force, where every person, every community is more autonomous and therefore more free, where everyone has more power and more responsibility. Like cells that must be healthy if the entire body is to function well, and are dependent on all the others. All these people are writing a new story. They tell us that it's not too late, but that we have to move, starting now.

We have so many things to do and so much potential to achieve them. Clean up the oceans; replant the forests; produce healthy food for all; revive the soil and ecosystems; ensure that every human being has shelter, health care, and education, so as to be able to live peacefully; produce abundant renewable energy; invent motors, cars, aircraft, machines; determine the most suitable recycling techniques—all to continue to live a long time on this small planet, without depleting the resources and interfering with the natural equilibrium. We know how to do all this; this is what we learned on our journey. Maybe not as well as we need to, but it's only a question of time and investment. We will succeed at what we decide to undertake. History has shown us this to be true, time and time again.

All this is possible if we redirect the money that is already in circulation, and if we find ways to create currencies that work toward these goals. All these activities could create hundreds of thousands of fascinating jobs. The question is knowing what we really want. Ultimately, what are we trying to defend by maintaining this consumerist, capitalist, and so-called free-exchange model. Our freedom? We saw, throughout our trip, just how alienating it is. Our comfort? Although we are lucky enough to be among the most privileged people on this planet, we know that this situation won't last. Our happiness? Who can truly say they are happy like this? That we find meaning and fulfillment in our lives as producers and consumers? I believe we are facing a paradoxical situation in which we all work to defend the privileges of a few, who are clever enough to get us to believe that we too enjoy these privileges. But what are they really worth, when they are leading us directly over the cliff?

Everything you have read in this book is true. Yet, like the film, it was written from a subjective point of view. I decided to concentrate on the positive and inspiring aspects of each initiative, without going into the problems and the contradictory opinions. I feel that too many articles are structured along this model: "These people are doing tremendous things, but here are all the limitations of their approach. Conclusion: it would obviously be amazing to do that, but there's no way it will happen." That was not the goal of this book. As I wrote in the introduction, the aim is to tell another story, to inspire, to make you want to dream the impossible. To change how we see the world. If you bring up these subjects among friends, among different types of people, you'll see that many of them will retreat behind a slew of responses: "It will never happen," "Yes, but the lobbies ...," "That's the job of politicians," "It's too small to really work," "What do you expect us to do?," "It's not going to change anything anyway," and the list goes on and on. But no one has ever changed the world starting with this type of reaction. No one crossed oceans, flew planes, launched rockets, found cures for diseases, wrote sonatas or symphonies, or overcame the worst ordeals by repeating these self-defeating mantras.

Today, we all need to mobilize as no community on Earth has ever done before. We need to deploy the very best we have in terms of creativity, solidarity, intelligence. Put our self-interests aside to embrace the collective interest. In a way, nothing is more exciting. This is a way to be heroes in a far more intelligent way than all the wars waged over millennia. All we have to do is to start telling this new story, together.

Now, imagine a world where the cities are all a reasonable size and located near nature. People could produce some of their food in containers available to all, in parks, and in shared or individual gardens. The rest would come from small permaculture farms in the suburbs and the surrounding countryside. All the waste would be recycled or composted. The compost from the city would be returned to the urban, peri-urban, or rural farms and added to their own compost. Hardly anyone would eat meat anymore, maybe once or twice a week, maximum. But it would be delicious meat, from animals raised with respect, living outdoors, fed by locally grown, organic feed. People will have learned how to cook a huge variety of delicious vegetables. The residents of these cities would get around by bike, on foot, in trams, metros, busses running on biofuel, hydrogen, or merely electricity. There would be hardly any more cars, but the few that remained would also have motors that don't emit gas or polluting elements. Most people would live in small buildings, a maximum of four or five stories high, surrounded by greenery that produced more energy than they consume. They would have green roofs and solar panels, they would harvest rainwater for non-food purposes, and recycle it via phyto-purification systems.

In these regions, an impressive diversity of local companies would meet the basic needs of the population. And in fact, a large proportion of the population would be entrepreneurs. The downtown areas would have thousands of small businesses and busy pedestrian centers, museums, bookstores, operas, theaters, concert halls. The residents would share multiple objects rather than purchase them.

Many of them would be made or repaired in the garages, homes, and fab labs that would have cropped up everywhere. There would be a diverse array of currencies, one for the city, one for the country or region's businesses, one for the nation, and one for international exchanges. Monetary creation would be transformed, with interest limited to the operation costs of the lending institutions. Companies would adhere to the principles of the circular economy and would no longer destroy resources, but would actively help to regenerate them. The wage differential in these companies would be limited, and governance would be participative. A large percentage of them would be cooperatives belonging to the employees. This would also be the case of banks, many of which would relocalize to the community. Speculation would be prohibited and stock markets would be transformed to make room for informed, useful, and sustainable shareholders. Most companies would operate according to the criteria of a triple-bottom line, and kids in schools would learn that its most important to discover their own specific talents and abilities, and to express them to solve our problems or contribute to their communities. Because they would be living their passions and interests, they would help to do good for others and for the planet. And to encourage that, they would learn to cooperate rather than to become the best.

These towns would be surrounded by a revived countryside, where the landscape would have fewer fields and more forests, hedges, woodlands. The residents would develop activities that can only thrive in natural environments. The population centers would be interconnected by trains fueled by renewable energies, while countries would be linked via aircraft and boats powered by clean engines. International trade would be based on equity, among territories that have acquired genuine autonomy, and with products, goods, and expertise specific to each country. Major businesses would continue to produce what only big businesses can implement: large-scale infrastructure, trains, boats, aircraft, roads, etc. But they would be restricted so that they could no longer become dominating or predatory forces over the entire economy. In terms of governance, citizen councils would be set up in our cities. At a national level, a parliament of elected citizens and a senate of citizens drawn by lots would work together to draw up and examine laws. A similar system would be set up on an international scale, consisting of heads of states and citizens from all countries, drawn by lots, who would take decisions concerning the entire planet. Cultures would no longer clash, but would be mutually enriching. Species would no longer disappear and would once again flourish in dense, rich, diverse ecosystems.

This world is only a dream, a story I tell myself, in the light of everything we have seen, heard, experienced. It is not meant to be exhaustive, nor the best solution. There are certainly thousands of other more intelligent, more human, more beautiful ones to imagine. And perhaps these worlds could coexist and reflect true diversity all around the globe. It's a story we can develop, even if it seems a bit utopian, because, as a man I've admired used to say:

You may say I'm a dreamer
But I'm not the only one
I hope someday you'll join us
And the world will live as one.[1]

1. "Imagine" © 1971 Lenono Music. Written by John Lennon. Reproduced with authorization / all rights reserved.

THE FILM

To find out more about *Tomorrow,* and find ways to act, to discover
other solutions, contact the people in the book and the film: www.
demain-lefilm.com.
The film *Tomorrow* was released on December, 2, 2015
Produced by Move Movie
A co-production with France 2 Cinéma, Mars Films, and Mely pro-
ductions
With support from the Agence Française de Développement
In association with Colibris, Agrinergia, Éditions Hozhoni, Johes,
Christophe Massot, APC—Affaires Publiques Consultants
With the participation of Akuo Energy fund
With the participation of OCS and France Télévisions
And crowdfunding by 10,266 KissBankers
Distributed by Mars Films

A film by Cyril Dion and Mélanie Laurent
Producer Bruno Lévy
Written by Cyril Dion
Original score by Fredrika Stahl
Editor Sandie Bompar
Director of Photography Alexandre Léglise
Digital color grading Jacky Lefresne
Sound recording Laurent Cercleux
Sound editors Alexis Place and Antoine Baudouin
Sound mixer Cyril Holtz
Graphics and animation La Brigade du Titre, Mathieu Decarli, and
Olivier Marquézy
Location manager Antoine Brétillard
Production manager Sylvie Peyre
Post-production manager Isabelle Morax

ACKNOWLEGEMENTS

An immense thanks to Aïté Bresson who supported me, reread and corrected my text, and encouraged me throughout this entire process. Thanks to Jean-Paul Capitani and Françoise Nyssen for their trust, enthusiasm, and unfailing friendship. Thanks to Mélanie for having undertaken this journey with me, made this adventure possible, and for devoting so much of her time and talent. Thanks to the entire film crew: Sylvie Peyre, Alexandre Léglise, Laurent Cercleux, Raphaël Dougé, Antoine Brétillard, Isabelle Morax, Julie Lescat (and all the others) and to our producer, Bruno Lévy, for everything you did for this project (no small affair). Thanks for having believed in this idea and in me, you are fantastic. And special thanks to Sandie Bompar, our editor, who deciphered many of these interviews and who, with great patience and enormous intelligence, created with me the narrative of the film, which was also the basis for the book. Thanks to Bénédicte Villain who carefully transcribed many of the interviews. Thanks to Pierre Rabhi for making me aware of all these issues. Thank you for being the extraordinary man that you are. And finally, thanks to Fanny, who has been supporting me, rereading my texts, cheering me up, and guiding me for more than fifteen years, and who has made me the person I am today.

RESOURCES

Introduction

Audrey Garric blog (website in French only): http://ecologie.blog.lemonde.fr/

Fairfield Osborn: http://nasonline.org/publications/biographical-memoirs/memoir-pdfs/osborn-henry-f.pdf

Club of Rome: https://www.clubofrome.org/

IPCC: https://www.ipcc.ch/

Colibris (website in French only): https://www.colibris-lemouvement.org/

Aproaching a state shift: http://mahb.stanford.edu/library-item/approaching-a-state-shift-in-earths-biosphere/

Worldwatch: http://www.worldwatch.org/

Earth Policy Institute: http://www.earth-policy.org/

1–Food for the Survival of the Species

Greening of Detroit: https://www.greeningofdetroit.com/

Keep Growing Detroit: http://detroitagriculture.net/

BALLE Network: https://bealocalist.org/about

Incredible Edible: https://www.incredible-edible-todmorden.co.uk/projects

Locality: http://locality.org.uk/

Ferme du Bec-Hellouin: http://www.fermedubec.com/

INRA: http://institut.inra.fr/en

Agro Paris Tech: http://www.agroparistech.fr/Presentation-of-AgroParisTech.html

2–Successful Energy Transition

Debate on fossil fuels: https://www.youtube.com/watch?v=0_a9
RP0J7PA
Negawatt: https://negawatt.org/en
Solagro: https://solagro.com/
Statistics Iceland: http://www.statice.is/statistics/environment/
emission/
Akuo Energy: https://www.akuoenergy.com/en/home.html
Dong Energy: http://www.dongenergy.com/en
Guardian article: https://www.theguardian.com/environment/2015/
jul/10/denmark-wind-windfarm-power-exceed-electricity-demand?
cmp=share_btn_fb
Triple Pundit: http://www.triplepundit.com/2011/06/top-10-globally-
resilient-cities/
Recology: https://www.recology.com/

3–An Economy for the Future

Oxfam report: https://www.oxfam.org/en/research/working-few
Guardian article: https://www.theguardian.com/environment/earth-
insight/2014/mar/14/nasa-civilisation-irreversible-collapse-study-
scientists
Pocheco: http://www.pocheco.com/?lang=en
Banque WIR (website in French, German, and Italian): https://www.
wir.ch/fr/
Bristol Pound: http://bristolpound.org/
SBN: http://www.sbnphiladelphia.org/
Woodstone: http://woodstone-corp.com/
Fab lab "Mount Eliot": http://www.uixdetroit.com/projects/mt-elliott.
aspx
Larry Burns's speech: https://www.ted.com/talks/reinventing_the_car

Foundation on Economic Trends' official website: http://www.
foet.org/

4–Reinventing Democracy

See the studies quoted by David Van Reybrouck:
http://www.bbc.com/news/blogs-echochambers-27074746
and
https://www.cambridge.org/core/journals/perspectives-on-politics/
article/div-classtitletesting-theories-of-american-politics-elites-interest-
groups-and-average-citizensdiv/62327F513959D0A304D4893B382B
992B

5–A New Story of Education

Finnish school system: https://finland.fi/life-society/with-free-high-
quality-education-for-all/

6–Getting Started

The Transition Network's website: http://transitionnetwork.org/